Lecturer in Russian Language,
Department of Language and Linguistics,
University of Essex

THE RUSSIAN VERB

A Guide to its Forms and Usage
for Advanced Learners

Edited by Elena Petrukhina,
Moscow State University

COLLETS
London & Wellingborough

CONTENTS

TABLES

PREFACE

This book aims to give a comprehensive guide to those forms and uses of the Russian verb which advanced learners of Russian find difficult. It is the result of the experience of teaching the problems of Russian grammar to generations of undergraduates of Russian and to students on the Norwich, and its successor, the Essex Russian Course. I have, where possible, avoided using technical language, preferring to explain everything in everyday language, as it is intended to be a practical guide to the Russian verb which can be used by students who are not studying linguistics.

The sections on the rules for forming the parts of the Russian verb have been made as comprehensive as possible: if the student follows the rules, he or she will produce the correct written form and from this the spoken form as well. The student will not end up being told so often, as I was as an undergraduate, the form he or she requires was an "exception". The book also aims to act as a reference guide and it is with this aim that the tables at the end of the chapters have been made as comprehensive as possible.

I am very grateful to Elena Petrukhina of Moscow State University who has made many valuable comments, which have been incorporated into the final version of the book; she is is the author of chapter 18, which I have edited and translated.

Elena Petrukhina and I have compiled a series of practical exercises, covering the main points in the book. This booklet will be available from Dr. R. Bivon, Department of Language and Linguistics, University of Essex, Wivenhoe Park, Colchester CO4 3SQ.

R. BIVON
APRIL 1992

ABBREVIATIONS

1PS	first person singular
2PS	second person singular
3PS	third person singular
1PP	first person plural
2PP	second person plural
3PP	third person plural
i	imperfective verb
ii	imperfective verb indeterminate
id	imperfective verb determinate
†	imperfective non-process verb (see p.82)
p	perfective verb
ip	verb having one form for both aspects
M	masculine
F	feminine
N	neuter
Pl	plural
A	accusative
G	genitive
D	dative
I	instrumental
P	prepositional

TABLES

imp	imperfective
perf	perfective

(про)**жи́ть** indicates that all verbs of the root -**жить** display the feature;

про**жи́ть** indicates that only the prefixed verb про**жи́ть** displays the feature.

CHAPTER 1. INTRODUCTION: THE RUSSIAN VERB SYSTEM

The Russian verb system has fewer forms than in the languages of Western Europe. It has two tenses: present and past. The forms of the future tense are discussed below. The present tense has six forms, which vary according to person and number. The past tense has four forms: three singular forms which change according to the gender of the subject: masculine, feminine and neuter and a single form used with a plural subject.

Unlike English, it has only one past tense, formed from both aspects (see below). This is the equivalent of the following English past tense forms:

wrote
was writing
have written
had written
have been writing
had been writing
used to write

The conditional (subjunctive) mood is formed by adding the particle бы to the past tense. It does not change for tense.

There are also special forms for the imperative mood and some special non-finite forms: participles (verbal adjectives) and gerunds (verbal adverbs). The participle is used either in relative clauses, in place of кото́рый and a tense form, or to form the passive voice of the verb in conjunction with the verb быть. The gerund is used to replace adverbial subordinate clauses beginning with когда́, е́сли, потому́ что, хотя́, etc.

The feature which distinguishes the Russian verb from the verb in Western European languages is the category of *aspect*. Most Russian verbs have two aspects: imperfective and perfective. The perfective is used to stress the completion or start of an action. The following verb forms are distinguished by aspect:

infinitive
past tense
future tense
imperative
conditional
participle
gerund

THE RUSSIAN VERB

Only the present tense has no contrast for aspect: it is always imperfective. Perfective verbs therefore have only past and future tenses.

A few verbs: *Verbs of Motion* have two imperfective forms, distinguished by the direction and frequency of the action.

The rules for forming the imperfective and perfective forms of the past tense, conditional mood and the imperative are the same for both aspects. The following parts of the verb are formed differently for the two aspects:

1) Future tense: the *imperfective* is formed by combining the future tense of the verb *быть* with the imperfective infinitive;

   the *perfective* is formed using the same rules as those for the present tense: the rules when applied to an imperfective verb produce the present tense, when applied to a perfective verb the result is the future tense.

2) Participles: the present active has no perfective form;

   the passive participles are formed differently for each aspect.

3) Gerunds: the two gerund forms are formed in different ways from each aspect.

The present and past tenses are formed from the infinitive. The present tense is the basis for forming the imperative mood, the present participles (active and passive) and the imperfective gerund. The past tense is the basis for the formation of the conditional mood, the past active participles and the perfective gerund. The past passive participle is normally formed directly from the infinitive. The following diagram shows the relationship between the forms:

1. INTRODUCTION: THE RUSSIAN VERB SYSTEM

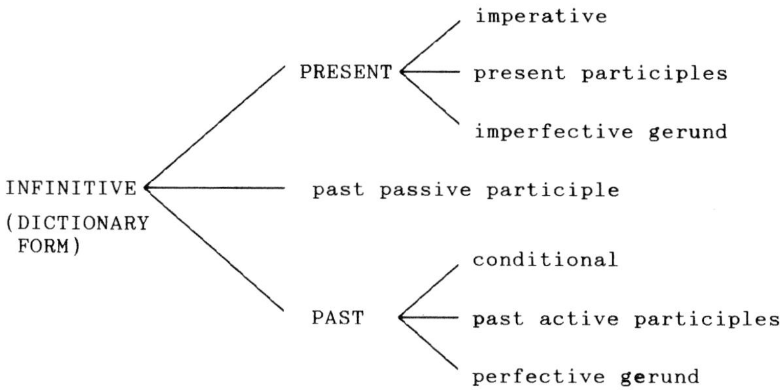

The rules for forming the present tense are complex and are explained in chapter 2; those for forming the past tense are much simpler, the past tense root is frequently the same as the infinitive. The details are given in chapter 3. Table 1 lists all the verbs forms from the verb чита́ть/прочита́ть *read.*

Prefixes and suffixes play an important role in the development of a variety of meanings in the Russian verb. Prefixes can add direction, or limit the action contained in the verb in a variety of ways. Both prefixes and suffixes can be used either to form the perfective aspect or to form verbs from adjectives and nouns.

The suffix -ся, which can be added on to many verbs, in origin had a reflexive meaning. It has now developed other meanings, such as forming the passive and creating intransitive verbs.

Part One of the book gives comprehensive rules for the formation of the finite verb forms: the tenses and the imperative. Part Two examines the formation and use of participles and gerunds. Part Three examines verb aspects, both formation and use, and discusses the special features of *Verbs of Motion.* Finally, Part Four examines verbal prefixes and suffixes.

Wherever possible, comprehensive rules are given with complete lists of exceptions and less common verb forms. In devising the rules and compiling tables of special forms and exceptions the following reference books have been used: Орфоэпи́ческий слова́рь ру́сского языка́, *Зализня́к*: Граммати́ческий слова́рь ру́сского языка́, *Ожегов*: Слова́рь ру́сского языка́. Full details are provided in the bibliography.

THE RUSSIAN VERB

TABLE 1	THE FORMS OF THE VERB ЧИТАТЬ	
	IMPERFECTIVE	PERFECTIVE
INFINITIVE	чита́ть	прочита́ть
PRESENT TENSE	я чита́ю ты чита́ешь он чита́ет мы чита́ем вы чита́ете они́ чита́ют	
FUTURE TENSE	я бу́ду чита́ть ты бу́дешь чита́ть он бу́дет чита́ть мы бу́дем чита́ть вы бу́дете чита́ть они́ бу́дут чита́ть	я прочита́ю ты прочита́ешь он прочита́ет мы прочита́ем вы прочита́ете они́ прочита́ют
PAST TENSE	он чита́л она́ чита́ла оно́ чита́ло они́ чита́ли	он прочита́л она́ прочита́ла оно́ прочита́ло они́ прочита́ли
IMPERATIVE	дава́й(те) чита́ть (ты) чита́й (вы) чита́йте пусть (пуска́й) он чита́ет они́ чита́ют	[дава́й(те)] прочита́ем (ты) прочита́й (вы) прочита́йте пусть (пуска́й) он прочита́ет они́ прочита́ют
CONDITIONAL (SUBJUNCTIVE)	он чита́л бы она́ чита́ла бы оно́ чита́ло бы они́ чита́ли бы	он прочита́л бы она́ прочита́ла бы оно́ прочита́ло бы они́ прочита́ли бы
PARTICIPLES ACTIVE PRESENT ACTIVE PAST PASSIVE	 чита́ющий чита́вший чита́емый	 прочита́вший прочи́танный
GERUNDS	чита́я	прочита́в

PART ONE THE FORMATION OF THE FINITE VERB FORMS

CHAPTER 2. FORMATION OF THE PRESENT/FUTURE TENSE

1) INTRODUCTION

A) CONJUGATION PATTERNS

There are two conjugation patterns in Russian for the present/future tense. With the exception of four verb roots: дать *give*, есть *eat*, бежáть *run* and хотéть *want*, all Russian verbs have either first or second conjugation endings. Imperfective verbs use the endings to form the present tense, perfective verbs use the same endings to form the future tense.

The two conjugations have much in common. 1PS ending is the same for both conjugations; the first conjugation has the vowel е in four of the six forms, while the second conjugation uses the vowel и in these forms. 3PP is, however, different: ют (ут) for the first conjugation, ят (ат) for the second.

B) DETERMINING CONJUGATION PATTERN FROM THE INFINITIVE

The following table summarises the relationship between infinitive ending and conjugation pattern:

INFINITIVE ENDING	CONJUGATION	COMMENTS
ать жать/чать/шать/щать + sound жать/чать/шать/щать not sound	1st 2nd 1st/2nd	 table 2 table 2
еть еть + sound	1st/2nd 2nd	table 3 table 3
ить monosyllabic root	2nd 1st	 table 5
оть	1st	type G
нуть	1st	type C
ыть	1st	types J, M
ять	1st	see below
ти, сть, зть	1st	type E
чь	1st	type F

Verbs ending in -ать, -еть and -ять in the infinitive are usually first conjugation. There are, however, a number of verb roots ending in -ать and -еть which are second conjugation. These include a large group ending in a sibilant (ж, ч, ш, щ) + ать, many of them having meanings indicating sounds. These are listed in tables 2 and 3. Two verb roots ending in -ять are second conjugation: боя́ться *be afraid* and стоя́ть *stand*, all the rest are first conjugation.

Verbs ending in -ить are usually second conjugation. A number of mainly monosyllabic verb roots are first conjugation. They are listed in table 5. Verbs with endings other than -ать, -еть, -ить and -ять in the infinitive are first conjugation.

C) SUFFIX -СЯ

The suffix -ся can be added after the present/future tense endings: there are two forms of this suffix: -ся is used after consonants, -сь after vowels. Thus 1PS and 2PP, which end in a vowel, add сь, the other forms add ся.

D) STRESS IN THE PRESENT/FUTURE TENSE

I) STEM STRESS in the infinitive

The same syllable will be stressed in the present/future tense as in the infinitive: eg ста́вить *put* (ста́влю, ста́вишь, ста́вит).

II) END STRESS in the infinitive

EITHER all the endings in the present/future tense will be stressed: eg чита́ть *read* (чита́ю, чита́ешь, чита́ет), говори́ть *say* (говорю́, говори́шь, говори́т...);

OR there is mobile stress: 1PS has end stress and the other forms have the stress on the preceding syllable: eg писа́ть *write* (пишу́, пи́шешь, пи́шет...), ходи́ть *go* (хожу́, хо́дишь, хо́дит...).

It is very rare for a verb stressed on the end in the infinitive to have stem stress in the present/future tense: one such verb is колеба́ться *shake* (коле́блюсь, коле́блешься, коле́блется...).

The stress pattern usually remains the same for all prefixed forms of a verb root. Note, however, that all perfective verbs with the prefix вы- have the stress on the prefix. Compare идти́ *go*, войти́ *enter*, уйти́ *leave* with вы́йти *go out*.

2) FIRST CONJUGATION

The endings of first conjugation verbs are:

	SINGULAR	PLURAL
1	Ю/У	ЕМ/ЁМ
2	ЕШЬ/ЁШЬ	ЕТЕ/ЁТЕ
3	ЕТ/ЁТ	ЮТ/УТ

The forms ю (1PS) and ют (3PP) are used after vowels, ь, л; they are also found after р in type G verbs (ending in -оть). Otherwise the forms у (1PS) and ут (3PP) are used. ё replaces е when the endings are stressed. The following table summarises the relationship between the infinitive and the present/future tense root:

TYPE	INFINITIVE	PRESENT/FUTURE
A	ать (ять, еть)	аю (яю,ею), аешь (яешь, еешь)
B	ать, ять	у (ю), ешь (ёшь)
C	нуть	ну, нешь (нёшь)
D	овать, евать евать	ую, уешь (уёшь) юю, юешь (юёшь)
E	ти, сть, зть	root consonant + у, ёшь (ешь)
F	чь	гу, жёшь (жешь), гут ку, чёшь, кут
G	оть	ю, ешь
H	ереть	ру, рёшь
I	авать	аю́, аёшь
J	ыть	о́ю, о́ешь
K	ить	ью́, ьёшь
L	нять (imp. нимать)	ниму, нимешь (йму, ймёшь)
M	ыть (ить)	ыву́ (иву́), ывёшь (ивёшь)
N	others	see table 8

Most of the present/future tense forms can be established by looking carefully at the infinitive ending and using the above table. However, it is not possible to forecast whether verbs ending in -ать and -ять will be type A or B. The vast majority are type A: these are usually labelled *regular* in most textbooks. A complete list of type B verbs ending in -ать is given in table 4. For verbs in -ять see the detailed comments below on type B verbs.

A) PRESENT/FUTURE TENSE WITH INFINITIVE VOWEL

Remove -ть from the infinitive
Add the first conjugation endings

2. FORMATION OF THE PRESENT/FUTURE TENSE

реша́ть	decide	реша́ю реша́ем	реша́ешь реша́ете	реша́ет реша́ют
сия́ть	shine	сия́ю сия́ем	сия́ешь сия́ете	сия́ет сия́ют
красне́ть	go red	красне́ю красне́ем	красне́ешь красне́ете	красне́ет красне́ют
дуть	blow	ду́ю ду́ем	ду́ешь ду́ете	ду́ет ду́ют

The following groups of verbs have this conjugation pattern:

I) The overwhelming majority of verbs ending in -ать and -ять. This includes all imperfective verbs formed from perfective verbs in -ить and almost all verbs ending in stressed -я́ть (see реша́ть *decide*, сия́ть *shine* above).

II) The majority of verbs ending in -еть including all verbs formed from adjectives (see красне́ть *go red* above).

III) Two verb roots ending in -уть: дуть *blow* and обу́ть /разу́ть *put shoes on/take shoes off*.

The stress in these verbs is fixed on the same syllable as in the infinitive. The endings are never stressed.

B) PRESENT/FUTURE TENSE WITHOUT INFINITIVE VOWEL

Remove the last 3 letters from the infinitive
Change the final consonant(s) of the root, as follows: г, д, з -- ж к, т -- ч с, х -- ш ск, ст, т -- щ б, м, п -- бл, мл, пл
Add the first conjugation endings

стона́ть	moan	стону́ сто́нем	сто́нешь сто́нете	сто́нет сто́нут
ла́ять	bark	ла́ю ла́ем	ла́ешь ла́ете	ла́ет ла́ют
смея́ться	laugh	смею́сь	смеёшься	смеётся

		смеёмся	смеётесь	смею́тся
ошиби́ться	be mistaken	ошибу́сь ошибёмся	ошибёшься ошибётесь	ошибётся ошибу́тся
сказа́ть	say	скажу́ ска́жем	ска́жешь ска́жете	ска́жет ска́жут
пла́кать	cry	пла́чу пла́чем	пла́чешь пла́чете	пла́чет пла́чут
писа́ть	write	пишу́ пи́шем	пи́шешь пи́шете	пи́шет пи́шут
иска́ть	look for	ищу́ и́щем	и́щешь и́щете	и́щет и́щут
колеба́ться	shake	коле́блюсь коле́блемся	коле́блешься коле́блетесь	коле́блется коле́блются

The following groups of verbs have this conjugation pattern:

I) *Verbs ending in -ать*. The verbs belonging to this group are mainly imperfective and form the perfective by prefixation. A few, such as сказа́ть are perfective. A complete list is given in table 4.

II) *Stem stressed verbs in -ять*. Two exceptions are found: смея́ться *laugh*, which belongs to this group despite end stress (see above) and ка́шлять *cough* which retains the vowel я (type A) despite stem stress (ка́шляю, ка́шляешь..).

III) *The following two verb roots*: реве́ть *roar* (реву́, ревёшь) and -шиби́ть, eg ошиби́ться *be mistaken* (see above).

Consonant alternation regularly takes place THROUGHOUT the present/future tense. A complete list is given in table 4. Note that the similar alternations which are found in second conjugation verbs take place in 1PS only. The following verbs, despite the final consonant of the root, do not undergo consonant alternation:

жа́ждать	thirst	ждать	wait
-шиби́ть: eg ошиби́ться	be mistaken	рвать	tear
реве́ть	roar	соса́ть	suck
ткать	weave		

The following stress patterns are observed:

I) In monosyllabic verb roots, соса́ть *suck*, реве́ть *roar* and смея́ться *laugh* the stress remains on the ending throughout the present/future tense.

II) In stem stressed verbs the stress remains fixed: eg ла́ять *bark*, пла́кать *cry*

III) In end stressed verbs, other than those in (I) above and колеба́ться *shake*, mobile stress is found (see сказа́ть *say*, писа́ть *write*, иска́ть *look for* above). колеба́ться *shake* has stem stress throughout the present tense.

C) INFINITIVE ENDING IN -НУТЬ

Remove -уть from the infinitive
Add the first conjugation endings

пры́гнуть	jump	пры́гну	пры́гнешь	пры́гнет
		пры́гнем	пры́гнете	пры́гнут
верну́ть	return	верну́	вернёшь	вернёт
		вернём	вернёте	верну́т
тону́ть	drown	тону́	то́нешь	то́нет
		то́нем	то́нете	то́нут

All verbs with the infinitive ending in -нуть are conjugated as above.

Most verbs have fixed stress: either end stress: see верну́ть *return*, or stem stress, see пры́гнуть *jump*. The following verb roots have mobile stress: (вз)гляну́ть *glance* (prefixed forms only), мину́ть *pass*, обману́ть *deceive*, тону́ть *drown*, тяну́ть *pull*.

D) INFINITIVE ENDING IN -ОВАТЬ OR -ЕВАТЬ

Remove -овать or -евать
Add у or ю
Add the first conjugation endings

сове́товать	advise	сове́тую	сове́туешь	сове́тует
		сове́туем	сове́туете	сове́туют
ночева́ть	spend the	ночу́ю	ночу́ешь	ночу́ет

	night	ночу́ем	ночу́ете	ночу́ют
воева́ть	wage war	вою́ю вою́ем	вою́ешь вою́ете	вою́ет вою́ют
плева́ть	spit	плюю́ плюём	плюёшь плюёте	плюёт плюю́т

у is added for verbs ending in -овать, or -евать preceded by ж, ч, ш, щ and ц; ю is added for other verbs ending in -евать.

Two groups of verb ending in -овать and -евать do not belong to this group. They are both type A:

I) the syllable ов or ев is part of the verb root: здоро́ваться *greet* (здоро́ваюсь, здоро́ваешься...) and зева́ть *yawn* (зева́ю, зева́ешь...), cf здоро́вый *healthy* and зево́к *yawn*;

II) a number of verbs where the imperfective ends in -евать and the perfective in -еть: eg одева́ть *dress* (одева́ю, одева́ешь...), cf perfective оде́ть.

Stem-stressed verbs have a fixed stress throughout the present/future tense (see сове́товать *advise*); end stress verbs almost always stress the inserted vowel у or ю (see ночева́ть *spend the night*, воева́ть *wage war* above). A few verbs stress the endings (see плева́ть *spit* above). Other such verbs are: блева́ть *puke*, жева́ть *chew*, клева́ть *peck*, кова́ть *forge*, основа́ть *found*, снова́ть *dash about* and сова́ть *shove*.

E) INFINITIVE ENDING IN -ТИ, -СТЬ, -ЗТЬ

Remove the last three letters from the infinitive
Add the root consonant
Add the first conjugation endings

The root consonant can be determined by finding another word connected with the verb:

вести́	*lead*	води́ть	*lead*	root consonant	д
цвести́	*flower*	цвето́к	*flower*	root consonant	т
лезть	*climb*	ла́зить	*climb*	root consonant	з
нести́	*carry*	носи́ть	*carry*	root consonant	с

2. FORMATION OF THE PRESENT/FUTURE TENSE

вести́	lead	веду́	ведёшь	ведёт
		ведём	ведёте	веду́т
цвести́	flower	цвету́	цветёшь	цветёт
		цветём	цветёте	цвету́т
лезть	climb	ле́зу	ле́зешь	ле́зет
		ле́зем	ле́зете	ле́зут
нести́	carry	несу́	несёшь	несёт
		несём	несёте	несу́т

A complete list of all verb roots of this type is given in table 6.

The final syllable is usually stressed. A few verbs in this group are stem stressed (see лезть). These verbs are marked in table 6.

F) INFINITIVE ENDING IN -ЧЬ

Remove the last two letters (чь) from the infinitive
Add EITHER к in 1PS and 3PP and ч elsewhere OR г in 1PS and 3PP and ж elsewhere
Add the first conjugation endings.

The choice of к/ч or г/ж can be determined by finding another word connected with the verb:

мочь	*be able*	могу́щество	*power*	use г/ж
течь	*flow*	тече́ние	*current*	use к/ч

течь	flow	теку́	течёшь	течёт
		течём	течёте	теку́т
мочь	be able	могу́	мо́жешь	мо́жет
		мо́жем	мо́жете	мо́гут

A complete list of all verb roots of this type is given in table 7.

мочь *be able* has mobile stress, лечь *lie down* has stem stress, all other verbs of this type have end stress.

G) INFINITIVE ENDING IN -ОТЬ

боро́ться	struggle	борю́сь	бо́решься	бо́рется
		бо́ремся	бо́ретесь	бо́рются
коло́ть	split	колю́	ко́лешь	ко́лет
		ко́лем	ко́лете	ко́лют

There are three further verb roots ending in -оть: моло́ть *grind*, (present: мелю́, ме́лешь....), поло́ть *weed* and поро́ть *thrash*. They all have mobile stress and all have ю and ют in 1PS and 3PP.

H) INFINITIVE ENDING IN -ЕРЕТЬ

умере́ть	die	умру́	умрёшь	умрёт
		умрём	умрёте	умру́т

There are two further verb roots of this type: тере́ть *rub* and -пере́ть: eg запере́ть *lock*. They are all end-stressed.

I) INFINITIVE ENDING IN -АВАТЬ

дава́ть	give	даю́	даёшь	даёт
		даём	даёте	даю́т

There are two further verb roots of this type: -знава́ть: eg узнава́ть *get to know* and -става́ть: eg встава́ть *stand up*. They are all end-stressed.

J) INFINITIVE ENDING IN -ЫТЬ, PRESENT/FUTURE IN -ОЮ, -ОЕШЬ

мыть	wash	мо́ю	мо́ешь	мо́ет
		мо́ем	мо́ете	мо́ют

There are four other verb roots of this type: выть *howl*, крыть *cover*, ныть *ache*, рыть *burrow*. All are stem-stressed.

K) INFINITIVE IN -ИТЬ, PRESENT/FUTURE IN -ЬЮ, -ЬЁШЬ

пить	drink	пью	пьёшь	пьёт
		пьём	пьёте	пьют

There are four other verb roots of this type: бить *hit*, вить *wind*, лить *pour*, шить *sew*. They are all end-stressed.

L) INFINITIVE IN PREFIX + -НЯТЬ, IMPERFECTIVE IN -НИМАТЬ

подня́ть	lift	подниму́	подни́мешь	подни́мет
		подни́мем	подни́мете	подни́мут
поня́ть	understand	пойму́	поймёшь	поймёт
		поймём	поймёте	пойму́т
приня́ть	receive	приму́	при́мешь	при́мет
		при́мем	при́мете	при́мут

Verbs with a prefix ending in a consonant form the future tense like подня́ть and have mobile stress; those with a prefix ending in a vowel (except приня́ть) form the future tense like поня́ть and are end-stressed.

M) INFINITIVE IN -ЫТЬ (-ИТЬ), PRESENT/FUTURE IN -ЫВ (-ИВ)

плыть	swim	плыву́ плывём	плывёшь плывёте	плывёт плыву́т
слыть	have a reputation	слыву́ слывём	слывёшь слывёте	слывёт слыву́т
жить	live	живу́ живём	живёшь живёте	живёт живу́т

N) OTHERS

A number of other verbs have roots in the present/future tense which are unpredictable. A complete list is given in table 8.

3) SECOND CONJUGATION

The endings of second conjugation verbs are:

	SINGULAR	PLURAL
1	Ю/У	ИМ
2	ИШЬ	ИТЕ
3	ИТ	ЯТ/АТ

A) FORMATION

Remove the last three letters from the infinitive (vowel + ть)
Add the second conjugation endings

говори́ть	say	говорю́ говори́м	говори́шь говори́те	говори́т говоря́т
по́мнить	remember	по́мню по́мним	по́мнишь по́мните	по́мнит по́мнят
учи́ться	learn	учу́сь у́чимся	у́чишься у́читесь	у́чится у́чатся
лежа́ть	lie	лежу́ лежи́м	лежи́шь лежи́те	лежи́т лежа́т
смотре́ть	look	смотрю́ смо́трим	смо́тришь смо́трите	смо́трит смо́трят
стоя́ть	stand	стою́ стои́м	стои́шь стои́те	стои́т стоя́т

B) <u>1PS AND 3PP ENDINGS</u>

In accordance with the spelling conventions of Russian, ю (1PS) and ят (3PP) are replaced by у (1PS) and ат (3PP) after the sibilants ж, ч, ш, щ (see учи́ться and лежа́ть above).

C) <u>STRESS</u>

If the infinitive has stem stress, the present/future tense also has the stress on the same syllable (see по́мнить above). If the infinitive has end stress,

EITHER the endings will be stressed throughout the present /future tense (see говори́ть, лежа́ть, стоя́ть above)

OR there will be mobile stress (see учи́ться, смотре́ть above)

D) <u>CONSONANT ALTERNATION</u>

A series of consonant alternations take place in 1PS only. In other forms the infinitive consonant is retained. The following table lists these alternations:

INFINITIVE CONSONANT	1PS CONSONANT
Д, З	Ж
С	Ш
Т	Ч
Т, СТ	Щ
Б В М П Ф	БЛ ВЛ МЛ ПЛ ФЛ

д/ж	ви́деть	see	ви́жу ви́дим	ви́дишь ви́дите	ви́дит ви́дят
з/ж	вози́ть	carry	вожу́ во́зим	во́зишь во́зите	во́зит во́зят
с/ш	проси́ть	ask	прошу́ про́сим	про́сишь про́сите	про́сит про́сят

т/ч	встре́тить	meet	встре́чу встре́тим	встре́тишь встре́тите	встре́тит встре́тят
т/щ	посети́ть	visit	посещу́ посети́м	посети́шь посети́те	посети́т посетя́т
ст/щ	прости́ть	forgive	прощу́ прости́м	прости́шь прости́те	прости́т простя́т
б/бл	люби́ть	love	люблю́ лю́бим	лю́бишь лю́бите	лю́бит лю́бят
в/вл	ста́вить	put	ста́влю ста́вим	ста́вишь ста́вите	ста́вит ста́вят
м/мл	корми́ть	feed	кормлю́ ко́рмим	ко́рмишь ко́рмите	ко́рмит ко́рмят
п/пл	спать	sleep	сплю спим	спишь спи́те	спит спят
ф/фл	графи́ть	rule (lines)	графлю́ графи́м	графи́шь графи́те	графи́т графя́т

Verbs whose root ends in т can have 1PS ending either in ч (see встре́тить above) or щ (see посети́ть above). The correct consonant alternation can be determined by referring to a connected word. In the above cases the imperfective demonstrates the same consonant alternation: встреча́ть /встре́тить (т/ч); посеща́ть/посети́ть (т/щ).

One verbs does not conform to the above alternations: чтить *honour* (1PS чту).

E) IRREGULARITIES

I) The verbs гнать and чтить

гнать *drive* has a present tense as follows:

гнать	drive	гоню́ го́ним	го́нишь го́ните	го́нит го́нят

The verb чтить *honour* has two forms for the 3PP; the regular чтят and the irregular чтут.

II) No first person singular

A few second conjugation verbs are never used in the first person singular form. They are listed in table 9.

4) VERBS BELONGING TO NEITHER CONJUGATION

A) MIXED CONJUGATION

Two verb roots have forms which are a mixture of the first and second conjugations:

хоте́ть	want	хочу́	хо́чешь	хо́чет
		хоти́м	хоти́те	хотя́т
бежа́ть	run	бегу́	бежи́шь	бежи́т
		бежи́м	бежи́те	бегу́т

B) ДАТЬ AND ЕСТЬ

These two verb roots show the remains of an archaic conjugation pattern:

дать	give	дам	дашь	даст
		дади́м	дади́те	даду́т
есть	eat	ем	ешь	ест
		еди́м	еди́те	едя́т

2. FORMATION OF THE PRESENT/FUTURE TENSE

TABLE 2		SECOND CONJUGATION -АТЬ VERBS			
A) NON-SOUND VERBS ENDING IN SIBILANT + -АТЬ					
держа́ть	hold	дрожа́ть	tremble	дыша́ть	breathe
лежа́ть	lie	мчать	rush	принадлежа́ть	belong
слы́шать	hear	торча́ть	protrude		
B) OTHER NON-SOUND VERBS					
гнать	drive	спать	sleep		
C) SOUND VERBS ENDING IN SIBILANT + -АТЬ					
бренча́ть	jingle	бурча́ть	mumble	брюзжа́ть	grumble
вереща́ть	chirp	визжа́ть	scream	ворча́ть	growl
дребезжа́ть	tinkle	жужжа́ть	buzz	журча́ть	babble
звуча́ть	sound	крича́ть	shout	мыча́ть	moo
молча́ть	be silent	пища́ть	squeal	рыча́ть	growl
стуча́ть	knock	треща́ть	crackle	урча́ть	rumble
шурша́ть	rustle				

TABLE 3		SECOND CONJUGATION -ЕТЬ VERBS			
A) NON-SOUND VERBS					
бдеть	watch	блесте́ть	shine	боле́ть	ache[1]
веле́ть	order	верте́ть	turn	ви́деть	see
висе́ть	hang	гляде́ть	look	горе́ть	burn
зави́сеть	depend	зреть	see	зуде́ть	itch
кипе́ть	boil	кише́ть	swarm	копте́ть	swot
корпе́ть	pore over	лете́ть	fly	ненави́деть	hate
оби́деть	offend	пестре́ть	strike eye[1]	пыхте́ть	pant
сиде́ть	sit	скорбе́ть	grieve	смотре́ть	look
терпе́ть	be patient				
1 боле́ть *be ill*, пестре́ть *become multi-coloured* are type 1A					
B) SOUND VERBS					
галде́ть	make a din	греме́ть	thunder	гуде́ть	buzz
дуде́ть	play pipes	звене́ть	ring	кряхте́ть	wheeze
свисте́ть	whistle	сипе́ть	croak	скрипе́ть	creak
сопе́ть	sniff	тарахте́ть	rattle	храпе́ть	snore
хрипе́ть	wheeze	хрусте́ть	crunch	шелесте́ть	rustle
шипе́ть	hiss	шуме́ть	be noisy		

TABLE 4	FIRST CONJUGATION TYPE B -АТЬ					
A) <u>NO CONSONANT ALTERNATION</u>						
	врать	lie	жа́ждать	thirst	ждать	wait
	жрать	eat	ора́ть	bawl	рвать	tear
	ржать	neigh	соса́ть	suck	стона́ть	moan
	ткать	weave				
B) <u>CONSONANT ALTERNATION</u>						
г-ж	бры́згать[1]	splash	дви́гать[2]	move		
д-ж	глода́ть[1]	gnaw				
з-ж	вяза́ть	tie	(по)каза́ть	show	лиза́ть	lick
	ма́зать	oil	низа́ть	thread	обяза́ть	oblige
	ре́зать[3]	cut	сказа́ть	say		
к-ч	кли́кать	call	курлы́кать[1]	gabble	мурлы́кать[1]	purr
	пла́кать	cry	скака́ть	jump	ты́кать[1]	prod
	хны́кать[1]	whimper				
т-ч	бормота́ть	mutter	гогота́ть	cackle	грохота́ть	crash
	клокота́ть	gurgle	куда́хтать	cackle	лепета́ть	babble
	лопота́ть	mutter	мета́ть	throw	пря́тать	hide
	рокота́ть	roar	стрекота́ть	chirp	топота́ть	stamp
	топта́ть	trample	хлопота́ть	bustle	хохота́ть	guffaw
	шепта́ть	whisper	щебета́ть	twitter	щекота́ть	tickle
с-ш	опоя́сать	gird	писа́ть	write	пля́сать	dance
	чеса́ть	scratch				
х-ш	бреха́ть	yelp	колыха́ть[1]	sway	маха́ть[1]	wave
	паха́ть	plough	пы́хать	blaze		
ск-щ	иска́ть	seek	плеска́ть[1]	splash	полоска́ть[1]	rinse
	ры́скать[1]	roam				
ст-щ	свиста́ть	whistle	хлеста́ть	lash	хлобыста́ть	lash
т-щ	клеве́та́ть	slander	ропта́ть	murmur	скрежета́ть	grit teeth
	трепета́ть	tremble				
б-бл	колеба́ться	shake				
м-мл	дрема́ть	doze				
п-пл	ка́пать[1]	drip	кра́пать[1]	spit	сы́пать[3]	strew
	трепа́ть	tousle	щипа́ть[1]	pinch		

1 also type A
2 дви́гать *move (physically)* type A; *move (emotions)* type B
3 ре́зать, сы́пать are type B when stem-stressed ; type A when end-stressed (only prefixed forms)

2. FORMATION OF THE PRESENT/FUTURE TENSE

TABLE 5	FIRST CONJUGATION -ИТЬ VERBS				
бить гнить пить (у)шиби́ть	hit rot drink injure	брить жить почи́ть[1] шить	shave live pass away sew	вить лить чтить	wind pour honour
1 Old-fashioned bookish style					

TABLE 6	FIRST CONJUGATION TYPE E -ТИ, -ЗТЬ, -СТЬ					
б	грести́	row, rake	скрести́	scrape		
д	блюсти́[1] грясти́[1] красть[2 3] сесть	guard approach steal sit down	брести́ идти́ пасть	stroll go fall	вести́ класть прясть	lead put spin
з	везти́ ползти́	transport crawl	грызть	gnaw	лезть[2]	climb
н	клясть	curse				
с	нести́ трясти́	carry shake	пасти́	graze	спасти́	save
ст	расти́	grow				
т	гнести́ плести́ (про)че́сть[4]	oppress weave read	мести́ рассвести́	sweep dawn	обрести́ цвести́	find flower

1 bookish: the infinitive (and past tense) is obsolete
2 stem stress
3 future tense: ся́ду, ся́дешь, ся́дет, ся́дем, ся́дете, ся́дут
4 present tense: -чту, -чтёшь, -чтёт, -чтём, -чтёте, -чтут

TABLE 7	FIRST CONJUGATION TYPE F -ЧЬ			
к/ч	влечь	drag	воло́чь	drag
	печь	bake	(из)ре́чь	speak
	сечь	flog	течь	flow
	толо́чь[1]	pound		
г/ж	бере́чь	keep	пренебре́чь	scorn
	жечь[2]	burn	лечь[3]	lie down
	мочь	be able	(за)пря́чь	harness
	стере́чь	watch	стричь	cut hair

1 present tense: толку́, толчёшь, толчёт, толчём, толчёте, толку́т
2 present tense: жгу, жжёшь, жжёт, жжём, жжёте, жгут
3 present tense: ля́гу, ля́жешь, ля́жет, ля́жем, ля́жете, ля́гут

The verb root -стичь: eg дости́чь *reach* has an alternative infinitive ending in -сти́гнуть and is conjugated in the future tense from this infinitive form (type C).

TABLE 8	FIRST CONJUGATION UNPREDICTABLE ROOT			
брать	take	беру́	берёшь	беру́т
брить	shave	бре́ю	бре́ешь	бре́ют
быть	be	бу́ду	бу́дешь	бу́дут
взять	take	возьму́	возьмёшь	возьму́т
гнить	rot	гнию́	гниёшь	гнию́т
(о)де́ть	dress	оде́ну	оде́нешь	оде́нут
драть	tear	деру́	дерёшь	деру́т
е́хать	go	е́ду	е́дешь	е́дут
жать	press	жму	жмёшь	жмут
жать	reap	жну	жнёшь	жнут
живописа́ть	depict	живопису́ю	живопису́ешь	живопису́ют
зача́ть	conceive	зачну́	зачнёшь	зачну́т
звать	call	зову́	зовёшь	зову́т
лгать	lie	лгу	лжёшь	лгут
мять	crumple	мну	мнёшь	мнут
нача́ть	begin	начну́	начнёшь	начну́т
петь	sing	пою́	поёшь	пою́т
почи́ть	pass away	почи́ю	почи́ешь	почи́ют
распя́ть	crucify	распну́	распнёшь	распну́т
слать	send	шлю	шлёшь	шлют
стать	become	ста́ну	ста́нешь	ста́нут
(за)стря́ть	stick	(за)стря́ну	(за)стря́нешь	(за)стря́нут
стыть	cool	сты́ну	сты́нешь	сты́нут

2. FORMATION OF THE PRESENT/FUTURE TENSE

TABLE 9	NO FIRST PERSON SINGULAR		
баси́ть	sing in deep voice	висе́ть	hang
голоси́ть	sing loudly	дерзи́ть	cheek
дуде́ть	play pipes	кипе́ть	seethe
очути́ться	find oneself	ощути́ть	sense
победи́ть	conquer	пылесо́сить	vacuum clean
убеди́ть	convince	чуди́ть	behave oddly

CHAPTER 3. FORMATION OF THE PAST TENSE

1) INTRODUCTION

The past tense of the Russian verb is formed from both aspects. Unlike the present/future tense it changes for gender and number, but not for person. It has four forms: masculine, feminine and neuter singular and a plural form. This is always used with the subject pronoun вы, whether it is referring to one or more people. It is in origin a participial form which used to be part of a compound past tense consisting of the participle plus a tense form of the verb "to be".

The suffix -ся may be added after the masculine form and -сь after the feminine, neuter and plural forms (see смеяться below).

2) REGULAR VERBS

A) <u>FORMATION</u>

Remove	ть	from the infinitive
Add	л	for a masculine singular subject
	ла	for a feminine singular subject
	ло	for a neuter singular subject
	ли	for a plural subject

читáть	read	читáл	читáла	читáло	читáли
писáть	write	писáл	писáла	писáло	писáли
смеяться	laugh	смеялся	смеялась	смеялось	смеялись
умéть	know how to	умéл	умéла	умéло	умéли
взяться	undertake	взялся	взялáсь	взялóсь (взялось)	взялúсь (взялись)
мыть	wash	мыл	мыла	мыло	мыли
быть	be	был	былá	было	были
говорúть	say	говорúл	говорúла	говорúло	говорúли
лежáть	lie	лежáл	лежáла	лежáло	лежáли
смотрéть	look	смотрéл	смотрéла	смотрéло	смотрéли
дать	give	дал	далá	далó (дáло)	дáли
выйти	go out	вышел	вышла	вышло	вышли
принять	receive	прúнял	принялá	прúняло	прúняли

3. FORMATION OF THE PAST TENSE

All verbs ending in a vowel plus ть, with the exception of those discussed in section 3 below, form the past tense in this way.

The past tense is always formed from the infinitive and not the present/future tense root. Compare the present/future tense roots of писáть (пишý), мыть (мóю), быть (бýду), etc with the past tense forms quoted above. The present/future tense conjugation pattern of the verb has no effect on the past tense: compare читáть and писáть (both first conjugation) with лежáть (second conjugation); умéть (first conjugation) with смотрéть (second conjugation).

B) STRESS

The past tense forms are normally stressed on the same syllable as in the infinitive. Perfective verbs with the prefix вы- always have the prefix stressed throughout the past tense (see вы́йти).

A few verbs, mainly with monosyllabic roots, have irregular stress patterns:

a) The feminine form is stressed on the ending (see быть, дать above); there is occasionally an alternative end stress in the neuter (see дать above). A complete list of these verb roots is given in table 10.

b) Verbs with a prefix containing a vowel may have this vowel stressed in the masculine, neuter and plural forms of the past tense (see принять above). Table 11 lists all such verbs.

c) A few verbs with the suffix -ся have stem stress in the masculine form and end stress in the remaining forms. There are optional stem stressed forms in the neuter and plural (see взяться above). Stress on the suffix -ся in the masculine is for most verbs now considered old-fashioned. Full details are given in table 12.

3) IRREGULAR VERBS

A) VERBS ENDING IN -ТИ, -ЗТЬ, -СТЬ

I) Formation

Remove the last three letters from the infinitive
EITHER add л for a masculine singular subject ла for a feminine singular subject ло for a neuter singular subject ли for a plural subject
OR add б, з or с for a masculine singular subject б, з or с + ла for a feminine singular subject б, з or с + ло for a neuter singular subject б, з or с + ли for a plural subject

вести́	lead	вёл	вела́	вело́	вели́
сесть	sit down	сел	се́ла	се́ло	се́ли
есть	eat	ел	е́ла	е́ло	е́ли
цвести́	flower	цвёл	цвела́	цвело́	цвели́
клясть	curse	клял	кляла́	кля́ло	кля́ли
грести́	row, rake	грёб	гребла́	гребло́	гребли́
лезть	climb	лез	ле́зла	ле́зло	ле́зли
нести́	carry	нёс	несла́	несло́	несли́

Verbs with a present/future tense root ending in д, т or н have a past tense masculine ending in л (see вести́, сесть, есть, цвести́ and клясть above), other verbs use the same root consonant (б, з or с) in the past tense as in the present/future tense (see грести́, лезть and нести́ above).

There are two past tense forms which do not conform to the above rules:

идти́	go	шёл	шла	шло	шли
расти́	grow	рос	росла́	росло́	росли́

II) Stress

Verbs ending in -ти are stressed on the final syllable throughout the past tense; those ending in -сть and -зть are stressed on the stem. The only exceptions are: the feminine form of клясть (кляла́) and the verb счесть (to consider): счёл, сочла́, сочло́, сочли́. The vowel е in the infinitive becomes ё when stressed in all verbs except лезть and сесть. Compare these two verbs with вести́, нести́.

B) VERBS ENDING IN -ЧЬ

I) Formation

Remove чь		
Add	г or к	for a masculine singular subject
	г or к + ла	for a feminine singular subject
	г or к + ло	for a neuter singular subject
	г or к + ли	for a plural subject

мочь	be able	мог	моглá	могló	моглú
стричь	cut (hair)	стриг	стрúгла	стрúгло	стрúгли
жечь	burn	жёг	жгла	жгло	жгли
печь	bake	пёк	пеклá	пекló	пеклú
толóчь	pound	толóк	толклá	толкló	толклú

e choice of г or к depends on the consonant found in 1PS and 3PP of the present/future tense: compare мочь, стричь and жечь with печь and толóчь. The vowel e always becomes ё when stressed in the masculine past tense (see жечь and печь).

Two verbs (жечь and толóчь) omit the vowel o or e in all forms except the masculine (see above). The verb достúчь forms the past tense from the alternative infinitive form достúгнуть. (see below).

II) Stress

Stress is on the final syllable throughout the past tense for all verbs except стричь, which has stem stress.

C) VERBS ENDING IN -НУТЬ

I) Formation

Verbs ending in -нуть may form the past tense as follows:

Remove нуть from the infinitive		
Add	nothing	for a masculine singular subject
	ла	for a feminine singular subject
	ло	for a neuter singular subject
	ли	for a plural subject

исчéзнуть	disappear	исчéз	исчéзла	исчéзло	исчéзли
свéргнуть	overthrow	сверг (свéргнул)	свéргла	свéргло	свéргли
достúгнуть	reach	достúг (достúгнул)	достúгла	достúгло	достúгли

This method of forming the past tense is typical of verbs which have an unstressed ending and do not indicate a single brief action. Some verbs have alternative masculine singular forms which retain the syllable нул. This syllable is never retained in the remaining forms (see свéргнуть and достúгнуть above).

The following two verbs add л to the root in the past tense:

сты́нуть	cool	стыл (сты́нул)	сты́ла	сты́ло	сты́ли
вя́нуть	fade	вял (вя́нул)	вя́ла	вя́ло	вя́ли

Verbs ending in -нуть may also form their past tense regularly (ie by removing ть and adding л). Such verbs are:

a) those stressed on the ending:

вернýть	return	вернýл	вернýла	вернýло	вернýли

b) those with the root ending in a vowel (except сты́нуть and вя́нуть):

кúнуть	throw	кúнул	кúнула	кúнуло	кúнули

c) those perfective verbs expressing the idea of a single brief action:

пры́гнуть	jump	пры́гнул	пры́гнула	пры́гнуло	пры́гнули

II) <u>Stress</u>

All verbs ending in -нуть have the same syllable stressed throughout the past tense as in the infinitive.

D) <u>THE VERBS -МЕРЕТЬ, -ПЕРЕТЬ, -ТЕРЕТЬ</u>

These three verb roots form their past tense as follows:

умерéть	die	ýмер	умерлá	ýмерло	ýмерли
заперéть	lock	зáпер	заперлá	зáперло	зáперли
терéть	run	тёр	тёрла	тёрло	тёрли

E) <u>THE VERB -ШИБИТЬ</u>

This verb root forms its past tense as follows:

ошибúться	be mistaken	ошúбся	ошúблась	ошúблось	ошúблись

3. FORMATION OF THE PAST TENSE

TABLE 10	PAST TENSE FEMININE END STRESS	
брать take	быть be	взять[1] take
вить wind	врать lie	гнать chase
гнить rot	дать[1] give	драть tear
жить live	жрать eat	зача́ть conceive
звать call	лгать lie	лить pour
нача́ть[2] begin	пить drink	плыть swim
рвать tear	роди́ть give birth (perf)	слыть have a reputation
созда́ть create	ткать[3] weave	
спать sleep		

1 Neuter may optionally be end-stressed
2 Stress is on the first syllable in the masculine, neuter and plural
3 Feminine may also be stem-stressed

TABLE 11	PAST TENSE STRESSED PREFIX	
(от)бы́ть[1] depart (при)ня́ть[4] accept	(за)да́ть[2] set	(про)жи́ть[3] live
THE FEMININE FORM IS END STRESSED (á)		

1 Only отбы́ть *depart*, побы́ть *stay*, прибы́ть *arrive* and убы́ть *decrease* have this stress pattern. побы́ть *stay* has optional mobile stress. забы́ть *forget* has the stress fixed on the stem. The remainder have mobile stress.
2 изда́ть *publish* has stem stress.
3 (про)жи́л, (про)жи́ло, (про)жи́ли are also found.
4 This root includes all verbs ending in -нима́ть in the imperfective and -нять in the perfective (present/future tense type 1L).

TABLE 12	PAST TENSE VERBS WITH SUFFIX -СЯ

M	stem stress (stress on ся́ is old-fashioned)
F	end stress
N, Pl	end or stem stress

бра́ться	undertake	ви́ться	wind	взя́ться	undertake
гна́ться	pursue	да́ться	be given	дра́ться	fight
жи́ться[1]	live	зва́ться	be called	нача́ться[2]	start
(под)ня́ться[3]	rise	пи́ться	be drunk	рва́ться	tear
роди́ться[4]	be born (perf)	созда́ться	be create	спа́ться[1]	sleep
		тка́ться[5]	be woven		

1 жи́ться and спа́ться are only used in the neuter form: жило́сь and спало́сь
2 начался́, начала́сь, начало́сь, начали́сь
3 поднялся́ or подня́лся, поднялáсь, подняло́сь (or подня́лось), подняли́сь (or подня́лись)
4 родился́ or роди́лся, родила́сь (or роди́лась), родило́сь (or роди́лось), родили́сь (or роди́лись)
5 тка́лся, ткала́сь (or тка́лась), ткало́сь (or тка́лось), тка́лись (or тка́лись)

CHAPTER 4. FORMATION OF THE IMPERATIVE

1) INTRODUCTION

There are three forms of the imperative in Russian:

PERSON	IMPERFECTIVE	PERFECTIVE	MEANING
1	дава́й(те) чита́ть	дава́й(те) прочита́ем OR прочита́ем	let's read
2	чита́й(те)	прочита́й(те)	read
3	пусть он чита́ет пуска́й он чита́ет пусть они́ чита́ют пуска́й они́ чита́ют	пусть он прочита́ет пуска́й он прочита́ет пусть они́ прочита́ют пуска́й они́ прочита́ют	let him read let them read

The first and third person imperatives are compound forms. The first person imperative (*let's read*) is formed by using дава́й (singular, familiar) or дава́йте (plural, formal) together with the imperfective infinitive or the first person plural of the perfective future tense. дава́й(те) is often omitted with the perfective future. A few verbs add -те to the 1PP of the future tense: eg пойдёмте.

The third person imperative (*let him read*) is formed by using пусть (or more colloquially пуска́й) together with the third person of the present or perfective future tense.

The second person imperative is a special form and the rest of this chapter will be devoted to its formation. It can be formed from both imperfective and perfective verbs. The form of the imperative is obtained by adding и (or й/ь) to 3PP root of the present/future tense; the вы form by adding те to the ты form.

The basic ending of the second person imperative is: и (*ты*) and ите (*вы*). This is reduced to:

A) *й/йте* after a vowel, unless the ending is stressed;
B) *ь/ьте* after a single consonant if the ending is unstressed.

Sections 2 to 4 give the full details.

The following table summarises the main endings:

ROOT ENDS IN	STRESS	ENDING ты	вы
single consonant/vowel	end	и	ите
single consonant	stem	ь	ьте
two or more consonants	end or stem	и	ите
vowel	stem	й	йте

The stress in the imperative is on the same syllable as in 1PS of the present/future tense. Thus for all verbs with mobile and end stress, the ending in the imperative is stressed. Only stem stressed verbs do not have the endings stressed.

The suffix -ся is added after й and ь, -сь after и and те.

2) IMPERATIVE ENDING IN -И AND -ИТЕ

Remove the final two letters from 3PP of the present/future tense
Add и for the ты form ите for the вы form

The following verbs form the imperative with these endings:

A) IMPERATIVE END STRESS -- ROOT ENDING IN A SINGLE CONSONANT

говори́ть	say	говори́	говори́те
сади́ться	sit down	сади́сь	сади́тесь
плати́ть	pay	плати́	плати́те
смотре́ть	look	смотри́	смотри́те
писа́ть	write	пиши́	пиши́те
идти́	go	иди́	иди́те
помо́чь	help	помоги́	помоги́те

Verbs in the above list, all stressed on the end in the imperative, have a present/future tense with either end (говори́ть, сади́ться, идти́) or mobile stress (плати́ть, смотре́ть, писа́ть, помо́чь).

B) IMPERATIVE STEM STRESS -- ROOT ENDING IN TWO OR MORE CONSONANTS

достúгнуть	reach	достúгни	достúгните
кóнчить	end	кóнчи	кóнчите

A few verbs have a possible alternative ending in -ь, ьте: see section 4 for details.

C) IMPERATIVE END STRESS -- ROOT ENDING VOWEL + ИТЬ

таúть	hide	тай	тайте
поúть	give to drink	пой	пойте

This is a small group of verbs which end in аúть or оúть in the infinitive.

D) PERFECTIVE VERBS WITH THE PREFIX ВЫ

Perfective verbs with the prefix вы́- always have this prefix stressed in all parts of the verb. The imperative is formed by analogy with the stress pattern in the basic verb or other prefixed forms of the verb root. A number of verbs will therefore end in -и, -ите in the imperative despite stem stress:

вы́йти	go out	вы́йди	вы́йдите

Compare идтú listed above.

3) IMPERATIVE ENDING IN -Й AND - ЙТЕ

Remove the final two letters from 3PP of the present/future tense
Add й for the ты form йте for the вы form

-й and -йте are added if the root ends in a vowel:

читáть	read	читáй	читáйте
одевáться	get dressed	одевáйся	одевáйтесь
объяснять	explain	объясняй	объясняйте
сметь	dare	смей	смéйте
целовáть	kiss	целýй	целýйте
плевáть	spit	плюй	плюйте
петь	sing	пой	пóйте

For verbs ending in -аúть or оúть see section 2C above.

4) IMPERATIVE ENDING IN Ь AND ЬТЕ

Remove the final two letters from 3PP of the present /future tense
Add ь for the ты form ьте for the вы form.

This ending is used when the imperative ending is not stressed and the root ends in a single consonant:

бро́сить	throw	брось	бро́сьте
гото́вить	prepare	гото́вь	гото́вьте
ста́вить	put	ставь	ста́вьте
пла́кать	cry	плачь	пла́чьте
встать	stand up	встань	вста́ньте
дви́нуться	move	дви́нься	дви́ньтесь
быть	be	будь	бу́дьте

If the ending is not stressed and the root ends in two or more consonants, the imperative ending will be -и and -ите (see 2B above). A few verbs with the ending unstressed in the imperative, whose root ends in two consonants, allow either -ь/-ьте or -и/-ите:

чи́стить	clean		чисть	чи́стьте
		OR	чи́сти	чи́стите
по́ртить	spoil		порть	по́ртьте
		OR	по́рти	по́ртите

Verbs ending in щ with an unstressed ending in the imperative can also have either -ь/-ьте or -и/-ите :

мо́рщить (лоб)	knit (brow)	OR	морщь	мо́рщьте
			мо́рщи	мо́рщите

5) IRREGULAR IMPERATIVES

A) <u>VERBS ENDING IN -ДАВАТЬ, -ЗНАВАТЬ AND -СТАВАТЬ</u>

дава́ть	give	дава́й	дава́йте	(3PP present даю́т)
встава́ть	get up	встава́й	встава́йте	(3PP present встаю́т)
узнава́ть	learn	узнава́й	узнава́йте	(3PP present узнаю́т)

These three verb roots form the imperative from the infinitive, and not the present tense, root.

4. FORMATION OF THE IMPERATIVE

B) <u>THE VERBS БИТЬ, ВИТЬ, ЛИТЬ, ПИТЬ, ШИТЬ</u>

These verbs (and their prefixed forms) have the following imperative forms:

бить	beat	бей	бéйте
вить	wind	вей	вéйте
лить	pour	лей	лéйте
пить	drink	пей	пéйте
шить	sew	шей	шéйте

C) <u>THE VERB ЕХАТЬ</u>

The verb éхать has the imperative forms: поезжáй, поезжáйте. Prefixed forms of éхать have one imperative for both aspects (formed from the imperfective), e.g. the verb приезжáть /приéхать has one form for both imperfective and perfective: приезжáй, приезжáйте.

D) <u>OTHERS</u>

дать	give	дай	дáйте
есть	eat	ешь	éшьте
лечь	lie down	ляг	лягте

PART TWO

PARTICIPLES AND GERUNDS

CHAPTER 5. FORMATION OF PARTICIPLES

1) INTRODUCTION

There are five participles in contemporary Russian:

Present	Active	Imperfective	(чита́ющий)
Past	Active	Imperfective	(чита́вший)
Past	Active	Perfective	(прочита́вший)
Present	Passive	Imperfective	(чита́емый)
Past	Passive	Perfective	(прочи́танный)

All participles are adjectives and decline like regular adjectives. The active participles do not have short forms, the passive participles have both long and short forms. Passive participles are only formed from transitive verbs.

The following table summarises the rules for forming participles:

5. FORMATION OF PARTICIPLES

PARTICIPLE	FROM	REMOVE	ADD
Present Active	3PP present чита́ют	т чита́ю	щий чита́ющий
Past Active	Past masculine чита́л	л чита́	вший чита́вший
Present Passive	1PP present чита́ем	-- чита́ем	ый чита́емый
Past Passive	Infinitive 1) (ать) прочита́ть	ть прочита́	нный прочи́танный
consonant change	2) (ить) получи́ть освободи́ть	ить получ освобод	енный, ённый полу́ченный освобо<u>жд</u>ённый
	3)monosyllabic нуть разби́ть заверну́ть	ь разби́т заверну́т	ый разби́тый завёрнутый

2) PRESENT PARTICIPLE ACTIVE (IMPERFECTIVE)

A) <u>FORMATION</u>

This participle is formed as follows:

Remove the last letter (т) from 3PP of the present tense
Add щий

чита́ть	read	чита́ют	чита́ющий
писа́ть	write	пи́шут	пи́шущий
целова́ть	kiss	целу́ют	целу́ющий
тону́ть	drown	то́нут	то́нущий
нести́	carry	несу́т	несу́щий
дава́ть	give	даю́т	даю́щий
мочь	be able	мо́гут	могу́щий
говори́ть	say	говоря́т	говоря́щий
смотре́ть	look	смо́трят	смотря́щий
люби́ть	like	лю́бят	лю́бящий
учи́ть	teach	у́чат	у́чащий

B) VERBS WITH SUFFIX -СЯ

Verbs retain the suffix -ся, even when it is preceded by a vowel. It is never abbreviated to сь:

смея́ться	laugh	смею́тся	смею́щийся
сади́ться	sit down	садя́тся	садя́щийся

C) STRESS

The stress in the present participle active is on the same syllable as in 3PP of the present tense for first conjugation verbs and on the same syllable as in 1PS of the present tense for second conjugation verbs. A few unprefixed second conjugation verbs are stressed on the syllable preceding the ending in contravention of these rules: see люби́ть above, and table 13 for a complete list.

The verb мочь (see above) also has an irregular stress pattern in the present participle active form.

3) PAST PARTICIPLE ACTIVE (IMPERFECTIVE AND PERFECTIVE)

A) VERBS WITH A REGULAR PAST TENSE

I) Formation

The past participle active is formed as follows:

Remove л from the masculine past tense
Add вший

5. FORMATION OF PARTICIPLES

IMPERFECTIVE

чита́ть	read	чита́л	чита́вший
целова́ть	kiss	целова́л	целова́вший
открыва́ть	open	открыва́л	открыва́вший
говори́ть	speak	говори́л	говори́вший
смотре́ть	look	смотре́л	смотре́вший
учи́ть	teach	учи́л	учи́вший
дава́ть	give	дава́л	дава́вший

PERFECTIVE

прочита́ть	read	прочита́л	прочита́вший
поцелова́ть	kiss	поцелова́л	поцелова́вший
откры́ть	open	откры́л	откры́вший
поговори́ть	speak	поговори́л	поговори́вший
посмотре́ть	look	посмотре́л	посмотре́вший
научи́ть	teach	научи́л	научи́вший
дать	give	дал	да́вший

II) Verbs with suffix -ся

Verbs retain the suffix -ся, even when it is preceded by a vowel. It is never abbreviated to сь:

смея́ться	laugh	смея́лся	смея́вшийся
верну́ться	return	верну́лся	верну́вшийся

III) Stress

The past participle active is stressed on the same syllable as in the infinitive.

B) VERBS WITH AN IRREGULAR PAST TENSE

I) No л in past tense masculine

a) Past tense masculine + -ший

The most common method of forming the past active participle is to add the ending -ший onto the past tense masculine:

нести́	carry	нёс	нёсший
привезти́	bring	привёз	привёзший
заже́чь	burn	зажёг	зажёгший
поги́бнуть	perish	поги́б	поги́бший
умере́ть	die	у́мер	уме́рший

This form is used:

1) for all verbs ending in -ти, -зть and -сть in the infinitive;
2) All *prefixed* verbs ending in -нуть in the infinitive (except исчéзнуть *disappear*, for which see below). *нуть* verbs with a regular past tense form the participle regularly, see вернýться *return* in section A above.

b) Infinitive formation

Other verbs form this participle by removing ть from the infinitive and adding вший:

гйбнуть	perish	гйбнувший
исчéзнуть	disappear	исчéзнувший
ушибйть	injure	ушибйвший

This form is used:

1) for all unprefixed verbs ending in -нуть in the infinitive, and the verb исчéзнуть *disappear*;
2) the verb root шибйть eg ушибйть *injure*.

II) <u>л in past tense masculine</u>

This group of verbs ends in -ти or -сть in the infinitive.

a) Participle ending in -вший

The verbs клясть *curse*, красть *steal*, пасть *fall*, прясть *spin* and сесть *sit down* form the past participle active regularly, replacing л in the past tense masculine with вший:

красть	steal	крал	крáвший
сесть	sit down	сел	сéвший

b) participle ending in -дший or -тший

All other irregular verbs ending in л in the past tense masculine replace this л with -дший or -тший in the past participle active. The choice of д or т depends on the final consonant in the root of the present/future tense:

прийти́	arrive	пришёл	прише́дший	(cf приду́)
вести́	lead	вёл	ве́дший	(cf веду́)
замести́	sweep up	замёл	замётший	(cf замету́)
расцвести́	flower	расцвёл	расцве́тший	(cf расцвету́)

Only the verbs мести́ *sweep* and плести́ *weave* retain the vowel ё in the past participle active. The remaining verbs replace ё with é (see прийти́, вести́ and расцвести́ above).

4) PRESENT PARTICIPLE PASSIVE (IMPERFECTIVE)

This participle is formed by adding ый to 1PP of the present tense. This participle is highly restricted in use and mainly formed from type 1A transitive verbs:

чита́ть	read	чита́ем	чита́емый
уважа́ть	respect	уважа́ем	уважа́емый

This form was more widely used in the nineteenth century when irregular forms ending in *-омый* were found: eg вести́ *lead* — ведо́мый, иска́ть *look for* — иско́мый. These forms are rarely used in the contemporary language.

5) PAST PARTICIPLE PASSIVE

The past participle passive is normally only formed from perfective verbs. It is only formed from transitive verbs, i.e. those which can have an object in the accusative case. There are two possible endings for the past participle passive. The most common ending is -нный; a few verbs end in -тый.

A) PARTICIPLES ENDING IN -ННЫЙ

I) Infinitive in -ать and -ять

a) Formation

This participle is formed as follows:

Remove ть from the infinitive
Add нный

прочита́ть	read	прочи́танный
услы́шать	hear	услы́шанный
потеря́ть	lose	поте́рянный
посе́ять	sow	посе́янный

There are two verbs with irregular forms, following rules for verbs ending in -ить

поколеба́ть	shake	поколе́бленный
защекота́ть	tickle	защеко́ченный

b) Stress

If the infinitive is stressed on the final syllable, the past participle passive is stressed on the syllable preceding the ending (see прочита́ть and потеря́ть above). Otherwise, the stress is on the same syllable as in the infinitive (see услы́шать and посе́ять above). In a few verbs with a monosyllabic root the prefix is stressed in the past participle passive (see table 14).

II) <u>Infinitive in -ить and -еть</u>

a) Formation

Remove the last three letters (-ить, еть)
Add енный (or ённый if the ending is stressed)

получи́ть	receive	полу́ченный
сохрани́ть	preserve	сохранённый
запо́лнить	fill in	запо́лненный
осмотре́ть	examine	осмо́тренный
преодоле́ть	overcome	преодолённый

b) Consonant Alternation

The final consonant of the verb root is subject to consonant alternation or to the addition of л. These consonant changes are very similar to those which take place in 1PS of the present /future tense of second conjugation verbs (see page 16). The following table lists these alternations:

5. FORMATION OF PARTICIPLES

INFINITIVE CONSONANT	PARTICIPLE CONSONANT
Д	Ж, ЖД
З	Ж
ЗД	ЖД
С	Ш
Т	Ч
Т, СТ	Щ
Б В М П Ф	БЛ ВЛ МЛ ПЛ ФЛ

д - ж	простуди́ть	let catch cold	просту́женный
	оби́деть	offend	оби́женный
д - жд	освободи́ть	liberate	освобождённый
з - ж	порази́ть	strike	поражённый
зд - жд	пригвозди́ть	nail	пригвождённый
с - ш	бро́сить	throw	бро́шенный
т - ч	встре́тить	meet	встре́ченный
	привертéть	screw tight	приве́рченный
т - щ	запрети́ть	forbid	запрещённый
ст - щ	опусти́ть	lower	опу́щенный
б - бл	осла́бить	weaken	осла́бленный
в - вл	поста́вить	put	поста́вленный
м - мл	утоми́ть	exhaust	утомлённый
п - пл	купи́ть	buy	ку́пленный
ф - фл	разграфи́ть	rule lines	разграфлённый

Where there is a choice of possible consonant alternations (д -- ж or жд; т -- ч or щ), the form of the imperfective will usually provide the same consonant alternation as in the past participle passive:

простуди́ть imperfective простужа́ть participle просту́женный
освободи́ть imperfective освобожда́ть participle освобождённый

встре́тить imperfective встреча́ть participle встре́ченный
запрети́ть imperfective запреща́ть participle запрещённый

Three verb roots do not conform to the above consonant alternations:

увйдеть	see	увйденный	(no consonant alternation)
изъéздить	traverse	изъéзженный	(alternation зд -- зж)
замы́слить	plan	замы́шленный	(alternation сл -- шл)

c) Stress

The stress in the participle is on the same syllable as the 3PP of the future tense. In end stressed verbs the ending is -ённый, in stem or mobile stressed verbs, the ending is -енный. A list of verbs not conforming to the regular stress pattern is given in tables 15 and 16.

III) Infinitive in -тй, -зть, -сть and -чь

a) Formation

The past participle passive from these verbs is formed from the 1PP of the future tense as follows:

Remove the last two letters (ем, ём, им)
Add енный (or ённый if the ending is stressed)

найтй	find	найдём	нáйденный
привестй	bring	приведём	приведённый
ввезтй	import	ввезём	ввезённый
укрáсть	steal	украдём	укрáденный
привлéчь	attract	привлечём	привлечённый
острйчь	cut hair	острижём	острйженный
съесть	eat	съедйм	съéденный

Note that no consonant alternations take place in this group of verbs.

b) Stress

The stress in the past participle passive is normally on the same syllable as in 1PP of the future tense. The following verbs have the syllable preceding the ending stressed: грызть *gnaw*, есть *eat*, красть *steal*, стричь *cut hair* in all their prefixed forms, and the verb идтй in two prefixed forms: найтй *find*, пройтй *pass*.

IV) <u>Short forms</u>

a) Formation

The short forms of the past participle passive for all verbs ending in -нный have a single н. The forms are:

Masculine	н
Feminine	на
Neuter	но
Plural	ны

прочи́танный	прочи́тан	прочи́тана	прочи́тано	прочи́таны
освобождённый	освобождён	освобождена́	освобождено́	освобождены́
приведённый	приведён	приведена́	приведено́	приведены́

b) Stress

For those participles ending in -ённый the stress is on the ending: -ён, -ена́, -ено́, -ены́ (see освобождённый and приведённый above). For all other verbs the stress is on the same syllable as in the long form (see прочи́танный above)

B) <u>PARTICIPLES ENDING IN -ТЫЙ</u>

This participle is normally formed from the infinitive as follows:

Remove ь from infinitive
Add ый

The following verbs have a participles ending in -тый:

I) <u>Infinitives ending in -нуть and -оть</u>

заверну́ть	wrap up	завёрнутый
све́ргнуть	overthrow	све́ргнутый
приколо́ть	nail	прико́лотый

If the infinitive is stressed on the stem (see све́ргнуть above), the stress remains on this syllable in the past participle passive; if the final syllable of the infinitive is stressed, the stress in the past participle passive is on the syllable preceding the ending (see заверну́ть, приколо́ть above).

II) Infinitive in -перéть and -терéть

The past participle passive for this group of verbs (present /future tense type 1H) is formed by adding the ending -тый to the past tense masculine (and not the infinitive):

заперéть	lock	зáпер	зáпертый
обтерéть	wipe	обтёр	обтёртый

The stress in the past participle passive is on the same syllable as in the past tense masculine.

III) Monosyllabic verb roots

Most monosyllabic verb roots, especially those with a present/future tense of types 1J, K, L, M or N, have a past participle passive ending in -тый. A complete list is given in table 17.

разби́ть	smash	разби́тый
закры́ть	close	закры́тый
начáть	begin	нáчатый
приня́ть	take	при́нятый

Note the irregular form: (прó)клятый from the verb (про)кля́сть *curse*.

The stress in the past participle passive is usually on the same syllable as in the infinitive. In a few cases the stress is on the prefix, if the prefix contains a vowel (see приня́ть and начáть above). Details of the stress pattern of all verbs in this group are given in table 17.

IV) Short forms

The short forms of the past participle passive ending in -тый are regular, ending in:

Masculine	т
Feminine	та
Neuter	то
Plural	ты

завёрнутый	завёрнут	завёрнута	завёрнуто	завёрнуты
зáпертый	зáперт	запертá	зáперто	зáперты
закры́тый	закры́т	закры́та	закры́то	закры́ты
при́нятый	при́нят	принятá	при́нято	при́няты

The stress is on the same syllable as in the long form with the exception of a few verbs where the feminine form is stressed on the ending (see заперта́ and принята́ above). The details of the stress pattern are given in table 17.

C) HISTORICAL NOTE

It is possible to form the past participle from a few imperfective verbs. This is restricted to simple unprefixed verbs which form the perfective by prefixation: e.g. писа́ть -- пи́санный *write*, чита́ть -- чи́танный *read*, бить -- би́тый *beat*, говори́ть -- говорённый *say*. The rules for forming them are the same as for perfecive verbs. Such verbs are only rarely used in the contemporary language.

TABLE 13	PRESENT PARTICIPLE ACTIVE -- STRESS				
SECOND CONJUGATION VERBS MOBILE stress in present tense STEM stress in present participle active					
беси́ть	enrage[1]	вари́ть	boil[1]	губи́ть	ruin
дразни́ть	tease	души́ть	strangle	дыша́ть	breathe
жени́ть	marry	лечи́ть	treat	лупи́ть	peel
люби́ть	love	мочи́ть	moisten	служи́ть	serve
суши́ть	dry	тащи́ть	drag	терпе́ть	suffer
учи́ть	teach	цени́ть	value	чини́ть	repair
1 stress on stem or ending (-я́щий)					

TABLE 14	PAST PARTICIPLE PASSIVE STRESS I				
MONOSYLLABIC VERB ROOTS ENDING IN -АТЬ STRESS ON PREFIX					
(со)бра́ть	gather	(за)гна́ть	drive	(пере)да́ть[1]	pass
(со)дра́ть	tear	(на)зва́ть	call	(по)сла́ть	send
(по)стла́ть	spread				
1 Short form feminine may have end stress: (пере)дана́					

TABLE 15	PAST PARTICIPLE PASSIVE STRESS II		
VERBS ENDING IN -ИТЬ MOBILE STRESS in future tense END STRESS (ЁННЫЙ) in participle			
взбеси́ть	enrage	влюби́ть	fall in love
(раз)дели́ть	divide	(за)дразни́ть	tease
(на)клони́ть	incline	(о)крести́ть	baptise
преломи́ть	refract	(пере)мени́ть	change
умоли́ть	beg	осве́домить	inform[1]
(об)суди́ть	discuss[2]	осади́ть	precipitate
(о)цени́ть	estimate	восхвали́ть	extol
1 Stem stress in future tense 2 Also присуди́ть *sentence*, осуди́ть *condemn* but not other prefixed forms			

5. FORMATION OF PARTICIPLES

TABLE 16	PAST PARTICIPLE PASSIVE STRESS III		
VERBS ENDING IN -ИТЬ END STRESS in future tense STEM STRESS (ЕННЫЙ) in participle			
(в)винти́ть	screw	(раз)двои́ть	bisect[1]
(под)зуди́ть	egg on	(с)коси́ть	squint[2]
(с)крои́ть	cut out	(раз)реди́ть	thin out[1]
(из)решети́ть	pierce[1]	(про)следи́ть	track down
затверди́ть	learn[1]	(при)торочи́ть	strap
(рас)труби́ть	trumpet		

1 End stress in participle (ённый) also found
2 The verb root коси́ть *cut* is regular

TABLE 17	PAST PARTICIPLE PASSIVE IN -ТЫЙ				
(по)би́ть	beat	(по)бри́ть	shave	(за)бы́ть	forget
взять	take	(раз)ви́ть	develop	(на)гре́ть	warm
(о)де́ть	dress	(на)ду́ть	inflate	(на)жа́ть	press
(с)жать	reap	(про)жи́ть	live	зача́ть	conceive
(про)кля́сть	curse	(по)кры́ть	cover	(на)ли́ть	pour
(по)мы́ть	wash	(с)мять	crumple	нача́ть	begin
(при)ня́ть	receive	(про)пе́ть	sing	(рас)пи́ть	drink up
(рас)пя́ть	crucify	(за)ры́ть	bury	(об)у́ть	put on shoes
(с)шить	sew				

STRESS

Stress is on the same syllable as in the infinitive except

(1) (про)кля́сть, нача́ть have stress on prefix, except end-stress on feminine short form

(2) (про)жи́ть разви́ть, (на)ли́ть (and other prefixed forms not mentioned in (3)) are identical with pattern 1 except that stress on stem is an alternative form in all forms apart from feminine short form

(3) взять, (об)ви́ть (and other prefixed forms except разви́ть), зача́ть, (рас)пи́ть, (пере/под/раз)ли́ть have stress as in infinitive, except for end-stress in feminine short form.

CHAPTER 6. FORMATION OF GERUNDS

1) INTRODUCTION

There are two gerunds in use in contemporary Russian:

Imperfective	(present)	(читáя)
Perfective	(past)	(прочитáв)

The labels *present* and *past* do not refer to their use but to the part of the verb from which they are normally formed.

The following table summarises the rules for forming gerunds:

GERUND	FROM	REMOVE	ADD
Imperfective	3PP present читáют говоря́т ýчат	ют/ут/ят/ат читá говор уч	я (а) читáя говоря́ учá
Perfective	past masculine прочитáл	л прочитá	в прочитáв

2) IMPERFECTIVE (PRESENT)

A) <u>FORMATION</u>

This gerund is formed from 3PP of the present tense as follows:

Remove the last two letters (ют, ут, ят, ат)
Add я (or *а* after *ж*, *ч*, *ш*, *щ*)

читáть	read	читáют	читáя
целовáть	kiss	целýют	целýя
нести́	carry	несýт	неся́
говори́ть	say	говоря́т	говоря́
смотрéть	look	смóтрят	смотря́
учи́ть	teach	ýчат	учá

B) VERBS WITH THE SUFFIX -СЯ

Verbs with the suffix -ся follow the usual rules and add ся after a consonant and сь after a vowel:

смея́ться	laugh	смею́тся	смея́сь
сади́ться	sit down	садя́тся	садя́сь

C) STRESS

The stress in the imperfective gerund falls on the same syllable as in 1PS of the present tense. The only exceptions to this stress rule are: глядéть *look* -- гля́дя, лежáть *lie* -- лёжа, сидéть *sit* - си́дя and стоя́ть *stand* -- сто́я.

D) IRREGULAR FORMATION

I) быть

The imperfective gerund is бу́дучи.

II) -давáть, -знавáть, -ставáть

These verb roots form the imperfective gerund from the infinitive:

давáть	give	давáя	(cf 3PP даю́т)
узнавáть	find out	узнавáя	(cf 3PP узнаю́т)
вставáть	get up	вставáя	(cf 3PP встаю́т)

E) LACK OF IMPERFECTIVE GERUND

First conjugation verbs, types C (-нуть), F (-чь), H (-ерéть) and K (-ить) do not have imperfective gerunds. Many other verbs, especially type 1B and 1N verbs either do not form an imperfective gerund or use it rarely (see tables 18 and 19).

3) PERFECTIVE (PAST)

A) VERBS WITH A REGULAR PAST TENSE

I) Formation

The perfective gerund is formed from the masculine past tense as follows:

Remove л Add в

прочита́ть	read	прочита́л	прочита́в
поцелова́ть	kiss	поцелова́л	поцелова́в
откры́ть	open	откры́л	откры́в
поговори́ть	speak	поговори́л	поговори́в
посмотре́ть	look	посмотре́л	посмотре́в
научи́ть	teach	научи́л	научи́в
дать	give	дал	дав

II) <u>Verbs with the suffix -ся</u>

Verbs with the suffix -ся replace *-лся* in the past tense masculine with вшись:

засмея́ться	laugh	засмея́лся	засмея́вшись
верну́ться	return	верну́лся	верну́вшись

III) <u>Stress</u>

The perfective gerund is stressed on the same syllable as the infinitive.

B) <u>VERBS WITH AN IRREGULAR PAST TENSE</u>

I) <u>Verbs ending in -ти, -зть, -сть</u>

Three endings are possible:

a) Gerund ending in в

Some verbs are formed regularly by removing *л* from the past tense masculine and adding в:

сесть	sit down	сел	сев
упа́сть	fall	упа́л	упа́в

b) Gerund ending in -ши

The perfective gerund is formed by adding -ши onto the past tense masculine.

зале́зть	climb	зале́з	зале́зши

The verb расцвести́ *flower* has the perfective gerund расцве́тши.

c) Gerund ending in я

The perfective gerund is formed from the future tense using the rules for the formation of the imperfective gerund, i.e. replacing the last two letters of 3PP with я:

уйти́	leave	уйду́т	уйдя́
привести́	bring	приведу́т	приведя́
ввезти́	import	ввезу́т	ввезя́
отнести́	take away	отнесу́т	отнеся́

Table 20 lists all the verb roots ending in -ти, -зть and -сть and indicates which method each verb root uses for forming the perfective gerund.

II) Verbs ending in -чь

The perfective gerund is formed by adding ши onto the past tense masculine:

зажéчь	burn	зажёг	зажёгши
испéчь	bake	испёк	испёкши

III) Verbs ending in -нуть

Verbs ending in -нуть with an irregular past tense form the perfective gerund from the infinitive by removing ть and adding в:

исчéзнуть	disappear	исчéзнув
подвéргнуть	subject	подвéргнув

Verbs with the suffix -ся, however, replace ся in the past tense masculine with шись:

подвéргнуться	undergo	подвéргся	подвéргшись

IV) The verbs -мерéть, -перéть and -терéть

The perfective gerund is formed from the infinitive by replacing ть with в:

умерéть	die	умерéв
заперéть	lock	заперéв
стерéть	erase	стерéв

Forms ending in -ши are also found: умéрши, зáперши, стёрши.

Perfective gerunds from verbs with the suffix -ся are usually formed by replacing ся in the past tense masculine with шись:

заперéться	lock	зáпер	запершúсь

Forms ending in -еревшись are also sometimes found, often with a different meaning:

заперéться refuse to speak about заперéвшись

V) <u>The verb -шибúть</u>

The perfective gerund, which is rarely used, is formed from the infinitive by replacing ть with в:

ушибúть	injure	ушибúв
ошибúться	be mistaken	ошибúвшись

Note that many perfective gerunds from verbs with an irregular past tense are rarely used.

4) HISTORICAL NOTE

The gerund forms have undergone a number of changes in recent times. Many verbs in the 19th century formed the perfective gerund using the rules for the imperfective gerund replacing the last two letters of 3PP with я or а. A few are still found today as alternative forms to the regular form in в, which are given in brackets:

увúдеть	see	увúдят	увúдя	(увúдев)
услы́шать	hear	услы́шат	услы́ша	(услы́шав)
замéтить	notice	замéтят	замéтя	(замéтив)

The perfective gerund was often formed by adding -вши on to the past tense root: прочитáл прочитáвши. These forms are now old-fashioned.

For many of the verbs with an irregular past, discussed in section 3B, older forms of the perfective gerund, consisting of the past tense masculine + -ши were often found.

In nineteenth century Russian it was also possible to form an imperfective gerund from the past tense root (eg читáв). This has been superseded by the imperfective formed from the present tense root (читáя).

6. FORMATION OF GERUNDS

TABLE 18	NO IMPERFECTIVE GERUND	
бежáть run	врать lie	есть eat
éхать go	жать press	жать reap
лгать lie	мять crumple	орáть bawl
петь sing	плясáть dance	стлать spread
стыть cool	ткать weave	

TABLE 19	IMPERFECTIVE GERUND RARE	
брехáть yelp	вязáть tie	гнить rot
ждать wait	жрать eat	лизáть lick
мáзать oil	низáть thread	пахáть plough
писáть write	рвать tear	рéзать cut
ржать neigh	стонáть moan	тесáть cut
хотéть want	чесáть scratch	

TABLE 20	PERFECTIVE GERUND VERBS IN -ТИ, -ЗТЬ -СТЬ	
a) Gerund in в		
(про)клясть swear[1]	(у)крáсть steal	(у)пáсть fall
(с)прясть spin	сесть sit down	
b) Gerund in ши		
(от)грестú row	(раз)грызть gnaw	(за)лéзть climb
(за)пастú store	(за)ползтú crawl	(вы́)расти grow
(на)скрестú scrape	спастú save	(рас)цвестú flower
(по)трястú shake		
c) Gerund in я		
(на)блюстú watch[1]	(за)брестú wander	(за)везтú carry
(за)вестú lead	(на)гнестú compress	(по)йтú go
(за)местú sweep	(за)нестú carry	обрестú find
(с)плестú weave	(про)чéсть read	
1 rarely used		

CHAPTER 7. USE OF PARTICIPLES AND GERUNDS

1) INTRODUCTION

A) PARTICIPLES

Participles, otherwise known as *verbal adjectives*, are adjectives formed from verbs; they decline like regular adjectives. They have three uses:

A) They are used instead of a relative clause, one which in Russian would otherwise begin with кото́рый.

B) The passive participles are used in conjunction with the verb быть to make up the passive of the verb.

C) The past passive participle is occasionally used in an adverbial function.

These meanings are discussed in detail in sections 2A-2C.

The decision to use кото́рый or a participle is one of style. Participles are not normally used in colloquial speech. They are are frequently used in more formal language. The more formal the language, the greater the frequency of occurrence of participles tends to be. Participle phrases preceding the noun are more formal than the equivalent phrase with the participle following the noun.

B) GERUNDS

Gerunds, otherwise known as *verbal adverbs*, are adverbs formed from verbs; like adverbs they have one form only. They are used to replace a variety of adverbial clauses beginning with words such as: когда́, потому́ что, е́сли, хотя́, etc.

Gerunds are also rarely used in colloquial speech. However, unlike participles, frequent use of gerunds is a feature of good style. They are much used in works of literature; the use of gerunds makes Russian prose sound more beautiful.

2) USE OF PARTICIPLES

There are five participles which differ according to tense, aspect and voice (active and passive):

7. USE OF PARTICIPLES AND GERUNDS

чита́ющий	PRESENT	IMPERFECTIVE	ACTIVE
чита́вший	PAST	IMPERFECTIVE	ACTIVE
прочита́вший	PAST	PERFECTIVE	ACTIVE
чита́емый	PRESENT	IMPERFECTIVE	PASSIVE
прочи́танный	PAST	PERFECTIVE	PASSIVE

A) REPLACEMENT OF RELATIVE (КОТОРЫЙ) CLAUSES

I) Tense and Aspect in Active Participles

a) Imperfective participles

There are two imperfective active participles labelled *present* and *past*. The present participle active (чита́ющий) is used to replace кото́рый + the present tense of the verb:

Студе́нт, чита́ющий кни́гу, зна́ет моего́ бра́та. — The student who is reading the book knows my brother.

cf Студе́нт, кото́рый чита́ет кни́гу, зна́ет моего́ бра́та.

If the sentence is set in the past tense and the action in the relative clause was going on at the same as the action in the main verb, either the present or past imperfective active participle (чита́ющий or чита́вший) may be used:

Студе́нт, чита́ющий кни́гу, зна́л моего́ бра́та. — The student who was reading the book knew my brother.

OR Студе́нт, чита́вший кни́гу, зна́л моего́ бра́та.

cf Студе́нт, кото́рый чита́л кни́гу, зна́л моего́ бра́та.

The imperfective past active participle (чита́вший) must be used if the time when the action in the relative clause takes place precedes the action in the main verb:

Студе́нт, чита́вший кни́гу, зна́ет моего́ бра́та. — The student who was reading the book knows my brother.

cf Студе́нт, кото́рый чита́л кни́гу, зна́ет моего́ бра́та.

Студе́нт, чита́вший кни́гу, зна́л моего́ бра́та.	The student who had been reading the book knew my brother.
cf Студе́нт, кото́рый чита́л кни́гу, зна́л моего́ бра́та.	

b) The Perfective Participle

The perfective active participle (прочита́вший) is always used when the action in the relative clause has been completed before the action in the main verb. This participle has been labelled *past*, because it always replaces кото́рый + past tense. It can be used to translate both the forms *have read* and *had read* in English.

Студе́нт, прочита́вший кни́гу, вы́шел из ко́мнаты.	The student who has (had) read the book left the room.
cf Студе́нт, кото́рый прочита́л кни́гу, вы́шел из ко́мнаты.	

II) Passive Participles

There are two passive participles in Russian: чита́емый and прочи́танный. They are usually labelled *present* and *past* respectively. However, neither of them really indicate tense. They are merely distinguished by aspect. If the action in the relative clause is or was being performed at the same as the the action in the main clause, the imperfective passive participle (чита́емый) is used:

Кни́га, чита́емая студе́нтом, о́чень интере́сная. cf Кни́га, кото́рую студе́нт чита́ет, о́чень интере́сная.	The book which the student is reading (which is being read by the student) is very interesting.
Кни́га, чита́емая студе́нтом, была́ о́чень интере́сная. cf Кни́га, кото́рую студе́нт чита́л, была́ о́чень интере́сная.	The book which the student was reading (which was being read by the student) was very interesting.

If the action in the relative clause is or was complete before the action in the main verb, the perfective passive participle (прочи́танный) is used:

Кни́га, прочи́танная студе́нтом, о́чень интере́сная. cf Кни́га, кото́рую студе́нт прочита́л, о́чень интере́сная.	The book which the student has read (which has been read by the student) is very interesting.

Кни́га, <u>прочи́танная</u> студе́нтом, была́ о́чень интере́сная.	The book which the student had read (which had been read by the student) was very interesting.
cf Кни́га, <u>кото́рую</u> студе́нт <u>прочита́л</u>, была́ о́чень интере́сная.	

Note that the imperfective passive participle (чита́емый) is not very commonly used and many verbs do not form one at all (see chapter 5, section 4). For the majority of verbs there is only one passive participle: the perfective (прочи́танный). Imperfective passives are usually relayed by кото́рый.

III) <u>Case Agreement</u>

Participles, like adjectives, must agree with a noun in case, number (singular or plural) and gender. All the examples in the previous sections have the participle in the nominative singular, either masculine, agreeing with студе́нт, or feminine, agreeing with кни́га. The following examples show the participles being used in other cases:

Я зна́ю студе́нта, <u>чита́ющего</u> кни́гу.	I know the student who is reading the book.
cf Я зна́ю студе́нта, <u>кото́рый</u> <u>чита́ет</u> кни́гу.	
Мы говори́м со студе́нтами, <u>прочита́вшими</u> кни́гу.	We talk to the students who have read the book.
cf Мы говори́м со студе́нтами, <u>кото́рые прочита́ли</u> кни́гу.	

Note that the case of the participle will not necessarily be the same as the case form of кото́рый. кото́рый agrees in number and gender with the preceding noun but not in case. The case of кото́рый is determined by its relationship with the verb in the relative clause. In all the examples above кото́рый is nominative when rephrasing active participles, and accusative, when rephrasing passive ones. The participle, on the other hand, is like an adjective, agreeing in number, gender <u>and</u> case with the noun.

IV) <u>Order and Punctuation</u>

Participles most frequently follow the noun with which they agree and are separated from the main clause by a comma. All the examples so far are of this type. Participle phrases may also precede the noun they agree with. In this case commas are not used.

В учреждённом в про́шлом году́ комите́те произошли́ измене́ния.	Changes had taken place in the committee set up last year.

This word order is typical of very formal Russian.

B) FORMATION OF THE PASSIVE VOICE

The passive voice may be conveyed in Russian by a number of constructions, one of which makes use of the passive participle. This section will examine the various constructions which Russian can use to translate the English passive voice.

I) Participial construction

The passive voice of the Russian verb is formed by combining the short form of the past passive participle with the verb быть:

Этот дом постро́ен на́шими рабо́чими.	The house has been built by our workers.
Эта кни́га была́ напи́сана в 1969 г.	This book was written in 1969.
Эти вопро́сы бу́дут обсуждены́ на конфере́нции.	These questions will be discussed at the conference.

The present tense of быть is often used to translate the English: *has been done*, as in the first example above.

The imperfective passive is occasionally formed by combining the short form of the present passive participle with the verb быть:

Он был уважа́ем все́ми.	He was respected by everyone.

This use is now restricted to a small number of verbs. It is usual to convey an imperfective passive idea into Russian by using verbs with the suffix -ся or an active construction (see IV below).

The short form of the passive participle *must* be used in the construction with a tense form of the verb *быть* and the passive participle. The long form is only used in place of *кото́рый* (see section A above). Compare the first two examples in this section with the following examples:

Дом, постро́енный на́шими рабо́чими, нахо́дится на э́той у́лице.	The house (which was) built by our workers is in this street.
Кни́га, напи́санная в 1969 г., ста́ла о́чень популя́рной.	The book (which was) written in 1969 has become very popular.

This construction predominates in formal written Russian.

II) Change of word order

Russian makes use of the active construction but places the elements of the sentence in the same order as in the English passive. The object (in the accusative case) is followed by the verb, which in turn is followed by the subject (in the nominative case).

Петербу́рг основа́л Пётр I.	St Petersburg was founded by Peter I.
Ле́кцию чита́л Ива́н Петро́вич.	The lecture was being given by Ivan Petrovich.

This construction can be used with both imperfective and perfective verbs, unlike the participle construction which, as explained in I above, is now usually only used with perfective verbs.

Делега́ция была́ встре́чена представи́телями моско́вской мэ́рии.	The delegation was met by representatives of the mayor of Moscow.
Вчера́ прие́хала моя́ ма́ма. Её встре́тил брат.	My mother arrived yesterday. She was met by her brother.

Stylistically, the active construction is less formal. In the examples above *была встречена* is appropriate for the first formal example, but would be totally inappropriate for the second example dealing with family life.

III) Third person plural impersonal construction

Меня́ всегда́ спра́шивают, где нахо́дится Большо́й теа́тр.	I am always being asked where the Bolshoi Theatre is.
Никола́ю поста́вили хоро́шую оце́нку.	Nikolai was given a good mark.

The 3rd person plural of the verb is used without the word они́. This is used instead of construction I or II when the person by whom the action was performed is not mentioned. Either aspect verb may be used.

IV) Verb with suffix -ся

Russian also makes use of the suffix -ся added to the verb to convey what would be conveyed in English by a passive verb form:

Этот па́мятник охраня́ется госуда́рством.	This monument is protected by the state.
Дом стро́ится рабо́чими из Англии.	The house is being built by workers from England.

This construction is largely restricted to imperfective verbs and is used to compensate for the lack of an imperfective passive participle for most verbs in Russian.

For other uses of the suffix -ся see chapter 15, section 5.

C) ADVERBIAL USE OF PAST PASSIVE PARTICIPLE

The past passive participle is very occasionally used to replace an adverbial clause, in much the same way as a gerund. This use is restricted to the nominative case of the long form of the past participle passive:

Освежённый, он пошёл да́льше.	Refreshed, he went on his way. *(i.e. when he had been refreshed)*

D) ADJECTIVES FROM PARTICIPLES

Some participles have developed into adjectives. Such words behave in all respects as adjectives and always precede the noun they are qualifying. Common examples are:

блестя́щий	brilliant	from блесте́ть	to shine
бы́вший	former	from быть	to be
люби́мый	favourite	from люби́ть	to love
определённый	definite	from определи́ть	to determine

The short form of adjectives formed from past passive participles may be different from the participial short form. Compare:

participle определённый: short form определён, определена́
adjective определённый: short form определёнен, определённа

3) USE OF GERUNDS

There are two gerunds in Russian, differing only in aspect:

IMPERFECTIVE	чита́я
PERFECTIVE	прочита́в

A) <u>AGREEMENT WITH SUBJECT</u>

The gerund can only be used if it has the same subject as that in the main clause:

Идя́ на рабо́ту, Ива́н чита́ет газе́ту.	Going to work, Ivan reads the paper.

The subject of идя́ is *Ivan* as he is the subject of the main verb (чита́ет).

In the following sentence, the English translation suggests that a gerund can be used, but because Russian uses an active construction, compared with the passive one in the English, the gerund is not possible.

Престу́пника пойма́ли, когда́ он перелеза́л че́рез сте́ну.	The criminal was caught climbing over the wall.

B) <u>USE OF ASPECT</u>

I) <u>The Imperfective Gerund</u>

The imperfective gerund is used as follows:

EITHER two actions are happening simultaneously; both verbs are imperfective:

Возвраща́ясь[i] домо́й, он разгова́ривал[i] со мной.	Returning home, he talked to me.

OR while the action expressed by the gerund is taking place, another complete action takes place; the main verb is perfective, the gerund is imperfective:

Идя́[i] на рабо́ту, он уви́дел[p] дру́га.	Going to work, he saw his friend.

II) The Perfective Gerund

The perfective gerund is used when two actions are happening in succession; the action expressed by the gerund is complete before the action in the main verb starts:

Верну́вшись[р] домо́й, он на́чал[р] рабо́ту.	Returning home, he started work.

In the first example in section I he has not yet reached home: he was talking on the way home. In the example in this section, he started work *after* he got home.

C) TENSE

Gerunds do not have tense, the tense can be worked out from the context. Imperfective gerunds have the same tense as the main verb (usually present or past):

Возвраща́ясь домо́й, мы разгова́риваем.	Returning home, we talk.
cf Когда́ мы возвраща́емся домо́й, мы разгова́риваем.	
Возвраща́ясь домо́й, мы разгова́ривали.	Returning home, we talked.
cf Когда́ мы возвраща́лись домо́й, мы разгова́ривали.	

Perfective gerunds are usually either past or future, again depending on the tense of the main verb:

Верну́вшись домо́й, он на́чал рабо́ту.	Returning home, he started work.
cf Когда́ он верну́лся домо́й, он на́чал рабо́ту.	
Верну́вшись домо́й, он начнёт рабо́ту.	Returning home, he will start work.
cf Когда́ он вернётся домо́й, он начнёт рабо́ту.	

D) POSITION OF GERUND CLAUSES

In all the examples so far, the gerund clause has preceded the main clause. Although this may be the most common position for the gerund clause, it is also frequently found in the middle of or following the main clause:

Студе́нт, сидя́ в библиоте́ке, чита́л кни́гу.	The student, sitting in the library, was reading the book.
Студе́нт сиде́л в библиоте́ке, чита́я кни́гу.	The student was sitting in the library, reading a book.

E) ADVERBIAL USES

In all the examples quoted above, the gerund is replacing a time clause and can be rephrased using the conjunction когда́. The gerund can, however, also replace other adverbial clauses.

I) because

Мы спеши́ли домо́й, боя́сь (потому́ что мы боя́лись) надвига́вшейся грозы́.	We rushed home, fearing (because we feared) the approaching storm.

II) if

Пообеща́в (Если он пообеща́л) прие́хать, он обяза́тельно прие́дет.	Promising (If he promised) to come, he will definitely come.

III) although

Прочита́в (Хотя́ он прочита́л) кни́гу, он всё-таки́ не зна́ет фами́лии гла́вного геро́я.	Reading (Although he has read) the book, he still does not know the surname of the main character.

IV) without (negative gerund)

Она́ вы́шла, не отве́тив.	She went out without answering

4) TRANSLATION OF PARTICIPLES AND GERUNDS

A) PARTICIPLES

I) Present/past imperfective active (чита́ющий/прочита́вший)

These two participles are either translated by the full form: *who is/was reading* or simply by the verb form in -ing: *reading*.

Студе́нт, чита́ющий (чита́вший) кни́гу, зна́л моего́ бра́та.	The student (who was) reading the book knew my brother.

II) Past perfective active (прочита́вший)

This participle is always translated in full:

Студе́нт, прочита́вший кни́гу, вы́шел из ко́мнаты.	The student who has (had) read the book left the room.

The translation: *having read the book* is not normally suitable, as it suggests an adverbial idea (and therefore a gerund in Russian) that first the student read the book and then left the room, rather than the (participial) idea of identifying which student left the room.

III) Passive participles

These participles are frequently translated without *who* or *which*, as follows:

Кни́га, чита́емая студе́нтом, о́чень интере́сная.	The book (which is) being read by the student is very interesting.
Кни́га, прочи́танная студе́нтом, о́чень интере́сная.	The book (which has been) read by the student is very interesting.

B) GERUNDS

I) Imperfective gerund

The imperfective gerund is translated by the verb form in -ing or by forms such as: *when doing, while doing*:

Возвраща́ясь домо́й, мы разгова́ривали.	(When/ While) Returning home, we talked.

II) Perfective gerund

The perfective gerund is translated in one of the following ways: the verb form in -ing, *having done*, *on doing*, *after doing*, *after having done*:

Верну́вшись домо́й, он на́чал рабо́ту.	Returning (Having returned, On returning, After returning, After having returned) home, he started work.

The form *(after) having returned* sounds somewhat stilted in English. It should not be used regularly to translate the perfective gerund, especially as the use of the gerund in Russian is a sign of good literary style.

III) <u>General</u>

Note that in Russian there is a choice of two alternatives:

(a) the gerund
(b) когда́, etc plus a tense form.

In English there are many more alternatives:

(a) the form in -ing
(b) the form *having done* (perfective gerund only)
(c) *when*, etc plus a tense form
(d) *when*, *while*, *after*, *on* plus a form in -ing.

In Russian you CANNOT use a gerund with a conjunction (such as когда́) or with a preposition (such as в or на).

The gerund is regularly translated into English by two main clauses:

Возвраща́ясь домо́й, мы разгова́ривали.	We were returning home and talking.
Верну́вшись домо́й, он на́чал рабо́ту.	He returned home and started work.

C) <u>ING</u>

The English verb form in -ing can be translated in the following ways into Russian:

I) <u>Tense forms</u>

Он чита́ет кни́гу.	He is reading the book.
Он чита́л кни́гу.	He was reading the book.

Russian NEVER uses participles or gerunds to translate such sentences.

II) <u>Gerunds</u>

The -ing form may require a gerund of either aspect, depending on the principles explained in section 3B:

Возвраща́ясь домо́й, мы разгова́ривали.	<u>Returning</u> home, we talked.

Верну́вшись домо́й, он на́чал рабо́ту.	Returning home, he started work.

III) Participles

The -ing form of the verb may translate an imperfective active participle:

Студе́нт, чита́ющий (чита́вший) кни́гу, зна́л моего́ бра́та.	The student reading the book knew my brother.

IV) Ambiguous Cases

When the form in -ing follows a noun, English displays a potential ambiguity, not present in the Russian; the translation into Russian may require either a participle or a gerund:

Студе́нт, сидя́/сидя́щий за столо́м, писа́л письмо́.	The student sitting at his desk was writing a letter.

If the sentence simply means that the student was sitting at his desk and (at the same time) was writing a letter, then a gerund (сидя́) should be used. If, on the other hand, you are trying to identify which student was writing a letter (the one sitting at his desk or the one standing in the corner), the participle (сидя́щий) is the correct translation. Although there is ambiguity in a sentence taken out of context, there is rarely any such ambiguity in a real situation.

PART THREE

ASPECTS

CHAPTER 8. FORMATION OF ASPECTS

1) INTRODUCTION

Unlike the other verb forms, it is not possible to produce precise rules for the formation of aspects. However, the vast majority of verbs do form their aspects according to a clear set of rules. The main methods are:

A) PREFIXATION

An unprefixed imperfective verb is made perfective by the addition of a prefix: писа́ть^{i} /написа́ть^{p} *write.*

B) CONJUGATION CHANGE

The perfective verb is second conjugation and ends in -ить, the imperfective is formed from it by changing the conjugation to first and the ending to -я́ть, or -а́ть for verbs ending in -жа́ть, -жда́ть, -ча́ть, -ша́ть or -ща́ть.

C) IMPERFECTIVE IN -ИВАТЬ/-ЫВАТЬ

The perfective verb ending is replaced in the imperfective by -ивать or -ывать. Typical aspect pairs are: imperfective -ивать, perfective -ить; imperfective -ывать, perfective ать.

These methods of aspect formation are examined in detail in sections 2A to 2C.

Verbs ending in -овать (type 1D) form their aspects either by methods A or C or have one form for both aspects. They are examined separately in section 2D.

The following table shows standard aspect formation:

section	IMPERFECTIVE	PERFECTIVE
A	basic verb *чита́ть*ⁱ	prefix + verb *прочита́ть*ᵖ
B	я́ть (а́ть) *объясня́ть*ⁱ	ить *объясни́ть*ᵖ
C	ивать *сра́внивать*ⁱ ывать *подпи́сывать*ⁱ	ить *сравни́ть*ᵖ ать *подписа́ть*ᵖ

There are a number of other verbs which form their aspects differently. These are largely verbs which retain patterns of aspect formation which are no longer current in the modern language. They also frequently have irregularities in the formation of other parts of the verb. The majority of them for example have a present/future tense types 1B to 1N. Such verbs are examined in section 3.

For the sake of clarity all the examples are given with the imperfective aspect preceding the perfective.

2) STANDARD FORMATION

A) <u>PREFIXATION</u>

Any imperfective verb which does not already have a prefix can form the perfective by the addition of a prefix. The prefixes which do not change the meaning of the verb are discussed in this section (see also chapter 9 section 1). The different forms that the prefixes can take are discussed in chapter 16. Other uses of prefixes which change the meaning of the basic verb in some way are discussed in chapters 17 and 18.

The most commonly used prefix is по-. Originally these prefixes had a concrete meaning: eg написа́тьᵖ *write on*, раста́ятьᵖ *melt in different directions*. In many verbs of this group the meaning of the prefix has been lost altogether: ви́детьⁱ/уви́детьᵖ *see*, де́латьⁱ/сде́латьᵖ *do*.

8. FORMATION OF ASPECTS

The following table lists the prefixes in alphabetical order.

вз (взо, вс)	взволнова́ть^{p}	excite
воз (вос)	воспо́льзоваться^{p}	use
вы	вы́пить^{p}	drink
за	заплати́ть^{p}	pay
из (изо, ис)	испе́чь^{p}	bake
на	написа́ть^{p}	write
о	опубликова́ть^{p}	publish
от (ото)	отпра́здновать^{p}	celebrate
пере	переночева́ть^{p}	spend the night
по	посмотре́ть^{p}	look
под (подо)	подгото́вить^{p}	prepare
при	присни́ться^{p}	dream
про	прочита́ть^{p}	read
раз (разо, рас)	раста́ять^{p}	melt
с (со)	сде́лать^{p}	make, do
у	уви́деть^{p}	see

Prefixation is used in aspect formation with the following groups of verbs:

I) Action verbs

Verbs conveying an action which will cause the object to change in some way use prefixation to form perfectives:

шить^{i} *с*шить^{p} (пла́тье) *sew (dress)*
учи́ть^{i} *вы́*учить^{p} (стихотворе́ние) *learn (poem)*

Some verbs may have a variety of prefixed perfective forms depending on the nature of the object:

бить^{i}
- *по*би́ть^{p} (ребёнка) *hit (child)*
- *раз*би́ть^{p} (посу́ду) *smash (crockery)*
- *с*бить^{p} (ма́сло) *churn (butter)*
- *про*би́ть^{p} (в ко́локол) *strike (bell)*
- *по*би́ть^{p} (ка́рту) *cover (card)*

II) Change of state

Prefixation is used with verbs having the meaning that the object or subject has changed state:

со́хнуть^{i} *вы́*сохнуть^{p} *dry out* старе́ть^{i} *по*старе́ть^{p} *grow old*

III) Verbs of speech, feelings, perception

Verbs introducing speech, referring to feelings, emotions and verbs of perception are subject to prefixation:

шути́ть^{i} *по*шути́ть^{p} *joke* звать^{i} *по*зва́ть^{p} *call*
жале́ть^{i} *по*жале́ть^{p} *regret* ви́деть^{i} *у*ви́деть^{p} *see*

B) CHANGE OF CONJUGATION

I) Formation

Imperfective Perfective	first conjugation second conjugation	-я́ть (-а́ть) -ить

The basic verb ends in -ить and is most commonly prefixed. The imperfective is formed by changing the ending from -ить in the perfective to -я́ть in the imperfective. The ending -а́ть is found after sibilants: ж, ч, ш, щ and after жд (see section IV on consonant alternation).

определя́ть[i]	определи́ть[p]	determine
объясня́ть[i]	объясни́ть[p]	explain
повторя́ть[i]	повтори́ть[p]	repeat
конча́ть[i]	ко́нчить[p]	end

II) Conjugation

The imperfective has type 1A endings in the present tense and the perfective second conjugation endings in the future.

III) Stress

The imperfective form in -я́ть (-а́ть) is always stressed on the final syllable. The perfective may be stem or end stressed.

IV) Consonant alternation

Consonant alternation, identical to that found in the past participle passive, is found when forming the imperfective aspect. Compare this table with one on p. 43.

IMPERFECTIVE CONSONANT	PERFECTIVE CONSONANT
Ж, ЖД	Д
Ж	З
ЖД	ЗД
Ш	С
Ч	Т
Щ	Т, СТ
БЛ	Б
ВЛ	В
МЛ	М
ПЛ	П
ФЛ	Ф

Ж -- Д	провожа́ть^{i}	проводи́ть^{p}	see off
ЖД -- Д	освобожда́ть^{i}	освободи́ть^{p}	liberate
Ж -- З	отража́ть^{i}	отрази́ть^{p}	reflect
ЖД -- ЗД	загроможда́ть^{i}	загромозди́ть^{p}	overload
Ш -- С	приглаша́ть^{i}	пригласи́ть^{p}	invite
Ч -- Т	замеча́ть^{i}	заме́тить^{p}	notice
Щ -- Т	обраща́ть^{i}	обрати́ть^{p}	turn
Щ -- СТ	помеща́ть^{i}	помести́ть^{p}	accommodate
БЛ -- Б	употребля́ть^{i}	употреби́ть^{p}	use
ВЛ -- В	представля́ть^{i}	предста́вить^{p}	present
МЛ -- М	изумля́ть^{i}	изуми́ть^{p}	amaze
ПЛ -- П	ослепля́ть^{i}	ослепи́ть^{p}	blind
ФЛ-- Ф	разграфля́ть^{i}	разграфи́ть^{p}	rule (lines)

Table 21 lists all verbs which have the consonant alternation ж/д, all other verbs have the consonant alternation жд/д. Table 22 lists all verbs with the consonant alternation ч/т, all other verbs have the consonant alternation щ/т. Note that after жд the ending -а́ть is found.

A few verbs do not conform to the above consonant alternation: table 23 lists all such verbs.

Two verb roots have irregular consonant alternations:

СК -- СТ	пуска́ть^{i}	пусти́ть^{p}	let
ШЛ -- СЛ	замышля́ть^{i}	замы́слить^{p}	plan

C) IMPERFECTIVE IN -ИВАТЬ OR -ЫВАТЬ

I) Formation

Imperfective	-ИВАТЬ/-ЫВАТЬ
Perfective	-ИТЬ/-АТЬ/-ЯТЬ/-ЕТЬ

The most common combinations are:

a) imperfective -ивать perfective -ить

скле́ивать^{i}	скле́ить^{p}	stick together
сра́внивать^{i}	сравни́ть^{p}	compare
сосредото́чивать^{i} (сосредота́чивать^{i})	сосредото́чить^{p}	concentrate

b) imperfective -ывать perfective -ать

расска́зывать^{i}	рассказа́ть^{p}	tell
подпи́сывать^{i}	подписа́ть^{p}	sign
обду́мывать^{i}	обду́мать^{p}	consider
опла́кивать^{i}	опла́кать^{p}	mourn

	поддéрживать[i]	поддержáть[p]	support
	зарабáтывать[i]	заработать[p]	earn

Other combinations are:

c)	скóвывать[i]	скова́ть[p]	forge
	зарисóвывать[i]	зарисовáть[p]	sketch
	арестóвывать[i]	арестовáть[p]	arrest
d)	рассмáтривать[i]	рассмотрéть[p]	examine
e)	осмéивать[i]	осмея́ть[p]	mock

II) <u>Imperfective in -ивать or -ывать</u>

Verbs with a perfective ending in -ить, -еть or -ять have the imperfective ending in -ивать (see groups a, d, e above). A few verbs ending in -ить in the perfective have an irregular imperfective ending in -ывать without the expected consonant alternation, discussed in V below. All such verbs are listed in table 24.

As can be seen in groups b and c above, perfective verbs ending in -ать have imperfective forms ending in -ывать, unless the root ends in a guttural (г, к, х) or a sibilant (ж, ч, ш, щ), when the usual spelling rules of Russian require и in place of ы.

III) <u>Conjugation</u>

The imperfective has type 1A endings in the present tense; the perfective has the following endings in the future:

-ить, -еть	second conjugation endings
-ать, -ять	first conjugation endings (type A or B)

Verbs ending in -овать (present tense type 1D) are discussed separately in section D.

IV) <u>Stress</u>

The syllable preceding the ending -ивать or -ывать in the imperfective is always stressed. The perfective may be stem or end stressed.

V) <u>Consonant Alternation</u>

Most of the consonant alternations found in 1PS of the present/future tense of second conjugation verbs are found when forming the imperfective aspect from perfective verbs ending in -ить or -еть. Note that perfective verbs ending in -ать form the imperfective in -ывать with *no consonant alternation.* Compare this table with the one on p. 16.

IMPERFECTIVE CONSONANT	PERFECTIVE CONSONANT
Ж	Д
Ж	З
Ш	С
Ч	Т
Щ	СТ
БЛ ВЛ МЛ ПЛ	Б В М П

Ж -- Д	усáживать^{i}	усади́ть^{p}	seat
	пересúживать^{i}	пересидéть^{p}	overstay
Ж -- З	заморáживать^{i}	заморóзить^{p}	freeze
Ш -- С	спрáшивать^{i}	спроси́ть^{p}	ask
Ч -- Т	закрýчивать^{i}	закрути́ть^{p}	twist
Щ -- СТ	нарáщивать^{i}	нарасти́ть^{p}	cultivate
БЛ -- Б	вдáлбливать^{i}	вдолби́ть^{p}	drum into
ВЛ -- В	останáвливать^{i}	останови́ть^{p}	stop
МЛ -- М	перекáрмливать^{i}	перекорми́ть^{p}	overfeed
ПЛ -- П	затáпливать^{i}	затопи́ть^{p}	light (a stove)

Table 24 lists all verbs ending -ить in the perfective which do not have consonant alternation.

Three verb roots have irregular consonant alternations:

К -- Ч	вскáкивать^{i}	вскочи́ть^{p}	jump up
	перекри́кивать^{i}	перекричáть^{p}	outshout
СК -- Щ	втáскивать^{i}	втащи́ть^{p}	drag in

VI) <u>a/o alternation</u>

Perfective verbs in which the syllable preceding the ending contains the vowel о change this to á in the imperfective, unless the vowel о in the perfective is stressed: see спроси́ть^{p}, вдолби́ть^{p}, останови́ть^{p}, перекорми́ть^{p}, затопи́ть^{p} and рассмотрéть^{p} above, where о changes to á, and сосредотóчить^{p}, where the о is usually retained in the imperfective, in accordance with the above rule. The verb сосредото́чить^{p} has a less common form of the imperfective: сосредота́чивать^{i}. The verbs заморо́зить^{p} and зарабо́тать^{p} change о to а́ despite the stress in the perfective. All such verbs where the imperfective compulsorily have the vowel а́ and the perfective has о́ are listed in table 25. For verbs ending in -овать (present tense type 1D) see section D.

D) <u>VERBS ENDING IN -ОВАТЬ/-ЕВАТЬ</u>

Verbs ending in -овать/евать (present tense type 1D) have three possible aspect formation patterns. Two of them have already been discussed above: prefixation (see section A) and imperfective in -ывать (see section C). Note that the vowel о is always retained in the imperfective. The following verbs have already been quoted:

section A (prefixation):
волнова́ть^{i} ночева́ть^{i} по́льзоваться^{i} пра́здновать^{i} публикова́ть^{i}

section C (-ывать)
арестова́ть^{p} скова́ть^{p} зарисова́ть^{p}

The third method is to have one form for both aspects:

легализова́ть^{ip}	legalise
аннули́ровать^{ip}	annul

For recently borrowed verbs the aspect forms of these verbs are still in a state of flux. When first borrowed into the language, verbs have a single form for both aspects. They then develop separate aspect forms using either prefixation or (for those verbs stressed on the final syllable) an imperfective in -ывать. For many verbs the process is far from complete, as illustrated in the following examples:

пакова́ть^{i} or (за)/(у)пако́вывать^{i}	
запакова́ть^{p} or упакова́ть^{p}	pack
организова́ть^{ip} (or организо́вывать^{i})	
сорганизова́ть^{p}	organise

пакова́ть has two possible prefixed perfective forms: *запакова́ть*^{p} or *упакова́ть*^{p}. From these forms two new imperfectives have developed: *запако́вывать*^{i} and *упако́вывать*^{i}. *организова́ть* is used as both an imperfective present and a perfective future form; in the past tense it is perfective only. Two other forms have developed: an imperfective *организо́вывать*^{i} and a perfective: *сорганизова́ть*^{p}.

3) NON-STANDARD FORMATION

A) PERFECTIVE VERBS ENDING IN НУТЬ

I) Formation

The ending -нуть may be used to form the perfective from verbs with a number of different imperfective endings. For many of them the meaning of the perfective is limited to that of a single action. Many authorities do not consider that verbs with this meaning should be considered the perfective form of the verb as they add an extra meaning.

The imperfective may end in -ать or -ять:

достига́ть^{i}	дости́гнуть^{p}	reach
привыка́ть^{i}	привы́кнуть^{p}	get used to
исчеза́ть^{i}	исче́знуть^{p}	disappear
щеголя́ть^{i}	шегольну́ть^{p}	flaunt

or in -ывать/-ивать:

заче́рпывать^{i}	зачерпну́ть^{p}	scoop
застёгивать^{i}	застегну́ть^{p}	button
вздра́гивать^{i}	вздро́гнуть^{p}	flinch
обма́нывать^{i}	обману́ть^{p}	deceive

The imperfective has a present tense type 1A and is stressed on the syllable preceding -ывать/-ивать.

There are a variety of other irregularities in the imperfective forms. A complete list is given in table 26.

II) Omission of final consonant

The final consonant of the verb stem is often omitted before the ending -нуть. The omitted consonant is underlined in the imperfective form:

дви́гать^{i}	дви́нуть^{p}	move
растя́гивать^{i}	растяну́ть^{p}	stretch
засыпа́ть^{i}	засну́ть^{p}	fall asleep
выгиба́ть^{i}	вы́гнуть^{p}	bend

A complete list of such verbs is given in table 27.

B) IMPERFECTIVE FORMED BY INSERTING -ВА

A number of verbs form their imperfective by inserting the syllable ва́ immediately before the ть of the perfective infinitive. The final syllable of the imperfective (-ва́ть) is always stressed. Such verbs are conjugated in the present tense as type 1A.

I) <u>Monosyllabic roots ending in -ить, -ыть, -еть, -уть</u>

The verbs in this group include all those with present/future tense types 1J, 1K and 1M and all other monosyllabic root verbs of type 1A and 1N with the above infinitive ending, as well as the second conjugation verb зреть *see*:

умыва́ть^{i}	умы́ть^{p}	wash	present type 1J	
вылива́ть^{i}	вы́лить^{p}	pour out	present type 1K	
прожива́ть^{i}	прожи́ть^{p}	live	present type 1M	
обува́ть^{i}	обу́ть^{p}	put shoes on	present type 1A	уть
одева́ть^{i}	оде́ть^{p}	dress	present type 1N	еть
загнива́ть^{i}	загни́ть^{p}	rot	present type 1N	ить
забыва́ть^{i}	забы́ть^{p}	forget	present type 1N	ыть
обозрева́ть^{i}	обозре́ть^{p}	survey	present 2nd conjugation	

II) <u>Perfective in -еть (present type 1A)</u>

одолева́ть^{i}	одоле́ть^{p}	overcome
овладева́ть^{i}	овладе́ть^{p}	take possession of
охладева́ть^{i}	охладе́ть^{p}	grow cool

Care should be taken not to confuse this type of verb ending in -евать with type 1D verbs such as ночева́ть *spend the night*.

Four other verb roots have -евать in the imperfective with irregular perfective forms: (о)вева́ть^{i}/(о)ве́ять^{p} *fan*, разева́ть^{i}/рази́нуть^{p} *open wide*, (за)сева́ть^{i} or (за)се́ивать^{i} /засе́ять^{p} *sow*, (за)стрева́ть^{i}/(за)стря́ть^{p} *stick*.

C) <u>INSERTION OF Ы OR И TO FORM IMPERFECTIVE</u>

A number of monosyllabic verb roots ending in -ать add the vowel ы or и between the consonants of the root to form the imperfective. With the exception of спать *sleep* they are all first conjugation (types B or N). The imperfective is always stressed on the final syllable (-а́ть) and has a type A first conjugation present tense.

собира́ть^{i}	собра́ть^{p}	gather
называ́ть^{i}	назва́ть^{p}	name

A complete list is given in table 28.

D) INFINITIVE ENDING IN -ТИ, -ЗТЬ, -СТЬ, -ЧЬ

Unprefixed imperfective verbs ending in -ти, -зть, -сть and -чь (present tense types 1E and 1F) form the perfective by adding a prefix:

красть^{i}	укра́сть^{p}	steal
мочь^{i}	смочь^{p}	be able

Prefixed verbs and unprefixed perfective verbs form the imperfective by adding the syllable -ать to the stem of 1PS of the future tense:

заплета́ть^{i}	заплести́^{p}	(1PS заплету́)	braid
спаса́ть^{i}	спасти́^{p}	(1PS спасу́)	save
помога́ть^{i}	помо́чь^{p}	(1PS помогу́)	help
запека́ть^{i}	запе́чь^{p}	(1PS запеку́)	bake

The imperfective is always stressed on the infinitive ending -ать and has a type 1A present tense.

The verbs of motion везти́ *transport*, вести́ *lead*, идти́ *go* and нести́ *carry* are discussed in section J. Other irregular forms are listed in table 29.

E) STRESS CHANGE

Two verb roots сы́пать *sprinkle* and ре́зать *cut* have the following forms when prefixed:

рассыпа́ть^{i}	рассы́пать^{p}	scatter
отреза́ть^{i}	отре́зать^{p}	cut off

The imperfective has type 1A present tense (-сыпа́ю, -сыпа́ешь...; -реза́ю, -реза́ешь...), the perfective -- type 1B with consonant alternation (-сы́плю, -сы́плешь...; -ре́жу, -ре́жешь).

F) INFINITIVE ENDING IN -ОТЬ

The imperfective of prefixed verbs ending in -оть (present tense type 1G) end in -ывать. The vowel о in the root of the verb changes to а and is stressed:

прока́лывать^{i}	проколо́ть^{p}	pierce
отпа́рывать^{i}	отпоро́ть^{p}	rip off

G) INFINITIVE ENDING IN -ЕРЕТЬ

The imperfective of these verb roots with type 1H future tense ends in -ира́ть and have a type 1A present tense:

(у)мира́ть^{i}	(у)мере́ть^{p}	die
(за)пира́ть^{i}	(за)пере́ть^{p}	lock
(с)тира́ть^{i}	(с)тере́ть^{p}	rub out

H) <u>PERFECTIVE IN -АТЬ, IMPERFECTIVE IN -АВАТЬ</u>

There are three verb roots in this group:

дава́ть^{i}	дать^{p}	give
(в)ставáть^{i}	(в)стать^{p}	stand up
(у)знава́ть^{i}	(у)зна́ть^{p}	get to know

The imperfective has type 1I present tense.

I) <u>IMPERFECTIVE IN -ИМАТЬ OR -ИНАТЬ</u>

Verbs in this group end in -ать or -ять in the perfective and have м or н in the future tense root. All verbs with a type 1L future tense (eg поня́ть *understand)* are in this group, as well the following type 1N verb roots: жать *press, reap*; зача́ть *conceive*; мять *crumple*; нача́ть *begin*; распя́ть *crucify*. All the type 1N verbs have imperfectives in -инать except жать in the meaning of *press*. The imperfective has the stress on the final syllable (-има́ть or ина́ть) and has a type 1A present tense.

понима́ть^{i}	поня́ть^{p}	understand
нажима́ть^{i}	нажа́ть^{p}	press

J) <u>VERBS OF MOTION</u>

Verbs of motion form aspects in a special way. The imperfective is formed by prefixing the indeterminate imperfective, the perfective by prefixing the determinate imperfective. Full details are given in chapter 14.

приходи́ть^{i}	прийти́^{p}	arrive
относи́ть^{i}	отнести́^{p}	take away

K) <u>IMPERFECTIVE AND PERFECTIVE FROM DIFFERENT ROOTS</u>

The following verbs form the two aspects from different roots, or from roots that, though related, appear to be different:

брать^{i}	взять^{p}	take
возвраща́ть^{i}	верну́ть^{p}	return
говори́ть^{i}	сказа́ть^{p}	say
класть^{i}	положи́ть^{p}	put
лови́ть^{i}	пойма́ть^{p}	catch
ложи́ться^{i}	лечь^{p}	lie down

садиться[i]	сесть[p]	sit down
становиться[i]	стать[p]	become

The verb возвращать[i] has an alternative regular perfective: возвратить[p].

The verb говорить also has standard aspect formation with a different meaning:

говорить[i]	поговорить[p]	have a talk

The verb класть[i]/положить[p] has the following forms when prefixed:

either	докладывать[i]	/доложить[p]	report
or	слагать[i]	/сложить[p]	compose (song)

Prefixed forms of говорить, сказать and ловить form imperfectives using standard method 2C (in -ивать or -ывать); возвращать has an alternative regular perfective возвратить; prefixed forms of вернуть are discussed in table 27; prefixed forms of брать uses method 3C; prefixed forms of сесть and лечь are discussed in table 29.

L) ONE FORM FOR BOTH ASPECTS

A few verbs use the same form for both aspects. This is very common for type 1D verbs ending in -овать and -евать and has already been discussed in section 2D. Other common verbs which do not differentiate for aspect are listed in table 30.

4) SECONDARY IMPERFECTIVISATION

A number of verbs which form the perfective by prefixation, form imperfectives from the prefixed form using one of the methods described in sections 2 (B, C or D) and 3. Many of these so called *secondary* imperfectives have the same meaning as the unprefixed imperfective. Examples of such verbs are:

пахать[i]	*вс*пахать[p]	вспах*и*вать[i]	*plough*
мести[i]	*под*мести[p]	подме*та*ть[i]	*sweep*
стыть[i]	*о*стыть[p]	осты*ва*ть[i]	*cool*

The formation of such secondary imperfectives is limited by reasons connected both with the form of the verb and its meaning.

THE RUSSIAN VERB

A) FORM RESTRICTIONS

Verbs ending in -и́ровать and -овать where the stress is not on the final syllable cannot form imperfectives ending in -о́вывать. Thus whereas a secondary imperfective is possible from группирова́ть^{i}, it is not from анализи́ровать^{ip} or расхо́довать^{i}:

группирова́ть^{i}	*с*группирова́ть^{p}	сгруппиро́в*ыв*ать^{i}	*classify*
анализи́ровать^{i}	*про*анализи́ровать^{p}	——	*analyse*
расхо́довать^{i}	*из*расхо́довать^{p}	——	*spend*

B) MEANING RESTRICTIONS

I) Spatial prefixes

If the prefix, like the basic verb, has a spatial element in its meaning, a secondary imperfective, most commonly ending in -ыва or -ива is found regularly with the prefixes вы-, на-, про-, раз-, с-:

поло́ть^{i}	*вы́*полоть^{p}	выпа́*лыв*ать^{i}	*weed*
ма́зать^{i}	*на*ма́зать^{p}	нама́з*ыв*ать^{i}	*spread (butter...)*
сверли́ть^{i}	*про*сверли́ть^{p}	просве́рл*ив*ать^{i}	*bore (hole)*
коло́ть^{i}	*рас*коло́ть^{p}	раска́л*ыв*ать^{i}	*crack (nuts)*
кле́ить^{i}	*с*кле́ить^{p}	скле́*ив*ать^{i}	*glue*

II) Non-spatial prefixes

a) The prefixes вы—, на-, про-, раз-, с-

Secondary imperfectives with these prefixes are formed from some verbs:

есть^{i}	*с*ъесть^{p}	съеда́ть†	*eat*
чита́ть^{i}	*про*чита́ть^{p}	прочи́т*ыв*ать†	*read*
пить^{i}	*вы́*пить^{p}	вып*ив*а́ть†	*drink*

The secondary imperfectives are however restricted in usage to describing a repeated action. The present tense is also used to depict actions in the past, as a stylistic device to make the event appear more vivid (the so-called *historic present*). Such verbs will be indicated with the symbol † to distinguish them from normal imperfectives:

По утра́м она́ выпива́ла† (пи́ла^{i}) лишь ча́шечку ко́фе и съеда́ла† (е́ла^{i}) бу́лочку.	In the morning she would only drink a cup of coffee and eat a roll.
Брат прочи́тывает† (чита́ет^{i}) письмо́ и выбега́ет^{i} на у́лицу.	My brother read the letter and ran out into the street.

Such secondary imperfectives cannot be used to indicate a lengthy process and cannot therefore be combined with words such as дóлго *for a long time*, or with сейчáс *at present* in the present tense.

b) The prefixes за-, о-, у-

These prefixes form secondary imperfectives with no restriction in usage:

кýтать^{i}	*закýтать*^{p}	закýт*ыв*ать^{i}	*muffle up*
чи́стить^{i}	*очи́стить*^{p}	очи*щ*áть^{i}	*peel*
паковáть^{i}	*упаковáть*^{p}	упакóв*ыв*ать^{i}	*pack*
or	*запаковáть*^{p}	*за*пакóв*ыв*ать^{i}	

A few have the restrictions described in section a:

ограблять†	*rob*	одурáчивать†	*make a fool of*
уберегáть†	*protect*		

c) The prefix по–

The prefix по– rarely forms secondary imperfectives. The follow verbs are exceptional:

ги́бнуть^{i}	*поги́бнуть*^{p}	погибáть^{i}	*die*
ви́снуть^{i}	*пови́снуть*^{p}	повисáть^{i}	*hang*
слать^{i}	*послáть*^{p}	пос*ы*лáть^{i}	*send*

Compare:

благодари́ть^{i}	поблагодари́ть^{p}	—	*thank*
вéрить^{i}	повéрить^{p}	—	*believe*
дари́ть^{i}	подари́ть^{p}	—	*give (present)*

TABLE 21	PERF -ДИТЬ (-ДЕТЬ) IMPERF -ЖАТЬ		
проводи́ть	see off	оби́деть	offend
опереди́ть	outstrip	сооруди́ть	erect
(раз)реди́ть	weed out	(на)ряди́ть	dress up
остуди́ть[1]	cool	ссуди́ть	lend

1 Other prefixed forms have -сту́живать in the imperfective

TABLE 22	PERF -ТИТЬ IMPERF -ЧАТЬ		
встре́тить	meet	(за)мети́ть	notice
отве́тить	answer		

TABLE 23	-АТЬ/ -ИТЬ NO CONSONANT ALTERNATION	
броса́ть[i]	бро́сить[p]	throw
(во)нза́ть[i]	(во)нзи́ть[p]	plunge
(за)купа́ть[i]	(за)купи́ть[p]	buy up[1]
(раз)руба́ть[i]	(раз)руби́ть[p]	chop
(по)ступа́ть[i]	(по)ступи́ть[p]	act
хвата́ть[i]	хвати́ть[p]	have enough[2]
(у)шиба́ть[i]	(у)шиби́ть[p]	injure

1 Note the irregular form: покупа́ть[i] /купи́ть[p]
2 Unprefixed form only

TABLE 24	-ЫВАТЬ/-ИТЬ (-ЕТЬ) NO CONSONANT ALTERNATION	
(вы)бра́сывать[i]	(вы́)бросить[p]	throw out
прогла́тывать[i]	проглоти́ть[p]	swallow
(раз)гля́дывать[i]	(раз)гляде́ть[p]	examine[1]
(при)ка́тывать[i]	(при)кати́ть[p]	roll up
(за)ку́сывать[i]	(за)куси́ть[p]	have a snack
(за)ла́мывать[i]	(за)ломи́ть[p]	break off
(о)хва́тывать[i]	(о)хвати́ть[p]	embrace

1 Some forms of this verb have a perfective in -гляну́ть: see table 27

8. FORMATION OF ASPECTS

TABLE 25	PERF -ó*$^{а}_{и}$ть		IMPERF -á*$^{ы}_{и}$вать
(под)готóвить	prepare	(за)дóбрить	cajole
удостóить	award	(за)кóнчить	finish
(за)морóзить	freeze	(за)рабóтать	earn
оспóрить	dispute	(у)стрóить	arrange

TABLE 26	IRREGULAR -НУТЬ VERBS	
восклицáть	воскли́кнуть	exclaim
вынимáть	вы́нуть	take out
(от)дыхáть	(от)дохну́ть	rest
(про)клёвывать	(про)клю́нуть[1]	peck through
(за)мыкáть	(за)мкну́ть	lock
разевáть	рази́нуть	open wide
(у)поминáть	(у)помя́нуть	mention
(за)сóвывать	(за)су́нуть	shove in
(с)плёвывать	(с)плю́нуть	spit
(за)стывáть	(за)сты́нуть[2]	congeal
(ис)сыхáть	(ис)сóхнуть	dry up
(за)тыкáть	(за)ткну́ть	plug

1 Alternative perfective ending in -клевáть
2 Alternative perfective ending in -стыть

TABLE 27	-НУТЬ VERBS: CONSONANT OMISSION	
блесте́ть	блесну́ть	shine
бры́згать	бры́знуть	splash
дви́гать	дви́нуть	move
дёргать	дёрнуть	pull
кида́ть	ки́нуть	throw
плеска́ть	плесну́ть	splash
пры́скать	пры́снуть	sprinkle
тиска́ть	ти́снуть	press
тро́гать	тро́нуть	touch
шепта́ть	шепну́ть	whisper
(про)блёскивать	(про)блесну́ть	shine through
(вз)бры́згивать	(вз)бры́знуть	splash
(по)вёртывать	(по)верну́ть	turn[1]
(у)вяда́ть	(у)вя́нуть	fade
(вы́)гибать	(вы́)гнуть	bend
(за)гля́дывать	(за)гляну́ть	glance
(про)двига́ть	(про)дви́нуть	move forward
(за)дёргивать	(за)дёрнуть	pull
(за)ки́дывать	(за)ки́нуть	throw
(за)плёскивать	(за)плесну́ть	splash
(с)пола́скиватъ	(с)полосну́ть	rinse
(вс)пры́скивать	(вс)пры́снуть	sprinkle
(за)сыпа́ть	(за)сну́ть	fall asleep
(за)ти́скивать	(за)ти́снуть	squeeze in
(у)топа́ть	(у)тону́ть	drown
(за)тра́гивать	(за)тро́нуть	touch
(рас)тя́гивать	(рас)тя́нуть	stretch

1 The root -верну́ть, when prefixed, has an alternative imperfective form -вора́чивать. When unprefixed the imperfective is formed from a different verb: возвраща́ть.

TABLE 28	IMPERFECTIVE BY INSERTING И OR Ы			
И	(со)бра́ть	gather	(при)вра́ть	make up
	(со)дра́ть	tear off	(вы́)ждать	wait for
	(по)жра́ть	devour	(по)пра́ть	trample
	(за)стла́ть	cover		
Ы	(на)зва́ть	name	(ото)рва́ть	tear off
	(по)сла́ть	send	(про)спа́ть	oversleep[1]

1 Many prefixed forms of спать have -сыпа́ть[i] /снуть[p] (see table 27)

TABLE 29	-ТИ,-ЗТЬ,-СТЬ,-ЧЬ IRREGULAR IMPERF	
(от)вола́кивать^{i}	(от)воло́чь^{p}	drag away
(за)жига́ть^{i}	(за)же́чь^{p}	light
(про)клина́ть^{i}	(про)кля́сть^{p}	curse
(рас)кра́дывать^{i}	(рас)кра́сть^{p}	loot
(за)лега́ть^{i}	(за)ле́чь^{p}	lie low
(пере)са́живаться^{i}	(пере)се́сть^{p}	change[1]
(о)седа́ть^{i}	(о)се́сть^{p}	settle[1]
счита́ть^{i}	счесть^{p}	count[2]
(пере)счи́тывать^{i}	(пере)счита́ть^{p} or (пере)че́сть^{p}	recount[2]
(пере)чи́тывать^{i}	(пере)чита́ть^{p} or (пере)че́сть^{p}	reread[2]

1 The verb сесть when prefixed has imperfectives either in -са́живаться or -седа́ть.
2 Apart from счита́ть^{i}/счесть^{p} the root -честь is a less common alternative perfective for either счита́ть or чита́ть.

TABLE 30	ONE FORM FOR BOTH ASPECTS		
веле́ть	order	венча́ть	crown
жени́ть(ся)	marry	казни́ть	execute
обеща́ть[1]	promise	ра́нить	wound
роди́ться	be borne	сочета́ть	combine

1 The perfective form пообеща́ть is also found

CHAPTER 9. USE OF ASPECTS

1) INTRODUCTION

Most Russian verbs have two aspects: *imperfective* and *perfective*. There is much discussion about the relationship between the two aspects, the most common view being that the two aspect forms express the same basic meaning but differ only for aspect usage. Most forms of the verb are contrasted for aspect: the past and future tenses, the infinitive, the imperative, the participles and gerunds (see table 1 on p. 4). Only the present tense does not have any aspect contrast.

A true aspect pair is one where one member of the pair can be replaced by the other if:

A) an action on a single occasion (perfective) is replaced by one which occurs repeatedly (imperfective);

Он проводи́л^{p} её до са́мого до́ма.	He took her all the way home.
Он всегда́ провожа́л^{i} её до са́мого до́ма.	He always took her all the way home.

B) if an action taking place on a single occasion in the past tense (perfective) is expressed by the *historic* present (imperfective);

Вчера́ де́ти прочита́ли^{p} объявле́ние и позвони́ли^{p} по ука́занному но́меру телефо́на.	Yesterday the children read the announcement and rang the number up.
Вчера́ де́ти прочи́тывают† объявле́ние и звоня́т^{i} по ука́занному но́меру телефо́на.	Yesterday the children read the announcement and rang the number up.

C) by changing the tense of an action from the present tense (imperfective) to the simple future (perfective);

Я пишу́^{i} отцу́ сейча́с.	I am writing to father now.
Я напишу́^{p} письмо́ отцу́ за́втра.	I will write father a letter tomorrow.

D) in the imperative form by making a positive command (perfective) into a negative one (imperfective).

Включи́^{p} телеви́зор!	Switch the television on.
Не включа́й^{i} телеви́зор!	Don't switch the television on.

A few unprefixed verbs of motion have three aspect forms: two imperfective and one perfective. The indeterminate and determinate imperfectives are used to indicate the direction of the movement and frequency of occurrence. They are discussed in chapter 14.

2) THE USE OF THE PERFECTIVE

The perfective is used when

I) an action occurring on a single occasion has EITHER been completed OR has begun AND

II) the speaker or writer considers it important to stress that the action has been completed or has begun.

BOTH halves of the above definition must apply for the perfective to be used. Thus an action *may* be complete on a single occasion, nevertheless the imperfective will be used, because the speaker or writer is interested in something else other than the completion or the beginning of the action. Choice of aspect allows a Russian to express his *attitude* to the real world.

Compare the following two sentences:

Милиционе́р до́лго объясня́л[i] нам доро́гу.	The policeman spent a long time explaining the way to us.
Мы легко́ нашли́ ваш дом, потому́ что милиционе́р объясни́л[p] нам доро́гу.	We found your house easily because the policeman explained the way to us.

In both sentences a complete action on a single occasion is being described: the policeman explained the way. The difference in aspect usage results from the fact that in the first sentence we are concentrating on how long it took to explain the way, whereas in the second the reason why we found the house so easily is because the policeman (successfully) explained the way to us. It is therefore important that the action was complete.

It will depend on the meaning of the verb whether the perfective indicates that the action has been completed, or whether the action has begun. The majority of perfective verbs indicate that the action has been completed. The following types of verbs indicate that the action has begun:

A) verbs with the meaning of *to see*, *hear*, *think*, *feel*, *want*, and those expressing emotions:

ви́деть^{i} /уви́деть^{p}	see
ду́мать^{i} /поду́мать^{p}	think
интересова́ть^{i} /заинтересова́ть^{p}	interest
люби́ть^{i} /полюби́ть^{p}	love
нра́виться^{i} /понра́виться^{p}	like
слы́шать^{i} /услы́шать^{p}	hear
чу́вствовать^{i} /почу́вствовать^{p}	feel
хоте́ть^{i} /захоте́ть^{p}	want

Я шёл по у́лице, когда́ уви́дел^{p} дру́га.	I was walking down the street, when I saw my friend.

In this example, we can see the point at which I caught sight of (i.e. started to see) my friend. Note that I did not stop seeing him: the action is not complete.

B) verbs which form the perfective with the addition of the prefix за-:

крича́ть^{i} /закрича́ть^{p} shout　　　смея́ться^{i} /засмея́ться^{p} laugh

Linguists disagree about whether such verbs are true perfectives. Some authorities consider that the prefix *за-* adds extra meaning (see chapter 17, section 2P). Using the criteria given in section 1 many do act as true aspect pairs:

В кабине́те у врача́ ребёнок закрича́л^{p}.	The child cried in the doctor's surgery.
В кабине́те у врача́ ребёнок всегда́ крича́л^{i}.	The child always cried in the doctor's surgery.

C) verbs of motion form the simple perfective by the addition of the prefix по-. These forms can be used either to stress the beginning or the completion of the action. Thus пое́хать^{p} can either mean: *to set off* or *to go somewhere (and get there).*

Я пое́хал^{p} в Росси́ю и в самолёте встре́тил ста́рого дру́га.	I set off for Russia and met an old friend on the plane.
Я пое́хал^{p} в Росси́ю и там навести́л ста́рого дру́га, кото́рый живёт в Москве́ де́сять лет.	I went to Russia and visited an old friend who has lived in Moscow for ten years.

In the first example the action has begun but is not complete: I have not yet got to Russia. In the second the action is complete: I met my friend in Russia.

3) THE USE OF THE IMPERFECTIVE

The imperfective is the neutral form: it simply states that the action has taken place or is to take place. It is used when the conditions for using the perfective outlined in the previous section are not fulfilled.

It is normal to attribute to the imperfective aspect a number of unconnected meanings. The more detailed the grammar of Russian, the more meanings the imperfective aspect seems to acquire. If the (negative) definition of the function of the imperfective is accepted, then all these unconnected uses can be easily explained.

The following sentences all contain imperfective verbs, because the actions are not complete on a single occasion and therefore condition I above is not fulfilled:

Он читáл^{i} кни́гу и слу́шал^{i} му́зыку.	He was reading the book and listening to music.
Ивáн пи́шет^{i} письмó.	Ivan is writing a letter.
Он чáсто приходи́л^{i} ко мне.	He used to come and see me often.
Он хóчет жить^{i} в Москвé.	He wants to live in Moscow.

In the first two sentences the action was not complete: at the end of the first sentence he was still reading the book and listening to music. The second sentence contains a present tense verb. The present tense of the Russian verb is always imperfective, as it can never be complete. In the third sentence the action took place on more than one occasion. The fourth sentence contains an imperfective infinitive жить^{i}: he wants to *be living* in Moscow. Such verbs are discussed below in section 4C.

There are however many occasions when the imperfective is used to indicate a complete action on one occasion. This is because the second condition for the use of perfective verbs has not been fulfilled: that the completeness/start of the action should be important for the speaker or writer. If attention is concentrated on some aspect of the sentence other than the fact that the action is complete, or has begun, the imperfective is used.

Милицionéр до́лго объясня́л^{i} нам доро́гу.	The policeman spent a long time explaining the way to us.
Вы чита́ли^{i} кни́гу? Чита́л^{i}.	Have you read the book? Yes, I have.
Вы прочита́ли^{p} кни́гу? Прочита́л^{p}.	Have you finished the book? Yes, I have.

In all three examples the actions are complete on a single occasion. The first two have imperfective verbs. The first example is repeated from the previous section, where it was fully discussed. The second example is a simple question, asking whether you have read the book or not. You confirm that you have. We are not interested in whether you have *finished* the book. The use of the perfective in the third example above, changes the meaning: the questioner knows that you have started reading the book and wants to know if you have *finished* (i.e. if the action is complete).

4) FACTORS INFLUENCING ASPECT CHOICE

The perfective aspect is used to *emphasise* that an action is complete or that it has begun. We now need to investigate the circumstances in which a Russian considers that there is sufficient emphasis to warrant the use of the perfective aspect.

As the general definition of aspects outlined above is put into practice, it will become clear that usage varies depending on the form of the verb (past or future tense, infinitive, imperative) and the meaning of the verb. The frequency with which the different aspects of particular verbs are used varies considerably. Some common examples are:

A) Verbs indicating movement from one place to another or a change from one state to another are more frequently used in the perfective:

Он вошёл^{p} в ко́мнату, сел^{p} и откры́л^{p} кни́гу.	He came into the room, sat down and opened his book.
Когда́ я вошёл^{p} в комна́ту, он стал^{p} серьёзным.	When I came into the room, he became serious.

The use of the imperfective would be far less usual, as the

actions are all clearly complete and of short duration. The imperfective would indicate that the actions were habitual:

Он входи́л^{i} в ко́мнату, сади́лся^{i} и открыва́л^{i} кни́гу.	He used to come into the room, sit down and open his book.
Когда́ я входи́л^{i} в комна́ту, он станови́лся^{i} серьёзным.	Whenever I came into the room, he would become serious.

B) Verbs such as ду́мать^{i} /поду́мать^{p} *think* and хоте́ть^{i} /захоте́ть^{p} *want* are usually found in the imperfective past.

Я ду́мал^{i} , что вы придёте.	I thought that you would come.
Я хоте́л^{i} уйти́.	I wanted to leave.

The perfective will only be used when the beginning of the action is made very clear. It is frequently used in conjunction with such words as вдруг (suddenly):

Я ходи́л по го́роду, когда́ вдруг захоте́л^{p} обе́дать.	I was walking round the town, when I suddenly wanted to have dinner.
Я посмотре́л на тебя́ и поду́мал^{p} , кака́я ты краси́вая!	I looked at you and thought how beautiful you were!

C) A group of common verbs only have one aspect: the imperfective. This is because the meaning of the verb, describing a static situation, prevents it from being used in the perfective.

Such verbs indicate:

I) activity

воева́ть	*wage war*	жить	*live*
рабо́тать	*work*	руководи́ть	*lead*
сиде́ть	*sit*		

II) relationship

принадлежа́ть	*belong*	противоре́чить	*contradict*
содержа́ть	*contain*	соотве́тствовать	*correspond*

III) location

быть	*be*	находи́ться	*be situated*

IV) possession

владе́ть	*possess*	име́ть	*have*

V) state (physical, psychological, mental)

боле́ть	*be ill*	знать	*know*
люби́ть	*love*	ненави́деть	*hate*

Some verbs of state and activity do form a perfective with the meaning *to begin to perform the action*. See section 2A.

Я сиде́л^{i} в ко́мнате и рабо́тал^{i}.	I sat in the room and worked.
Он знал^{i}, что бу́дет жить^{i} в Санкт-Петербу́рге.	He knew that he was going to live in St Petersburg.

These verbs are sometimes found with the prefixes по- or про-. However, they are not true perfectives as the meaning changes: посиде́ть^{p} means: *to sit for a short time*, просиде́ть^{p} means: *to sit for a specified period of time* (see chapter 17, sections 2P, 2U and chapter 18, section 2C).

Он посиде́л^{p} в ко́мнате и ушёл^{p}.	He sat in the room for a short time and left.
Он прожи́л^{p} в Санкт-Петербу́рге три ме́сяца, пото́м перее́хал в Москву́.	He lived in St Petersburg for three months, then moved to Moscow.

D) Some verbs can be both transitive or intransitive. Their use as intransitive verbs is restricted to the imperfective aspect:

Я мно́го чита́л^{i}.	I read a lot.
Я чита́л^{i} кни́гу вчера́.	I was reading the book yesterday.
Я прочита́л^{p} кни́гу вчера́.	I read the book yesterday.
Вчера́ она́ вяза́ла^{i} и ши́ла^{i}.	Yesterday she was knitting and sewing.
Вчера́ она́ связа́ла^{p} ша́почку и сши́ла^{p} ю́бку.	Yesterday she knitted a hat and sewed a skirt.

In these examples the verbs чита́ть^{i}/прочита́ть^{p} *read*, вяза́ть^{i}/связа́ть^{p} *knit*, шить^{i}/сшить^{p} *sew* can only be used without a direct object when imperfective. When perfective, the object cannot be omitted.

In chapters 10-13 we shall look separately at the use of aspects in the past and future tenses, in the infinitive and the imperative. The use of aspect in participles and gerunds has already been discussed in chapter 7.

CHAPTER 10. ASPECTS IN THE PAST TENSE

1) INTRODUCTION

The perfective is used in the past tense when the speaker or writer wishes to stress that the action has been completed or has begun. It is found when describing a series of actions each happening in succession; when the verb describes an action, the result of which is important for what follows; when describing the point at which an action begins. All of these actions occur on a single occasion. This is examined in detail in section 2.

The imperfective is found when the action was not complete: it describes a process that was taking place but was not finished. It is also normally used when the action takes place on more than one occasion, whether complete or not. These uses are discussed in section 3.

The imperfective is also found when the action was complete on a single occasion but when there were other factors of greater interest to the speaker. The imperfective is used: if he is merely confirming or denying that the action took place; if the centre of attention is on who performed the action or to whom, or when or where the action was performed; if the result of the action no longer applied at the time of speaking; if the action was scheduled to take place but has not yet taken place; if he has tried to perform the action (but not succeeded). Further details are given in section 4.

In negative sentences in the past tense the imperfective is commonly used. This is examined in section 5.

2) THE USES OF THE PERFECTIVE

A) <u>ACTIONS IN SUCCESSION</u>

A narrative in which actions happen on one occasion in succession will make use of the perfective:

Рабо́чий верну́лся^{p} домо́й, поу́жинал^{p} и засну́л^{p}.	The worker returned home, had supper and fell asleep.

Action 1 *(returned home)* is complete before action 2 *(had supper)* starts; action 2 *(had supper)* is complete before action 3 *(fell asleep)* starts.

Когда́ он оде́лся[p], он вы́шел[p] в сад.	When (After) he had got dressed, dressed, he went out into the garden.

когда́ + a perfective verb often translates the English *after.*

Как то́лько он прие́хал[p] в Москву́, он посети́л[p] Кремль.	As soon as he arrived in Moscow, he visited the Kremlin.

Because these actions are clearly all taking place in succession, the use of the imperfective in these sentences could only convey the meaning that the actions were happening on more than one occasion (see section 3B).

B) <u>RESULT</u>

If an action has taken place and the result of this action is significant for the following context, the perfective will be used:

Я бы, наве́рное, не нашёл Ната́шу, но мне помо́г[p] почтальо́н.	I would probably not have found Natasha but I was helped by the postman.
Звоно́к буди́льника разбуди́л[p] меня́, и я сра́зу же встал.	The alarm clock woke me up and I got up straight away.

The result of the postman's help is crucial: I have found Natasha; the alarm clock woke me up with the result that I got up. To use the imperfective, it would be necessary to change the second half of the sentence.

The perfective often indicates success while the imperfective often conveys the idea of: *attempting to perform the action (but not succeeding).* Further details are given in section 4D.

C) <u>START OF AN ACTION</u>

For those verbs where the perfective indicates the start of an action (see section 2 of chapter 9), the perfective past will be used whenever the verb indicates that the action has started:

Как то́лько я уви́дел[p] его́ лицо, я сра́зу поду́мал[p], что случи́лось что-то неприя́тное.	As soon as I saw his face, I immediately thought that something unpleasant had happened.

Он вошёл в кóмнату, посмотрéл^{p} на меня́ и улыбну́лся.	He came into the room, looked at me and smiled.
Онá вздохну́ла и замолчáла^{p}.	She sighed and fell silent.
Он был возбуждён, и егó глазá заблестéли^{p}.	He was excited and his eyes sparkled.

All of the verbs marked ^{p} above indicate the point at which the action commenced. The action did not stop: in the first example I did not stop seeing his face, nor did I stop thinking that something unpleasant had happened.

Мне óчень понрáвился^{p} фильм о Росси́и.	I liked the film about Russia a lot.

(по)нрáвиться *like* is usually in the perfective past if you liked one thing: you have taken a liking to *(begun to like)* it.

Он поéхал^{p} в Австрáлию вчерá.	He set off for Australia yesterday.

Verbs of motion with the prefix по- often indicate the start of the action. Further details are given in chapter 14.

For many verbs the start of an action is conveyed by стал or нáчал + the imperfective infinitive (see chapter 18 section 2A):

Он нáчал^{p} читáть^{i} э́ту кни́гу.	He started reading this book.
Он стал^{p} рабóтать^{i} в Москвé.	He began working in Moscow.

3) THE IMPERFECTIVE: INCOMPLETE/REPEATED ACTION

A) INCOMPLETE ACTION

An incomplete action is always expressed by an imperfective verb:

Лёжа в постéли, он ду́мал^{i} о кни́ге, котóрую писáл^{i}.	Lying in bed, he was thinking about the book he had been writing.

Вчера́ он сиде́л[i] до́ма и гото́вился[i] к экза́менам.	Yesterday he stayed at home and prepared for the examinations.
В про́шлом году́ он сиде́л до́ма и гото́вился[i] к экза́менам.	Last year he had stayed at home and had prepared for the examinations..

In the first example all three actions are incomplete. In the second and third examples Russian uses imperfective verbs because there is no time limit set on staying at home or preparing for the examination. The perfective would only be used if the examination preparation had a clear result, as in the following sentence:

Вчера́ он подгото́вился[p] к экза́мену и хорошо́ отве́тил на все вопро́сы.	Yesterday he had prepared for the examination and answered all the questions well.

We can see the result of his preparation: he answered all the questions well. This use of the perfective is discussed above in section 2B.

Note that the English verb forms in the first example: *was lying, thinking, had been reading* indicate an incomplete action in progress and will therefore result in the use of the imperfective aspect in Russian. There is however no such correlation between the English verb forms *prepared* and *had prepared* and the choice of aspect. Compare the verb forms in the final three examples.

когда́ with the imperfective verb is the equivalent of the English: *as, while* (see the first example in this section).

B) <u>REPEATED ACTION</u>

Рабо́чий возвраща́лся[i] домо́й, у́жинал[i] и засыпа́л[i].	The worker used to return home, have supper and fall asleep.
Он ча́сто ложи́лся[i] спать о́чень по́здно.	He often went to bed very late.
Когда́ он заходи́л[i] ко мне, он говори́л[i] по-ру́сски.	Whenever he came to see me, he would speak Russian.

Russian normally uses an imperfective verb to convey a repeated action. English uses either the forms: *used to* (example 1), *would* (example 3) or the simple past (example 2). There is no special word to translate *whenever*: the repetition conveyed by this word is clear because Russian makes use of imperfective verbs to convey actions occurring in succession, instead of the expected perfective (see section 2A).

There are special circumstances when Russian uses a perfective aspect to convey a repeated action. Compare the following two sentences:

Он перечитáл^{p} письмó два рáза и заплáкал.	He read the letter twice and burst out crying.
Он перечи́тывал^{i} «Войнý и мир» два рáза.	He read "War and Peace" twice.

In the first example although he read the letter twice (and the action was therefore repeated), it is interpreted as a single action; it is the first in a series of two actions in succession, identical to those discussed in section 2A. In the second example reading a novel the length of "War and Peace" twice cannot have taken place on a single occasion and verb is therefore imperfective.

4) THE IMPERFECTIVE -- COMPLETE ACTION: SINGLE OCCASION

A) STATEMENT OF FACT

If the aim of the sentence is to state that the action did or did not happen, the imperfective is often used:

Вы смотрéли^{i} фильм? Смотрéл^{i}.	Have you seen the film? I have.
Хотя́ ещё рáно, но мы сегóдня ужé обéдали^{i}.	Although it is still early, we have already had dinner today.
Вчерá по рáдио передавáли^{i}, что сегóдня бýдет дождь.	They forecast yesterday on the radio that it would rain today.

In the first example, I am being asked if I have seen the film: I confirm that I have. The fact that the action is complete is not relevant. In the second example, dinner may be over but the point of the sentence is merely to state that we have had it. The third example is merely a report of what was said on the radio.

Мы пообéдали^{p} и поéхали в гóрод.	We had dinner and went to town.
Я посмотрéл^{p} фильм «Андрéй Рублёв» и объясни́л всем идéи Таркóвского.	I saw the film "Andrei Rublyov" and explained to everyone Tarkovsky's ideas.

The above examples demonstrate when perfective verbs should be used. They are not merely stating the fact that something has happened. The first example has two actions in succession (*having dinner* and *going to town*): this is discussed in section 2A. In the second example I can only explain Tarkovsky's ideas if I had seen the film (see section 2B).

As explained in chapter 9 the perfective is only used if the action is complete on one occasion and the speaker wishes to stress this fact. All five examples have complete actions one a single occasion; only the last two stress the completeness of the action.

If some other element in the sentence is being heavily stressed, the imperfective is often used, as the speaker is no longer stressing the completeness of the action.

— Кто сего́дня убира́л[i] ко́мнату? Почему́ так мно́го пы́ли?	"Who cleaned the room today? Why is there so much dust?"
— Я убира́л[i] её вчера́, а кто убира́л[i] её сего́дня, не зна́ю.	"I cleaned it yesterday, but I don't know who cleaned it today."

In this conversation, we are discussing *who* cleaned the room — all the verbs are imperfective. The fact that the action is complete is not important.

Он пыта́лся вспо́мнить, где же он встреча́л[i] его́.	He tried to remember where on earth he had met him.

The emphasis here is on the place where he had met him rather than on the action itself.

B) <u>ACTION CANCELLED</u>

If an action happened but by the time the speaker reports it, the result of the action has been cancelled, the imperfective is used because attention cannot be focused on the completeness of the action.

К вам приходи́л[i] Ива́н Петро́вич: он сказа́л, что придёт опя́ть за́втра.	Ivan Petrovich has been to see you: he said he would come and see you again tomorrow.

Ivan Petrovich came to see me but went away again. Compare this with the perfective usage:

К вам пришёл[p] Ива́н Петро́вич: он вас ждёт в гости́ной.	Ivan Petrovich has come to see you: he is waiting for you in the lounge.

The result of the action is clear: Ivan Petrovich is in the lounge.

Утром мы открыва́ли[i] окно́, но сейча́с в ко́мнате ду́шно.	We opened the window this morning, but the room is stuffy now.

The window had been opened and closed again.

Он е́здил[i] в Росси́ю в про́шлом году́.	He went to Russia last year.

He is now back home again. This usage is typical of indeterminate verbs of motion expressing *action there and back*. There are further examples in chapter 14.

C) <u>SCHEDULED ACTION</u>

If the action was scheduled to happen, but had not actually happened, the imperfective is used, as the speaker cannot be stressing the completeness of an action that has not yet taken place:

Мы пришли́ к дру́гу, кото́рый сего́дня ложи́лся[i] в больни́цу.	We went to see our friend who was going into hospital today.

The use of the perfective лёг (in place of ложи́лся) would mean that he had already gone into hospital

D) <u>ACTION ATTEMPTED</u>

A number of verbs are used in the imperfective to convey the idea that an attempt was made to perform the action, the perfective had the meaning of successfully achieving the result.

Он угова́ривал[i] меня́ уе́хать, но не уговори́л[p].	He tried to persuade me to leave but failed.
Мы до́лго реша́ли[i] зада́чу и наконе́ц реши́ли[p] её.	We spent a long time trying to solve the problem and at last we solved it.

The imperfective and perfective forms are contrasted by the lack of result in the imperfective and achievement (or non-achievement) of a result in the perfective. As in the above examples, this idea is often made explicit by repeating the verb, first in the imperfective and then in the perfective:

Occasionally, English will have to make use of two different verbs:

Он сдава́л^{i} экза́мен но не сдал его́.	He *took* the examination but did not *pass* it.

He tried to pass the examination but did not succeed.

5) NEGATIVE SENTENCES

The imperfective is more commonly used in negative sentences than in the equivalent positive sentences because the aim of a negative sentence is often simply to deny that the action took place. Whether the action was complete or not is of lesser importance than the fact that the action did not take place. It is the negative equivalent of the *statement of fact* usage discussed in section 4A.

Мой брат не приходи́л^{i} сего́дня.	My brother didn't come today.
Студе́нт сказа́л, что он не писа́л^{i} сочине́ния.	The student said that he hadn't done the essay.

Both of these sentences are merely stating that the actions had not taken place.

Мой брат не пришёл^{p}. Не зна́ю, что случи́лось: он обеща́л прийти́.	My brother hasn't come. I don't know what has happened: he promised to come.

The perfective is used because he promised but has not actually managed to come.

Студе́нт сказа́л, что он ещё не написа́л^{p} сочине́ния, что допи́шет его́ во вто́рник.	The student said that he hadn't completed the essay yet, he would finish it on Tuesday.
Студе́нт сказа́л, что он ещё не написа́л^{p} сочине́ния, потому́ что был бо́лен.	The student said that he hadn't done the essay yet because he had been ill.

In first of these two examples the negative perfective is used because he had started the essay but not completed it, in the second he was aware that he should have written it but was explaining why had not managed to do it.

Thus the imperfective is used when merely reporting that an event had not taken place. The perfective is used if one of the following undertones is present: an expected event did not take place (*my brother did not come*), the action had begun but was not complete (*the student had not finished the essay*), the action should have been performed but was not (*the student was ill and did not write the essay*).

CHAPTER 11. ASPECTS IN THE FUTURE TENSE

1) INTRODUCTION

There are two aspect forms in the future tense: the perfective future formed like the present tense but from a perfective verb and the imperfective future formed by combining the future tense of the verb *to be* (бу́ду, бу́дешь...) with the imperfective infinitive.

The perfective form is more commonly used. If the action will happen on one occasion and will be complete (or, depending on the verb, will have started), the perfective is almost certain to be used. These uses are examined in section 2.

The imperfective is used, as in the past tense, in cases when the action will be in progress but will not be complete and when the action will be repeated. This is discussed in section 3.

The imperfective is also occasionally used when the action will take place on a single occasion and will be complete if the speaker is expressing his intention to do something; if the speaker is merely stating that the action will take place; if it is not worthwhile performing the action. For further details, see section 4.

2) THE USES OF THE PERFECTIVE

The perfective future is almost always used to convey an action that will happen on one occasion in the future:

Он придёт[p] ко мне за́втра в два часа́.	He will come to see me tomorrow at 2-00.
Он пое́дет[p] за́втра в Москву́.	He is going to Moscow tomorrow.
Если она́ позвони́т[p], попроси́те её верну́ться домо́й в сре́ду.	If she rings, ask her to return home on Wednesday.

The actions (*will come*, *is going*, and *rings*) will happen on one occasion in the future. Note that in *if* and *when* clauses English uses the present tense, Russian the future tense. Verbs of motion are used almost exclusively in the perfective.

The idea of completion is sometimes very clearly expressed:

Он прочитáет^{p} статью́ ко втóрнику.	He will finish the article by Tuesday.

3) THE IMPERFECTIVE: INCOMPLETE/REPEATED ACTION

A) <u>INCOMPLETE ACTION</u>

An incomplete action in the future requires an imperfective verb:

Я бýду жить^{i} в Москвé и изучáть^{i} рýсский язы́к.	I will live in Moscow and study Russian.
— Что вы бýдете дéлать^{i} зáвтра. — Я бýду читáть^{i} «Войнý и мир».	"What are you going to do tomorrow?" "I'm going to read *War and Peace*".

All of the actions in the above sentences will be in progress: I will not finish living in Moscow, studying Russian or reading "War and Peace".

B) <u>REPEATED ACTION</u>

If you are conveying a repeated or habitual action in the future, the imperfective will be used:

Когдá мы поéдем^{p} на Чёрное мóре, кáждый день бýдем вставáть^{i} в дéсять часóв, читáть^{i} кни́ги и отдыхáть^{i} от рабóты.	When we go to the Black Sea, we will get up every day at 10-00, read books and get away from work.

The first verb (поéдем) is perfective, as this will happen only once and will be complete; the remaining verbs are imperfective, as we are explaining what our daily routine will be.

4) THE IMPERFECTIVE -- COMPLETE ACTION: SINGLE OCCASION

A) <u>INTENTION</u>

If the future tense expresses an intention to perform an action, the imperfective is often used:

Если бу́дете открыва́ть[i] окно́, убери́те с подоко́нника цветы́.	If you are going to open the window, take the flowers off the window sill.
Вы бу́дете выходи́ть[i] ?	Are you getting off?
Вы бу́дете пить[i] чай и́ли ко́фе?	Do you want tea or coffee?

The first example clearly expresses intention. Compare this with the *if* sentence in section 2, where there is no expression of intention. The second example is a standard phrase heard on a Russian bus and is enquiring whether you are intending to get off at the next stop. The third example is asking what you intend to do: have tea or coffee.

B) <u>STATEMENT OF FACT</u>

The use of the imperfective future simply to state that action will happen is much more restricted than in the past tense. It is limited to simple unprefixed verbs and the perfective can also be used without any change in meaning:

Я бу́ду звони́ть[i] ему́ за́втра. OR Я позвоню́[p] ему́ за́втра.	I will ring him tomorrow.

The imperfective aspect is more typical of informal colloquial language.

C) <u>NOT WORTH WHILE</u>

Не бу́дем спо́рить[i] .	Let's not quarrel.
Не бу́дем заде́рживаться[i] , пойдёмте!	Let's not delay, let's go!

These sentences have the meaning: *let's not do it/it is not worthwhile doing it*. A similar use of the imperfective is found with the infinitive.

CHAPTER 12. ASPECTS IN THE INFINITIVE

1) INTRODUCTION

A) INFINITIVE CONSTRUCTIONS

The infinitive is used in a variety of dependent constructions. It is commonly found after words with the meaning of:

I) obligation: на́до, ну́жно, приходи́ться^{i} /прийти́сь^{p} *must*; до́лжен *should*; сле́довать^{i} *ought*; необходи́мо *necessary*; вы́нужден *forced*; обя́зан *obliged.*

II) possibility: мочь^{i} /смочь^{p} *be able*; мо́жно *possible*; невозмо́жно, нельзя́ *impossible*; име́ть^{i} возмо́жность *have the possibility*; уме́ть^{i} /суме́ть^{p} *know how to*; спосо́бен *capable*

III) desire: хоте́ть^{i} /захоте́ть^{p} *want*; жела́ть^{i} /пожела́ть^{p} *desire*

IV) attempt: стара́ться^{i} /постара́ться^{p}, пыта́ться^{i} /попыта́ться^{p}, про́бовать^{i} /попро́бовать^{p} *try, attempt*

It is also used after a variety of verbs which have a dependent infinitive construction, such as: проси́ть^{i} /попроси́ть^{p} *ask*, реша́ть^{i} /реши́ть^{p} *decide*; сове́товать^{i} /посове́товать^{p} *advise*; люби́ть^{i} /полюби́ть^{p} *love*; after impersonal constructions with words ending in -o, such as: тру́дно *it is difficult to*, хорошо́ *it is good to* and after a few conjunctions, such as: что́бы *in order to.* The infinitive is also used on its own or with a subject in the dative, this construction is commonly found in the spoken language.

B) ASPECT CHOICE

The perfective is used when you want to (must, can...) perform a single complete action on one occasion. It can also be used with words such as все́гда *always* to convey the idea that an action can potentially take place and when warning someone not to perform an action. These meanings are examined in section 2.

The imperfective is used: (a) to convey an action that you want to (must, can...) be in the process of performing;
(b) in cases where the action is to be performed repeatedly or habitually.

Such meanings are discussed in section 3.

The imperfective is also used when one wants to (must, can) perform one action on a single occasion. It is obligatory in sentences conveying the meaning that an action is prohibited, must not be performed. It is commonly used in sentences expressing the idea that you do *not wish* to perform an action; that it is *time to* perform it; when there is a sense of *urgency* that the action must be performed; when an action is *scheduled* to happen. It is also used when simply *stating the fact* that something should be done, though this use is considerably rarer than in the past tense. Full details are given in section 4.

Following certain verbs there is a strict use of verb aspect: such cases are discussed in section 5.

2) USES OF THE PERFECTIVE

A) SINGLE ACTION, ONE OCCASION

The following examples display the infinitive used in a variety of constructions. All of the infinitives are perfective because they all refer to a single action to be performed on a single occasion.

Я хочу́ прийти́^{p} за́втра.	I want to come tomorrow.
Вам на́до прочита́ть^{p} э́ту кни́гу.	You have to read this book.
Мо́жно купи́ть^{p} тако́й стол в ГУМе.	You can buy this table in GUM.
Он постара́лся позвони́ть^{p} мне.	He tried to telephone me.
Я попроси́л его́ откры́ть^{p} окно́.	I asked him to open the window.
Тру́дно отве́тить^{p} на мой вопро́с.	It is difficult to answer my question.
Она́ пошла́ в ко́мнату, что́бы оде́ться^{p} к обе́ду.	She went to her room to dress for dinner.

B) POTENTIAL ACTION

The perfective is used to express an action that may be potentially performed. The fact that the action may be completed on a single occasion is being stressed:

Если вы хоти́те, вы всегда́ мо́жете прийти́[p] ко мне в суббо́ту.	If you want to, you can always come and see me on Saturday.

The perfective infinitive is being used because the suggestion is made that you can potentially come on a Saturday: it is not assumed that you will come every Saturday.

Ты мо́жешь иногда́ загляну́ть[p] к нам?	Can you drop in to see us sometime?

Once again, repetition is not assumed: you can drop in on some occasion(s), if you wish.

Some verbs, which by virtue of their meaning usually combine with the imperfective, may be found with a perfective infinitive if the idea of a potential action is suggested:

Мой брат, е́сли ну́жно, уме́ет испе́чь[p] хлеб.	My brother, if necessary, can bake bread.
Я люблю́ в выходно́й день отдохну́ть[p] на пля́же.	I like to spend my holidays on the beach.

In the second example the perfective is used if it has the meaning: if I have the chance I will spend my holidays on the beach. If the meaning was simply that I always spend my holidays on the beach, the imperfective (отдыха́ть) would be used.

3) THE IMPERFECTIVE: INCOMPLETE/REPEATED/HABITUAL ACTION

A) <u>INCOMPLETE ACTION</u>

The following sentences all display imperfective infinitives conveying the idea of an action in progress:

Я хочу́ жить[i] в Москве́.	I want to live in Moscow.
За́втра мне придётся сиде́ть[i] весь день в библиоте́ке.	I've got to stay in the library all day tomorrow.
Мо́жно всю неде́лю отдыха́ть[i].	You can have a week's holiday.

B) <u>REPEATED ACTION</u>

In each of the following sentences the action is to happen repeatedly:

Я хочу́ приходи́ть^{i} к вам по су́бботам.	I want to come and see you on Saturdays.
Студе́нты должны́ чита́ть^{i} книги ка́ждый день!	Students should read books every day.
Он ча́сто мо́жет де́лать^{i} нену́жные поку́пки.	He can often do unnecessary shopping.
Прошу́ вас писа́ть^{i} нам поча́ще.	Please write to us more often.
Он стара́лся звони́ть^{i} мне два ра́за в день.	He tried to ring me twice a day.

In deciding whether an imperfective infinitive should be used in cases of repetition, care must be taken to ensure that the repetition applies to the infinitive and not just to the preceding word.

Я всегда́ хоте́л^{i} стать^{p} преподава́телем.	I have always wanted to become a teacher.
Он два ра́за стара́лся^{i} позвони́ть^{p} мне.	He tried to ring me twice.

In both of these sentences the past tense verb is imperfective and the infinitive perfective, as the repetition applies only to the past tense: he always wanted to become a teacher once, he tried twice to have one phone conversation with me. Contrast this with the sentences above where the repetition applies either to the whole sentence or just to the infinitive.

C) <u>HABITUAL/GENERALISED ACTION</u>

If the infinitive is used to describe an action which happens habitually or has general application, the imperfective will be used:

Он уме́ет хорошо́ пла́вать^{i}.	He can swim well.
Мы стара́емся писа́ть^{i} интере́сные сочине́ния.	We try to write good essays.
Кни́ги ну́жно сдава́ть^{i} в библиоте́ку во́время!	Books must be returned to the library on time.

These three statements do not apply to a single occasion: the first sentence has general application, the second is what we habitually try to do and the third is an encouragement habitually to return books on time.

4) THE IMPERFECTIVE -- COMPLETE ACTION: SINGLE OCCASION

A) <u>PROHIBITION</u>

Any phrase which has the meaning that something is not allowed, not necessary always has an imperfective infinitive. The meaning also extends to phrases with the idea that something is not worthwhile. Attention is focused on the word or phrase preceding the infinitive; the infinitive is therefore placed in the neutral form -- the imperfective.

Не нáдо помогáть[i] мне.	You don't need to help me.
Не стóит откла́дывать[i] наш разговóр.	It isn't worth putting off our conversation.
Вам нéзачем приходи́ть[i] рáно.	There's no reason for you to arrive early.
При крáсном свéте нельзя́ переходи́ть[i] у́лицу.	When the lights are red you must not cross the road.

All of the above sentences express the idea that it was neither necessary, worthwhile nor permissible to perform the action. Any other phrase that acquires this undertone will require the use of an imperfective infinitive. The imperative also uses the imperfective for sentences with a similar meaning (see chapter 13, section 4B).

Special attention should be paid to the word нельзя́ as it is used in both meanings of the English word *cannot*. If it means: *it is not possible* the infinitive will be in the same aspect as with мóжно. Compare the final example above with the following one, which makes use of a perfective infinitive:

Здесь стрóят подзéмный перехóд, в э́том мéсте у́лицу нельзя́ перейти́[p].	They are building a subway here, you can't cross the road at this point.

The former example tells us what we *may not* do, the latter example tells us what we *physically cannot* do.

B) <u>NOT WANT</u>

The imperfective infinitive is most commonly used after verbs expressing the idea of not wanting to perform the action:

Он не хотéл приходи́ть[i].	He didn't want to come.

C) <u>START OF ACTION</u>

In phrases indicating the point at which an action commenced, the imperfective verb is used. на́до, ну́жно, мо́жно, etc are close in meaning to пора́ *time to*:

Уже́ 9 часо́в: на́до включа́ть[i] телеви́зор.	It is already 9-00: we must put the television on.
До нача́ла спекта́кля оста́лось 40 мину́т, мы должны́ выходи́ть[i].	There are 40 minutes left till the start of the show. We should leave.
Мо́жно налива́ть[i] чай?	Can I pour the tea?
Мо́жно нали́ть[p] вам чай и́ли ко́фе?	Can I pour you some tea or coffee?

In the first example we presumably want to watch the news, which starts at 9-00. We know that we have to switch the television on: this sentence is telling us to do it *now*. Similarly, in the second sentence if we are going to the theatre, we clearly have to leave the house: this sentence tells us to perform the action *now*.

The third and fourth sentences take place when visiting friends or relations. In the third sentence the tea is prepared and the host is asking if his guests are ready to drink some tea. In the fourth sentence a perfective infinitive is used because it is no longer asking when to start performing an action, but whether the host can pour you tea or coffee.

The imperfective is used because attention is focused on *when* we should perform the action rather than on the action itself. A similar use is noted for the imperative (see chapter 13, section 4AI)

D) <u>SCHEDULED ACTION</u>

If the idea that action *has to* happen does not indicate obligation, but simply that the action is scheduled to happen in the future, both aspects are found with до́лжен, на́до and ну́жно; the imperfective is obligatory when using a dative + infinitive construction:

Я ещё до́лжен скла́дывать[i] /сложи́ть[p] ве́щи.	I still have to pack my things.

Мне ещё скла́дывать[i] ве́щи. I still have to pack my things. The above sentence simply indicates a future task: packing my things. Used with до́лжен the imperfective is more typical of colloquial Russian; used simply with a dative case the imperfective is compulsory. This construction is very commonly found in colloquial Russian.

Compare this usage with a similar usage in the past tense (see section 4C of chapter 10).

E) URGENT ACTION

If there is great stress on the absolute necessity of performing an action, the imperfective infinitive is frequently used. The obligation word (на́до, придётся...) is heavily stressed, so much so that the very fact that the action *has to* be performed is more important than the action itself: thus the infinitive is in the neutral, imperfective, aspect.

Больно́му ста́ло ху́же, на́до вызыва́ть[i] врача́!	The patient has got worse, we *must* call the doctor.
Мы у́же опа́здываем, хо́чешь — не хо́чешь, на́до брать[i] такси́.	We are already late, whether we like it or not, we'll *have to* take a taxi.

F) STATEMENT OF FACT

The use of the imperfective infinitive simply to state that you should perform an action is highly restricted and certainly not as widespread as in the past tense. It is used in informal colloquial language in questions where the words with the meaning of *must, should* have been omitted; the action itself is obvious from the context and the speaker is questioning what he should do, or when, where, how he should do it:

— Напеча́тай[p] мне па́ру страни́ц. — Хорошо́. Что печа́тать[i]?	"Type a couple of pages for me." "Fine. What should I type?"
— Мне на́до попа́сть[p] на Белору́сский вокза́л. Где мне выходи́ть[i]?	I've got to get to the Byelorussky Station. Where should I get off?

In the first example the verb is first given in the perfective imperative (напеча́тай) and then repeated in the imperfective infinitive (печа́тать). The second example takes place on a bus — it is obvious that I want to get off but what I am asking is *where* I should get off.

5) SPECIAL VERB USAGES

A) <u>VERBS REQUIRING THE IMPERFECTIVE</u>

I) <u>Beginning, Continuing, Finishing</u>

Any verb which has the above meaning is always followed by an imperfective infinitive. The *beginning, continuing, finishing* verb will be in either aspect, the infinitive is merely naming the action that has begun, was continuing or was finished. The following verbs are commonly found:

BEGIN	
начина́ть^{i} /нача́ть^{p}	begin
стать^{p}	begin
приступа́ть^{i} /приступи́ть^{p}	set about
принима́ться^{i} /приня́ться^{p}	set about
пуска́ться^{i} /пусти́ться^{p}	set about
CONTINUE	
продолжа́ть^{i} /продо́лжить^{p}	continue
остава́ться^{i} /оста́ться^{p}	remain (sitting...)
FINISH	
конча́ть^{i} /ко́нчить^{p}	finish
зака́нчивать^{i} /зако́нчить^{p}	finish
ока́нчивать^{i} /око́нчить^{p}	finish
перестава́ть^{i} /переста́ть^{p}	stop, cease
прекраща́ть^{i} /прекрати́ть^{p}	stop, cease
броса́ть^{i} /бро́сить^{p}	give up

Он на́чал чита́ть^{i} .	He started reading.
Мы продолжа́ли говори́ть^{i} .	We continued reading.
Он переста́л приходи́ть^{i} к нам.	He stopped coming to see us.

II) <u>Habitual Action</u>

The following verbs express the idea that you are in the habit of, acquire or lose the habit of performing an action. They are always followed by imperfective verbs:

привыка́ть^{i} /привы́кнуть^{p}	get used to
отвыка́ть^{i} /отвы́кнуть^{p}	lose the habit of
приуча́ть^{i} /приучи́ть^{p}	train
отуча́ть^{i} /отучи́ть^{p}	break (habit)
учи́ться^{i} /научи́ться^{p}	learn
надоеда́ть^{i} /надое́сть^{p}	be tired of (doing)
устава́ть^{i} /уста́ть^{p}	become tired
избега́ть^{i}	avoid[1]
полюби́ть^{p}	love[2]
понра́виться^{p}	like[2]
разлюби́ть^{p}	stop loving

1 The perfective is never used with an infinitive
2 The imperfective can be used with a perfective infinitive (see section 2B)

III) Prohibition

Verbs with the meaning of *to prohibit, forbid* (запреща́ть^{i} /запрети́ть^{p}, воспреща́ть^{i} /воспрети́ть^{p}) and negative forms of the verbs with the meaning of *to allow* (разреша́ть^{i} /разреши́ть^{p}, позволя́ть^{i} /позво́лить^{p}) are always followed by an imperfective infinitive. This is the same aspect usage as that discussed in section 4A.

Он запреща́ет мне поступа́ть^{i} в университе́т.	He forbids me to go university.
Он не разреши́т сы́ну е́хать^{i} в Ло́ндон.	He won't allow his son to go to London.

B) VERBS REQUIRING THE PERFECTIVE

Verbs which require the perfective infinitive all have the meaning of *to succeed, manage*. Only the perfective forms of the verbs require the perfective infinitive. The verbs which are commonly found are: успе́ть^{p} *manage, have time to*; уда́ться^{p} *succeed*; суме́ть^{p} *manage, have gained the ability*, смочь^{p} *be able to*. The imperfective of the first two verbs may be used with an imperfective infinitive in cases of repetition.

Я успе́л прие́хать^{p} во́время.	I managed to arrive on time.
Мне удало́сь прочита́ть^{p} кни́гу.	I managed to read the book.

CHAPTER 13. ASPECTS IN THE IMPERATIVE

1) INTRODUCTION

The imperative is used to order, advise or request someone to perform an action. The negative imperative will forbid someone from performing the action or warn them to be careful. The use of apsects in the imperative parallels very closely their usage in the infinitive.

The perfective imperative is used when ordering, advising or requesting someone to perform a single action on a single occasion. It is also used when warning someone not to perform the action.

The imperfective is used when ordering, advising or requesting someone to perform a continuous action, when the action is to be repeated or to have general application.

The imperfective is also used to convey a single action on a single occasion when you are being encouraged to perform an action that is known from the context: the start of the action may be stressed, you may be using the language of polite invitation, or you may be expressing your impatience that the action has not been performed. The imperfective is also used when forbidding someone to perform an action.

2) USES OF THE PERFECTIVE

A) <u>SINGLE ACTION, ONE OCCASION</u>

The perfective is used when ordering, advising, requesting someone to perform one specific action on one occasion:

Откро́йте^{p} окно́, пожа́луйста.	Open the window, please.
Зайди́те^{p} ко мне за́втра в 9 часо́в.	Come and see me tomorrow at 9-00.

In both of these sentences you are being asked to perform one complete action: *open the window*, *come and see me*.

B) <u>WARNING</u>

If you are warning someone not to perform an action (or there will be unfortunate consequences), the perfective imperative is used:

Здесь ско́льзко. Смотри́те не упади́те^{p}.	It's slippy here. Watch you don't fall over.

Не потеря́йте[p] кни́гу, она́ из библиоте́ки.	Don't lose the book. It's from the library.
Не забу́дьте[p] прийти́ в два часа́.	Don't forget to come at 2-00.

All of these examples can be paraphrased: *be careful or you will fall over/lose the book/forget to come.* You are not ordering someone *not to fall over/lose the book or forget to come.* They can be also expressed in Russian using a perfective future:

Осторо́жно, а то вы упадёте[p]
потеря́ете[p] кни́гу
забу́дете[p] прийти́

Compare this use of the negative imperative with the use of the imperfective in the meaning of *prohibition* discussed in section 4B.

3) THE IMPERFECTIVE: INCOMPLETE/REPEATED/HABITUAL ACTION

A) <u>INCOMPLETE ACTION</u>

Сто́йте[i] здесь, никуда́ не уходи́те.	Stand here, don't go anywhere.
Смотри́те[i] всё вре́мя вперёд.	Keep looking forwards all the time.

Both of these examples tell you to keep on performing the action. There is no time limit set on how long you should perform the action and the action that you are expected to perform is not complete.

B) <u>REPEATED ACTION</u>

Чита́й[i] газе́ту ка́ждый день.	Read the newspaper every day.
Когда́ вы вхо́дите в ко́мнату, открыва́йте[i] окно́, пожа́луйста.	Whenever you come into the room, open the window, please.

Both of these sentences express repetition. In the first sentence it is clearly expressed by the phrase: ка́ждый день; in the second by the use of е́сли + a present tense. The English *whenever* conveys the repetition.

C) <u>HABITUAL/GENERALISED ACTION</u>

Пиши́[i] интере́сные сочине́ния!	Write interesting essays.
Сдава́йте[i] кни́ги в библиоте́ку во́время.	Return the books to the library on time.
Встава́йте[i] в 7 часо́в утра́, ложи́тесь[i] спать в 10 часо́в ве́чера!	Get up at 7-00 in the morning, go to bed at 10-00 in the evening.

These sentences all advise people to perform the action as a general rule: you should *always* write interesting essays, hand back books on time and get up at 7-00 and go to bed at 10-00. The same use is observed with the infinitive (see chapter 12, section 3C).

4) THE IMPERFECTIVE-- COMPLETE ACTION: SINGLE OCCASION

A) <u>ENCOURAGEMENT TO PERFORM KNOWN ACTION</u>

If the action that you are being told to perform is known, either because it has already been mentioned or because it is clear from the context, the imperfective is used. This is similar to the *Statement of Fact* usage in the past tense (chapter 10, section 4A). We shall examine below the most common situations when this use of the imperative occurs:

I) <u>Start of action</u>

In all of the following sentences you are being told when to commence the action, that you should perform the action *now*:

Уже 9 часо́в: включа́йте[i] телеви́зор!	It's 9-00, put the television on.

This is identical with the usage already noted with the imperfective infinitive (see chapter 12, section 4C): we want to watch the news programme, which begins at 9-00. We know we have to switch the television on: we now know that it is time to switch it on.

Пиши́те[i] !	Start writing!

This is said by an examiner at the start of a written examination. You all know that you have to write the examination: you are being told when to start.

Платите[i] в кассу!	Pay at the cash desk.

This is said in a Russian shop. You have chosen your goods; you are being dismissed by the assistant and told to go to the next stage in the proceedings: paying for them.

Вы хотели меня о чём-то спросить? Спрашивайте[i].	Did you want to ask me any questions? Go on, ask them.

You are being encouraged to ask your questions at that point in time.

II) <u>Continuation of an action</u>

This usage is very similar to the previous one: you have started to perform the action, have stopped for some reason and are now being encouraged to continue:

Что же вы замолчали? Говорите[i]!	Why have you stopped speaking? Carry on.
Почему вы остановились? Продолжайте[i].	Why have you stopped? Carry on.

III) <u>Polite Invitation</u>

If you using the language of polite invitation, the imperfective will be used, as the actions to be performed are clear from the context:

Заходите[i], заходите[i]! Снимайте[i] пальто! Проходите[i]. Садитесь[i], берите[i] печенье, наливайте[i] сами кофе!	Come in, come in. Take your coat off. Go through. Sit down, take a biscuit, pour yourself some coffee.

To use perfective aspects in the above example would sound rude: it would assume that your visitors were not familiar with social etiquette.

Contrast this usage with the second example in section 2A, repeated here for convenience:

Зайдите[p] ко мне завтра в 9 часов.	Come and see me tomorrow at 9-00.

This could be a request from a teacher to a student to come and see him: its purpose is to impart the information that the student should come and see him at 9.00. As such, it is perfectly polite. By contrast, the imperfective *заходите* in the previous sentence states the obvious: what else do visitors expect to do, when they arrive at a friend's house?

IV) Impatient Repetition

(*Кто-то стучи́т в дверь*) — Войди́те![p] (*Молча́ние*) — Входи́те[i], входи́те[i]!	(*Someone knocks at the door*) "Come in." (*Silence*) "Come in, come in."
— Запиши́[p] мой телефо́н, ну, запи́сывай[i], запи́сывай[i]! Я о́чень тороплю́сь!	"Write down my telephone number, number, come on, write it down. I'm in a great hurry."

On first mention, the instruction is given using a perfective imperative. When repeated, the imperfective is used, as the speaker assumes that the information has already been given, the repetition is merely encouragement to perform the action quickly.

B) PROHIBITION

When a negative imperative is used to express the idea that you should not perform or are prohibited from performing the action, the imperfective is always used:

Не открыва́йте[i] окно́, пожа́луйста. Здесь хо́лодно.	Don't open the window, please. It's cold here.
Не приходи́[i] за́втра. Мы о́чень за́няты.	Don't come tomorrow. We are very busy.

This usage is identical with the use of the infinitive with words such as не на́до *must not*, не до́лжен *should not* (see chapter 12, section 4A).

CHAPTER 14. VERBS OF MOTION

1) INTRODUCTION

There are fourteen *Verbs of Motion* in Russian which have the following special properties:

A) The unprefixed forms have two imperfectives: *determinate* and *indeterminate*. These forms indicate the direction in which the actions take place and the frequency with which they occur (see section 3);

B) They use prefixes in a unique way to form verbs indicating motion in a specified direction (see section 4).

2) THE VERBS AND THEIR MEANINGS

Not all verbs indicating motion have these properties. The following is a complete list:

Indeterminate	Determinate	Meaning
ходи́ть хожу́, хо́дишь PAST	идти́ иду́, идёшь шёл, шла	go (on foot)
езди́ть е́зжу, е́здишь IMPERATIVE	е́хать е́ду, е́дешь поезжа́й(те)	go (by vehicle)
носи́ть ношу́, но́сишь PAST	нести́ несу́, несёшь нёс, несла́	carry (on foot)
води́ть вожу́, во́дишь PAST	вести́ веду́, ведёшь вёл, вела́	lead (on foot)
вози́ть вожу́, во́зишь PAST	везти́ везу́, везёшь вёз, везла́	carry (by vehicle)
бе́гать бе́гаю, бе́гаешь	бежа́ть бегу́, бежи́шь ...бегу́т	run
пла́вать пла́ваю, пла́ваешь	плыть плыву́, плывёшь	swim, sail, float

Indeterminate	Determinate	Meaning
лета́ть лета́ю, лета́ешь	лете́ть лечу́, лети́шь	fly
по́лзать по́лзаю, по́лзаешь PAST	ползти́ ползу́, ползёшь полз, ползла́	crawl
ла́зить ла́жу, ла́зишь PAST	лезть ле́зу, ле́зешь лез, ле́зла	climb
гоня́ть гоня́ю, гоня́ешь	гнать гоню́, го́нишь	drive, chase
таска́ть таска́ю, таска́ешь	тащи́ть тащу́, та́щишь	drag
ката́ть ката́ю, ката́ешь	кати́ть качу́, ка́тишь	roll
броди́ть брожу́, бро́дишь PAST	брести́ бреду́,бредёшь брёл, брела́	stroll, wander

The verb ходи́ть[ii], идти́[id] not only means *to go (on foot)* but is also used commonly of buses and cars. Compare:

Я е́ду[id] на авто́бусе.	I go by bus.
Вот идёт[id] авто́бус.	Here comes the bus.

The verb носи́ть[ii], нести́[id] is used when someone is carrying something on foot; води́ть[ii], вести́[id] indicates that two people/animals are involved, both on foot: one is leading the other; вози́ть[ii], везти́[id] is always used when something or someone is being carried by vehicle:

Он идёт[id] по у́лице и *несёт*[id] кни́гу.	He is walking along the street and carrying a book.
Вот они́ иду́т[id]. Ми́ша *ведёт*[id] бра́та в шко́лу.	Here they come. Misha is taking his brother to school.
Ми́ша *везёт*[id] бра́та в шко́лу на маши́не.	Misha is taking his brother to school by car.

пла́вать[ii], плыть[id] has a much more general meaning than any equivalent English verb: it is used of any activity on water -- *sailing, swimming, floating.*

The verb ла́зить^{ii} has a less common alternative form: ла́зать^{ii} (ла́заю, ла́заешь).

броди́ть^{ii}, брести́^{id} is comparatively rarely used: the verb ходи́ть^{ii}, идти́^{id} is often preferred.

The first and second person singular of the present tense are given for all verbs. Verbs with irregularities in the past tense and the imperative have these forms listed. Further details can be found in chapters 2-4.

3) USE OF INDETERMINATE AND DETERMINATE IMPERFECTIVE

The determinate imperfective is used when motion takes place in a clearly specified direction on a single occasion. The indeterminate imperfective can have a variety of meanings involving motion in more than one direction or on more than one occasion. The indeterminate imperfective is the unmarked member of the two imperfectives: it is used when the speaker does *not* wish to emphasise that the action is taking place in a single direction and on a single occasion.

A) DETERMINATE IMPERFECTIVE

These verbs are used when the direction is clearly specified and occurs on one occasion:

Мы сего́дня идём^{id} в университе́т.	We are going to the university today.
За́втра я е́ду^{id} на ры́нок.	I am going to the market tomorrow.
Ло́дка плывёт^{id} по реке́.	The boat is sailing down the river.
Па́па ведёт^{id} сы́на к врачу́.	The father is taking his son to the doctor's.
Ло́шадь та́щит^{id} в го́ру тяжёлый груз.	The horse drags the heavy load up the mountain.

The determinate verb may occasionally be used even when the action is repeated. This will only occur if the direction is very clearly specified:

Ка́ждое у́тро я иду́[id] ми́мо ва́шего до́ма на рабо́ту.	Every morning I go past your house to work.

Compare the first example of section II of the indeterminate imperfective verbs.

B) <u>INDETERMINATE IMPERFECTIVE</u>

I) <u>No Single Direction Specified</u>

Мы до́лго е́здили[ii] по го́роду на на́шей маши́не.	We drove round town in our car for a long time.
Оте́ц но́сит[ii] сы́на по ко́мнате.	The father is carrying his son round the room.
Где лета́ют[ii] пти́цы? Они́ лета́ют[ii] над по́лем.	Where are birds flying? They are flying over the field.

All of these sentences indicate *in what place* the action was taking place, but not where the subject was going to. All of these sentences could answer questions with the question word *где* (see the third example above).

II) <u>Repeated Action</u>

Мы хо́дим[ii] в универсисте́т ка́ждый день.	We go to the university every day.
Раз в ме́сяц учи́тель во́дит[ii] дете́й в теа́тр.	Once a month the teacher takes the children to the theatre.
Мы ре́дко бе́гаем[ii] домо́й.	We rarely run home.

These examples indicate how often the action took place.

III) <u>Habitual Action</u>

Я о́чень люблю́ е́здить[ii] на велосипе́де.	I like riding a bicycle a lot.

It is clear from this sentence that I habitually ride my bicycle.

IV) <u>General Ability to Perform an Action</u>

Этот ребёнок ещё не хо́дит[ii].	This child isn't walking yet.
Я уме́ю пла́вать[ii].	I can swim.
Такси́ст хорошо́ во́дит[ii] маши́ну.	The taxi-driver drives the car well.

All of these sentences show that the subject does or does not have the ability to walk, swim or drive a car.

V) <u>Action There and Back</u>

Вчера́ я ходи́л^{ii} в кино́.	I went to the cinema yesterday.
Утром он бе́гал^{ii} в апте́ку.	He ran to the chemist's in the morning.
На́ши студе́нты е́здили^{ii} в Санкт-Петербу́рг в про́шлом году́.	Our students went to St Petersburg last year.

Each of these sentences indicate that you went somewhere and came back: the subject has returned from the cinema, the chemist's or St Petersburg: we are not told what happened at the cinema, at the chemist's or in St Petersburg.

4) USE OF PREFIXED FORMS

There are three ways in which prefixes can be used with verbs of motion:

A) <u>THE PREFIX ПО-</u>

The prefix по- is added to the determinate imperfective to create a perfective verb without specifying the direction in which the action took place.

Он пошёл^{p} в теа́тр.	He has gone to the theatre. *or* He has set off for the theatre.
Мы пое́дем^{p} в Москву́ за́втра.	We are going to Moscow tomorrow.
Мы хоти́м пое́хать^{p} в Новосиби́рск.	We want to go to Novosibirsk.
Снача́ла он шёл^{id} пря́мо, пото́м он пошёл^{p} нале́во.	At first he walked straight on, then he went to the left.
Дождь усили́лся, и она́ побежа́ла^{p} быстре́е.	The rain got heavier and she started running faster.

Perfective verbs of motion with the prefix по- either indicate that the action has been completed or that it has started. The first example above may have either interpretation depending on whether in the sentence following there is a description of the play (*has gone to the theatre*) or the next sentence discusses what happened on the way there (*has set off for the theatre*). The second two examples express our intention to go to Moscow or Novosibirsk (and to get there). The final two examples indicate the start of the action.

B) DIRECTIONAL PREFIXES

I) The Prefixed Forms

Directional prefixes are added to the indeterminate verbs of motion to form a new *imperfective* verb and to the determinate verbs to form the corresponding *perfective* form. The table lists all the verbs of motion with the addition of the prefix при-. In a few verbs the prefixed forms differ from the unprefixed ones. Such forms are underlined in the table.

IMPERFECTIVE	PERFECTIVE
приходи́ть	прийти́
приезжа́ть	прие́хать
приноси́ть	принести́
приводи́ть	привести́
привози́ть	привезти́
прибега́ть	прибежа́ть
приплыва́ть	приплы́ть
прилета́ть	прилете́ть
приполза́ть	приползти́
прилеза́ть	приле́зть
пригоня́ть	пригна́ть
прита́скивать	притащи́ть
прика́тывать	прикати́ть
прибреда́ть	прибрести́

The forms which differ when prefixed are:

- (a) the verb идти́ is always written -йти;
- (b) -езжа́ть replaces е́здить;
- (c) the stress is on the final syllable in -бега́ть;
- (d) -плыва́ть replaces пла́вать;
- (e) the stress is on the final syllable in -полза́ть;
- (f) -леза́ть replaces ла́зить;
- (g) -та́скивать replaces таска́ть;
- (h) -ка́тывать replaces ката́ть;
- (i) -бреда́ть replaces броди́ть.

II) Variations in the Spelling of Prefixes

(a) The root -йти́ must have a prefix ending in a vowel. All prefixes ending in a consonant add a filler vowel o: e.g. войти́^{p}, подойти́^{p}.

(b) Prefixes ending in a consonant add a hard sign (ъ) when preceding the root: -езжа́ть/-е́хать: e.g. въезжа́ть^{i}/въе́хать^{p}, подъезжа́ть^{i}/подъе́хать^{p}.

(c) The prefixes раз-, вз- and из- are spelt рас-, вс- and ис- respectively in front of the following verb roots: ходи́ть, -плыва́ть, плыть, -ползать, ползти́, -та́скивать, тащи́ть, -ка́тывать, кати́ть.

(d) The prefix об has the alternative form о, which is used with the verbs beginning with б or п: бежа́ть, плыть, ползти́.

Further details can be found in the chapter 16.

III) The Meanings of the Prefixes

This section lists the major meanings of the directional prefixes with the verbs of motion. When prefixed with a directional prefix, verbs of motion only have a single imperfective. Where applicable, for each prefix the prepositional usage is given and an example, if possible with ходи́ть^{ii}/идти́^{id}. Further details of the meanings of these prefixes can be found in chapter 17.

a) INTO/OUT OF

INTO	в	входи́ть^{i}/войти́^{p}	в +A
OUT OF	вы	выходи́ть^{i}/вы́йти^{p}	из +G

Я вошёл^{p} в ко́мнату. — I went into (entered) the room.

Я вы́шел^{p} из ко́мнаты. — I came out of (left) the room.

b) ARRIVAL/DEPARTURE

ARRIVE	при	приходи́ть^{i} /прийти́^{p}	в/на +A, к +D
DEPART	у	уходи́ть^{i} /уйти́^{p}	из/с/от +G
GO ON WAY TO	за	заходи́ть^{i} /зайти́^{p}	в/на +A, к +D

Я пришёл^{p} в университе́т.	I arrived at the university.
на вокза́л.	I arrived at the station.
к вам.	I came to see you.

Я ушёл^{p} из университе́та.	I left the university.
с вокза́ла.	I left the station.
от вас.	I left you.

Я зашёл^{p} в магази́н.	I called in at the shop.
на по́чту.	I called in at the post-office.
к вам.	I called in to see you.

за- suggests that you called in somewhere or to see someone on the way somewhere else; при- does not have this undertone.

With the verbs носи́ть/нести́, води́ть/вести́, вози́ть/везти́ the prefix от- is usually used in sentences indicating the direction something is taken away:

Я отнёс^{p} кни́гу в библиоте́ку.	I took the book off to the library.
Я отвёл^{p} его́ домо́й.	I took him off home.
Я отвёз^{p} его́ за́ город.	I took him off to the country.

The prefix от- is also used with the verbs идти́, е́хать, лете́ть, and плыть to indicate the time when a vehicle or an official group of people depart:

Авто́бус отхо́дит^{i} в 10 часо́в.	The bus departs at 10-00.
Делега́ция отъезжа́ет^{i} в 7 часо́в утра́.	The delegation departs at 7-00 in the morning.

The perfective infinitives пройти́^{p} and прое́хать^{p} are used when asking for directions to a place:

Как пройти́^{p} на Кра́сную пло́щадь?	How do I get to Red Square?

c) MOVEMENT TOWARDS/AWAY FROM

MOVEMENT TOWARDS	под	подходи́ть^{i}/подойти́^{p}	к	+D
MOVEMENT AWAY	от	отходи́ть^{i}/отойти́^{p}	от	+G

Я подошёл^{p} к вам.	I went up to you.
к две́ри.	up to the door.
Я отошёл^{p} от вас.	I moved away from you
от две́ри.	away from the door.

d) MOVEMENT UP/DOWN

UP	вз	всходи́ть^{i}/взойти́^{p}	на	+A
	в	въезжа́ть^{i}/въе́хать^{p}	на	+A
DOWN	с	сходи́ть^{i}/сойти́^{p}	с	+G

Я въе́хал^{p} на́ гору.	I drove up the mountain.
Я сошёл^{p} с горы́.	I came down the mountain.

The prefix вз- is used with the following verbs: всходи́ть^{i}/взойти́^{p}, взбега́ть^{i}/взбежа́ть^{p}, взлета́ть^{i}/взлете́ть^{p} and всплыва́ть^{i}/всплыть^{p}; the prefix в- with the verbs: въезжа́ть^{i}/въе́хать^{p}, влеза́ть^{i}/влезть^{p}, вка́тывать^{i}/вкати́ть^{p}, втаскивать^{i}/втащи́ть^{p}, вноси́ть^{i}/внести́^{p}, ввози́ть^{i}/ввезти́^{p}. The form вбега́ть^{i}/вбежа́ть^{p} is sometimes found as a synonym of взбега́ть^{i}/взбежа́ть^{p}.

The verbs всходи́ть^{i}/взойти́^{p} and сходи́ть^{i}/сойти́^{p} are less frequently used than the verbs поднима́ться^{i}/подня́ться^{p} *go up* and спуска́ться^{i}/спусти́ться^{p} *come down*.

e) MOVEMENT TOGETHER/APART

TOGETHER	с (+ ся)
APART	раз (+ ся)

Мы все съе́хались^{p} в университе́т.	We all gathered at the university.
Мы свели́^{i} всех детей в зал.	We led all the children into the hall.
Мы все разошли́сь^{p} в ра́зные сто́роны.	We all went in different directions.
Почтальо́н разно́сит^{i} пи́сьма по дома́м.	The postman delivers the letters round the houses.

The suffix -ся is added to all verbs that do not have a direct object in the accusative case.

f) MOVEMENT AS FAR AS

AS FAR AS	до	доходи́ть^{i} /дойти́^{p}	до +G

Я дошёл^{p} до две́ри.	I got as far as (up to) the door.

Do not confuse the prefix до- with the prefix под-. под- simply indicates motion in the direction of the object or person, до- stresses how far you got.

g) MOVEMENT AROUND

AROUND	об	обходи́ть^{i} /обойти́^{p}	вокру́г +G +A (no preposition)

Я обошёл^{p} вокру́г до́ма.	I walked round the house.
Я обошёл^{p} дом.	I went round (avoided) the house.

When used with the preposition вокру́г the word *round* should be taken in its literal sense: he walked round the outside of the house and inspected it. Used with the accusative case without a preposition, it can be less literal: it can often mean: *to avoid.*

h) MOVEMENT PAST

PAST	про	проходи́ть^{i} /пройти́^{p}	ми́мо +G +A (no preposition)

Я прошёл^{p} ми́мо ва́шего до́ма	I went past your house.
Я прое́хал^{p} остано́вку.	I went past (missed) the stop.

Used with the preposition ми́мо the meaning is literally *to go past*; used with the accusative case without a preposition the meaning is: *to go past and miss.*

14. VERBS OF MOTION

i) MOVEMENT THROUGH

THROUGH	про	проходи́ть^{i}/пройти́^{p}	че́рез +A сквозь +A

Мы прошли́^{p} че́рез лес.	We walked through a forest.
Мы прошли́^{p} сквозь густу́ю толпу́.	We walked through a dense crowd.

The preposition сквозь is used when there is great difficulty in getting through. Otherwise че́рез is used. The verb is occasionally used with the accusative case without a preposition.

j) MOVEMENT ACROSS

ACROSS	пере	переходи́ть^{i}/перейти́^{p}	че́рез +A +A (no preposition)

Я перешёл^{p} (че́рез) у́лицу.	I crossed the street.

че́рез is optional with all verbs of motion except: везти́, вести́, нести́ and лезть. Verbs with the prefix пере- are also used with prepositions meaning *to* or *from*:

Я перевёз^{p} все кни́ги из до́ма в университе́т.	I took all the books from home to the university.

k) MOVEMENT FAR INTO

FAR INTO	за	заходи́ть^{i}/зайти́^{p}	в/на +A

Мы зашли́^{p} глубоко́ в лес.	We went deep into the forest.

l) DIRECTION

DIRECTION	за	залеза́ть^{i}/зале́зть^{p}	в/на +A

Я зале́з^{p} на де́рево.	I climbed up the tree.
Я завёл^{p} лошаде́й в коню́шню.	I led the horses to the stable.

The prefix за- is used with the verbs везти́, вести́, нести́, лезть, ползти́, гнать, кати́ть and тащи́ть to indicate that movement took place in a direction, dependent on the verb.

m) MOVEMENT BEHIND

BEHIND	за	заходи́ть^{i} /зайти́^{p} за +А

Я зашёл^{p} за де́рево. — I went behind the tree.

C) PREFIXES LIMITING THE EXTENT OF THE ACTION

Prefixes limiting the extent of the action can be added either to the determinate or indeterminate imperfective to form a perfective, which retains the meaning of the imperfective form but limits it, usually in time or space. When such prefixes are added to the indeterminate imperfective, the original form of the indeterminate imperfective is retained. Thus the verbs е́здить, бе́гать, пла́вать, ла́зить, по́лзать, таска́ть, ката́ть and броди́ть are found with prefixes.

I) Prefixes added to the determinate imperfective

a)

action for a specific time/distance	про

Он прошёл^{p} два киломе́тра. — He walked for two kilometres.
два часа́. — for two hours.

b)

action by/to a quantity	на

Налете́ли^{p} му́хи. — A swarm of flies flew in.

Он навёл^{p} госте́й в дом. — He brought a lot of guests to the house.

Verbs that do not have a direct object in the accusative case indicate that a quantity of the subject performed the action (see натете́ть^{p} above); those verbs that have a direct object indicate that the action is happening to a quantity of the object (see навести́^{p} above).

c)

movement round many objects	об

Учи́тель обошёл^{p} всех ученико́в и прове́рил дома́шнее зада́ние. — The teacher went round all the pupils and checked their homework.

II) <u>Prefixes added to the indeterminate imperfective</u>

All of the prefixed forms listed below retain the meaning of either an action in no specific direction or an action there and back.

a)

action for a (short) time	по

Мы походи́ли^{p} полчаса́ о́коло до́ма, верну́лись и легли́ спать.	We walked up and down for half an hour near the house, returned and went to bed.

b)

action for a specific time	про

Я проходи́л^{p} по па́рку це́лый день.	I walked round the park for a whole day.

The same prefix is used with determinate verbs of motion (see Ia above) to indicate action in one direction for a specified time.

c)

action started	за

Он встал и в волне́нии заходи́л^{p} по ко́мнате.	He got up and in anxiety started pacing the room.

d)

action round the whole of an object	из об

Мы исходи́ли^{p} весь парк, но не нашли́ фотоаппара́т.	We went round the whole park but couldn't find the camera.
Он объе́здил^{p} три райо́на.	He travelled round all three regions.

Indeterminate verbs prefixed with из- have a very similar meaning to verbs prefixed with об-. If the prefix об- indicates motion in one direction round a number of objects, the prefix is added to the determinate verb (see section Ic above). из- always retains the non-directional idea in the indeterminate verb.

e)

distance covered in a specific time	на

За год шофёр нае́здил^{P} 80,000 км без ремо́нта маши́ны.	During the year the driver did 80,000 km without any repairs to his car.

f)

motion there and back -- perfective	с

Я до́лжен сходи́ть^{P} к врачу́.	I must go to the doctor's.
Мы съе́здили^{P} на ры́нок и сейча́с гото́вим обе́д.	We went to the market and are now cooking dinner

This prefix is used to form the perfective aspect of indeterminate verbs having the meaning: *to go and come back.* It is regularly used in the infinitive to express the idea that you have to or want to make a round trip (*to the doctor's* in the first example above). In the past tense it is only used, when the result of the action is clear: in the second example as a result of going to market, we are cooking dinner.

PART FOUR

VERBAL PREFIXES AND SUFFIXES

CHAPTER 15. PREFIXES AND SUFFIXES

1) INTRODUCTION

Prefixes and suffixes play an important role in the Russian verbal system. Prefixes are added at the beginning of the verb, most suffixes are added at the end of the verb but before the inflections. One suffix -ся is added after the inflections.

This chapter will examine the role played by prefixes and suffixes in the Russian verbal system. Chapter 16 will examine the rules for producing the correct forms of prefixes, chapter 17 investigates the major meanings of each prefix, chapter 18 looks at the modifications in meanings that can be made by the addition of prefixes and suffixes.

Prefixes and suffixes have the following roles:

A) <u>ASPECT FORMATION</u>

Both prefixes and suffixes play an important role in the formation of aspects. This has already been discussed fully in chapter 8: *The Formation of Aspects*.

B) <u>FORMATION OF NEW VERBS</u>

Prefixation and suffixation are an important means of increasing the number and variety of verbs in Russian. This may be done as follows:

I) Adding prefixes, sometimes combined with suffixes, including the suffix -ся, to already existing verbs;
II) Formation of new verbs from other parts of speech *either* by the addition of a suffix on its own, *or* by the simultaneous addition of a prefix and suffix.

All of these uses will be examined in more detail below. The suffix -ся, when used on its own, has a variety of functions, which will be discussed in section 5 below.

2) PREFIXATION

The role of prefixation in the formation of aspects has already been discussed in chapter 8. This section will concentrate on the role of prefixation in the formation of new verbs.

The most commonly used system for the creation of new verbs in Russian is to add a prefix to an *imperfective* verb to produce a *perfective* verb. Prefixation causes the regular modifications in the meaning of the basic verb which are discussed in chapters 17 and 18.

писа́ть^{i}	*write*	——	*под*писа́ть^{p}	*sign*
дели́ть^{i}	*divide*	——	*от*дели́ть^{p}	*separate*

A few *perfective* verbs may also produce new verbs by this method, in which case there is no change in aspect:

дать^{p}	*give*	——	*пере*да́ть^{p}	*pass*
реши́ть^{p}	*decide*	——	*раз*реши́ть^{p}	*allow*

In a few cases, an imperfective verb, when prefixed, may not change aspect. This often happens with two prefixes of Church Slavonic origin со- and, less commonly, пред- The origin of prefixes is discussed in chapter 16, section 2A.

чу́вствовать^{i}	*feel*	——	сочу́вствовать^{i}	*sympathise*
ви́деть^{i}	*see*	——	предви́деть^{i}	*foresee*

Verbs of Motion are unique in their method of forming new verbs: they add a prefix to the indeterminate imperfective verb and form a new imperfective verb; the same prefix added to the determinate imperfective produces the perfective:

ходи́ть^{ii}, идти́^{id}	*go*	——	*при*ходи́ть^{i} /*при*йти́^{p}	*arrive*

See chapter 14: *Verbs of Motion* for further details.

It is usual in Russian to add only a single prefix to any one verb root. If two prefixes are used, the first one will most commonly be one limiting the action in time or expressing repetition (*re*). The use of two prefixes often produces verbs typical of informal colloquial Russian.

Occasionally, situations have developed where a combination of prefix plus verb becomes a new verb root in itself and this new verb root behaves in the contemporary language as a separate verb, combining with prefixes of all kinds: сказа́ть *say* is derived from the root -каза́ть *show* by prefixation. Both roots now form new verbs as if they were completely independent words:

-каза́ть	—	*показа́ть*ᴾ	*show*,	*указа́ть*ᴾ	*indicate*
сказа́тьᴾ	—	*рассказа́ть*ᴾ	*say*,	*вы́сказать*ᴾ	*pronounce*

Most prefixes are productive: they can be combined freely with already existing verb roots to form new verbs. As a result, the dictionary can never list all the prefixed forms in current use. An analogous situation is found in English, where the prefix *re-* can be added to almost any verb in the language, but only a small proportion of these are listed in the standard dictionaries.

3) SUFFIXATION

The addition of a suffix may play one of the following roles:

A) CHANGE OF ASPECT

Suffixation will change the aspect: from perfective to imperfective. This may be achieved by the addition of a suffix between the stem and an already existing suffix. This happens in those perfective verbs formed by means of prefixation mentioned above in section 2:

подписа́тьᴾ	*sign*	——	подпи́*сы*ватьⁱ
переда́тьᴾ	*pass*	——	переда*ва́*тьⁱ

Alternatively, the perfective suffix *-ить* may be replaced by the imperfective suffix *-ять* (*-ать*):

объясн*и́*тьᴾ	explain	——	объясн*я́*тьⁱ
разреш*и́*тьᴾ	allow	——	разреш*а́*тьⁱ

B) FORMATION OF NEW VERBS

Verbs can be formed from adjectives and nouns by the addition of a suffix:

серебро́	*silver*	——	серебр*и́ть*ⁱ	*silver*
чёрный	*black*	——	черн*е́ть*ⁱ	*be/become black*
слепо́й	*blind*	——	сле́п*нуть*ⁱ	*go blind*

The suffix *-ить* forms transitive verbs with the meaning: *to make something have the quality of the root word*. It is most commonly combined with a prefix (see section 4). The suffix *-еть* (and, less commonly, *-нуть*) are used to form intransitive verbs with the meaning: *to be or become the quality of the root word*.

4) PREFIXATION AND SUFFIXATION

New perfective verbs can be formed from adjectives or nouns by the simultaneous addition of *either* the prefix о (об) *or* у and the suffix -ить:

я́сный	*clear*	*объясни́ть*^{p}	*explain*
свобо́дный	*free*	*освободи́ть*^{p}	*free*
лу́чший	*better*	*улу́чшить*^{p}	*improve*
вели́кий	*great*	*увели́чить*^{p}	*increase*

The meaning of such words is: *to make something have the quality of the root word.*

5) THE SUFFIX СЯ

The suffix -ся is in origin a truncated form of the reflexive pronoun себя́. It has the following meanings:

A) <u>REFLEXIVE</u>

It retains the original meaning of the reflexive pronoun: the verb assumes the action is performed to itself:

Он умыва́ется^{i} и одева́ется^{i}.	He washes and dresses himself.

B) <u>EACH OTHER</u>

The action is reciprocal, -ся is a replacement for друг дру́га *each other:*

Мы встре́тились^{p} в Москве́.	We met each other in Moscow.

C) <u>INTRANSITIVE</u>

The suffix -ся converts a transitive verb into an intransitive one:

Дверь откры́лась^{p} и мы вошли́^{p}.	The door opened and we went in.
Заня́тия начина́ются^{i} в 10 часо́в.	Lessons begin at 10 o'clock.

Compare these sentences with transitive ones:

Я откры́л^{p} дверь и вошёл^{p}.	I opened the door and went in.
Мы на́чали^{p} заня́тия в 10 часо́в.	We began lessons at 10 o'clock.

D) PASSIVE

The suffix -ся is used as one means of forming the passive voice:

Этот вопро́с сейча́с обсужда́ется^{i} все́ми студе́нтами.	This question is now being discussed by all the students.

Further details can be found in chapter 7, section 2B IV.

E) IMPERSONAL VERBS

The suffix -ся is sometimes used to form an impersonal verb. Such verbs are only used in the the third person singular of present and future tenses and in the neuter form of the past tense. The subject, when present, is in the dative case.

Мне не спи́тся^{i}.	I can't sleep.
Нам не хоте́лось^{i} занима́ться ру́сским языко́м.	We didn't feel like studying Russian.

F) VERBAL MODIFICATION

The suffix -ся may be used in combination with a number of prefixes to modify the meaning of the verb: *вду́маться think carefully*, *дозвони́ться get (on the phone)*, *засиде́ться stay too long*, *нае́сться eat one's fill*, etc. Further details can be found in chapters 17 and 18.

G) MISCELLANEOUS

A few verbs are used with the suffix -ся for no apparent reason. Common examples are: боя́ться^{i} *be afraid of*; улыба́ться^{i} *smile*; смея́ться^{i} *laugh*; ложи́ться^{i} *lie down*; сади́ться^{i} *sit down*; станови́ться^{i} *become*. The last three have perfectives without -ся: лечь^{p}, сесть^{p} and стать^{p}.

CHAPTER 16. THE FORMATION OF VERBAL PREFIXES

1) INTRODUCTION

Prefixes often have two or more forms. This may be a result of Russian orthography attempting to imitate pronunciation or the insertion of a vowel to avoid difficult consonant combinations.

It may also be a result of the influence of Church Slavonic, the language of the Russian Orthodox church. The Orthodox church was largely responsible for the development of literacy in medieval Russia and as a result Church Slavonic, a language of the Southern Slavs closely related to Russian, had a widespread influence on the development of the language. Some prefixes have two forms, one of Church Slavonic origin and the other from Old Russian (eg пере *Old Russian*; пре *Church Slavonic*).

2) THE FORMS OF THE PREFIXES

A) <u>THE PREFIXES AND THEIR ORIGINS</u>

Table 31 lists all the prefixes used with verbs in modern Russian with their alternative forms.

The prefixes may come from one of three sources: Russian, Church Slavonic or they may be of foreign origin. The majority of the prefixes are of Russian origin and many of them are highly productive.

The Church Slavonic forms tend to be more formal in usage and less literal in meaning. They are not productive in the modern language, no longer combining to form new verbs. The Church Slavonic forms are normally close in form to the equivalent Russian prefixes: the only exceptions being: *вы* (Russian), *из* (Church Slavonic); *с* (Russian), *низ* (Church Slavonic)

The foreign prefixes are very limited in usage in modern Russian. They always combine with foreign verb roots with the suffix: -овать. The meaning of the foreign prefixes is the same as in the language from which they have been borrowed. It is often difficult to decide whether they are really prefixes in Russian or whether they have been borrowed as a unit together with the root. The presence of foreign verb roots which combine with a variety of prefixes of both foreign and Russian origin supports their inclusion as prefixes. An example of such a verb is: организова́ть *organise*, which combines with the foreign prefixes *ре-* and *дез-*, as well as with the Russian prefixes: *пере* and *с*. A list of other similar verb roots listed in the four volume *Словарь русского языка* compiled by the Russian Language Institute of the Academy of Sciences in 1981-4 is given in table 32.

B) ALTERNATIVE FORMS

I) Insertion of o

The vowel o is inserted before verb roots normally beginning with two or more consonants mainly as an aid to pronunciation. It is found after the following prefixes ending in a consonant: в, вз, из, над, низ, об, от, под, раз, с. Most of the verbs concerned are monosyllabic first conjugation verb roots:

идти́^{i}	*go*	войти́^{p}	*enter*
брать^{i}	*take*	взобра́ться^{p}	*climb up*
драть^{i}	*tear*	изодра́ть^{p}	*tear to pieces*
рвать^{i}	*tear*	надорва́ть^{p}	*tear slightly*
слать^{i}	*send*	отосла́ть^{p}	*send off*
греть^{i}	*warm*	подогре́ть^{p}	*warm slightly*
гнать^{i}	*chase*	разогна́ть^{p}	*drive away*
лгать^{i}	*lie*	солга́ть^{p}	*lie (perf)*

The inserted vowel is found in all forms of the verb except where the initial combination of consonants changes between the infinitive and present/future tense. Compare:

Compare	войти́^{p}	войду́
	надорва́ть^{p}	надорву́
with	взобра́ться^{p}	взберу́сь
	разогна́ть^{p}	разгоню́

With prefixed forms of the verb roots бить^{i} *beat*, вить^{i} *wind*, лить^{i} *pour*, пить^{i} *drink*, шить^{i} *sew*, жечь^{i} *burn* and честь^{i} *consider, read* the prefix in the infinitive never has an inserted o, whereas the present/future tense does when the prefix ends in a consonant:

вшить^{p}	вошью́
поджéчь^{p}	подожгу́
счесть^{p}	сочту́

The past tense (feminine, neuter, plural) also have an inserted *o* when the verb roots *жечь* and *честь* are preceded by a prefix ending in a consonant:

поджéчь^{p}	поджёг	подожглá	подожглó	подожгли́
счесть^{p}	счёл	сочлá	сочлó	сочли́

Although ease of pronunciation is clearly a factor, it is not the only factor determining the insertion of the vowel. Compare:

взбрóсить^{p}	*throw up*	взобрáться^{p}	*climb up*
издроби́ть^{p}	*pulverise*	изодрáть^{p}	*tear to pieces*
подгрести́^{p}	*rake up*	подогрéть^{p}	*warm up*

A list of verb roots which insert the vowel о is given in table 33.

In one prefix *с* there is an extra complicating factor: the Russian and Church Slavonic forms of the prefix differ by the insertion of the vowel о. The prefix *со* is found very frequently where there is clearly no pronunciation difficulty in the meaning of *accompanying*. In fact two verbs may exist side by side, one with the prefix *с* and the other with the prefix *со*. The verb совершáть^{i}/соверши́ть^{p} *accomplish* has a less common form свершáть^{i}/сверши́ть^{p}. Compare:

содержáть^{i}	*contain*	сдержáть^{p}	*hold back*

In such verbs the form *со* is retained in all forms:

Compare	взобрáться^{p}	*climb up*	взберу́сь
with	собрáть^{p}	*gather*	соберу́

The form *во* is also occasionally found in a few formal verbs, where there is no justification on grounds of difficulty of pronunciation: eg воображáть^{i}/вообрази́ть^{p} *imagine*.

II) Alternation of з and с

The prefixes whose basic form ends in *з* change this to *с* before an unvoiced consonant. Thus the prefixes вз, воз, из, низ, обез and раз are written вс, вос, ис, нис, обес and рас before the following consonants: к, п, с, т, ф, х, ц, ч, ш, щ. Before all other consonants and all vowels they are written with a final *з:*

вски́нуть^{p}	*throw up*	взойти́^{p}	*go up*
воспитáть^{p}	*educate*	возвращáть^{i}	*return*
избежáть^{p}	*avoid*	исполня́ть^{i}	*carry out*
низвергáть^{p}	*overthrow*	ниспослáть^{p}	*send down*
обезболи́ть^{p}	*anaesthetise*	обесси́лить^{p}	*weaken*

The alternation occasionally takes place within a single verb. This is caused by the insertion of the vowel *о*, as discussed in I above, in the present/future tense:

расче́сть^{p} *calculate* разочту́
испи́ть^{p} *drain* изопью́

Note that prefixes with a basic form ending in *с* (с and дис) never change this to *з*, although such a spelling would convey more accurately the pronunciation: спроси́ть^{p} *ask* and сде́лать^{p} *do* are both spelt with the letter *с* although the latter is pronounced as if it were spelt with the letter *з*.

III) Addition of ъ

After any of the prefixes ending in a consonant a hard sign (ъ) is inserted before verbs beginning with *е*, *ю* or *я*:

разъе́хаться^{p} *disperse* объясня́ть^{i} *explain*

IV) Alternation of и/ы

Verb roots beginning with the vowel *и* change this to *ы* when preceded by a prefix ending in a consonant:

иска́ть^{i} *look for* обыска́ть^{p}
игра́ть^{i} *play* сыгра́ть^{p}

V) The prefix о/об

The two forms of this prefix are both used before consonants. Occasionally the vowel *о* is inserted after об under conditions described in I above. Before vowels *обо* is used with the verb обойти́^{p} *go round*, otherwise *о* is used:

обнажи́ть^{p} *expose* освети́ть^{p} *illuminate*
обучи́ть^{p} *teach (perf)* оборва́ть^{p} *tear off*

Occasionally pairs of verbs exist with two different meanings, one with the prefix *о*, the other with *об*:

обсуди́ть^{p} *discuss* осуди́ть^{p} *condemn*

Verb roots beginning with the consonant *в* may omit this consonant after the prefix *об*:

об + вора́чивать^{i}/верну́ть^{p} *turn round*
becomes: обора́чивать^{i}/оберну́ть^{p}.

TABLE 31	THE ORIGIN OF VERBAL PREFIXES				
RUSSIAN		CHURCH SLAVONIC		FOREIGN	
BASIC FORM	ALTERNATIVE FORM	BASIC FORM	ALTERNATIVE FORM	BASIC FORM	ALTERNATIVE FORM
в	во				
вз	взо вс	воз	вос		
вы		из	изо ис		
				де	дез
				дис	
до					
за					
				ин	им
на					
над	надо				
недо					
о	об обо				
обез	обес				
от	ото				
пере		пре			
по					
под	подо				
		пред			
при					
про					
		противо			
раз	разо рас				
				ре	
с	со (*with*)	со			
с	со (*down*)	низ	низо нис		
у					
				экс	

TABLE 32	FOREIGN PREFIXES
де (дез before vowels)	
деблоки́ровать	raise blockade
дегази́ровать	decontaminate
дегенери́ровать	degenerate
дезинформи́ровать	misinform
дезорганизова́ть	disorganise
дезориенти́ровать	disorient
демаски́ровать	unmask
демилитаризова́ть (демилитаризи́ровать)	demilitarise
демобилизова́ть	demobilise
денатурализова́ть	denaturalise
детони́ровать	sing out of tune
деформи́ровать	deform
децентрализова́ть	decentralise
дешифрова́ть	decode
дис	
дисгармони́ровать	be out of tune
дисквалифици́ровать	disqualify
дискредити́ровать	discredit
дискримини́ровать	discriminate
ин (им before м, п)	
иммигри́ровать	immigrate
иммобилизова́ть	immobilise
импони́ровать	impress
импорти́ровать	import
инкримини́ровать	incriminate
интони́ровать	intone
ре	
регенери́ровать	regenerate
реконструи́ровать	reconstruct
ремилитаризова́ть (ремилитаризи́ровать)	remilitarise
реорганизова́ть	reorganise
репатрии́ровать	repatriate
ретрансли́ровать	rebroadcast
реформи́ровать	reform
реэвакуи́ровать	reevacuate
экс	
экспатрии́ровать	expatriate
экспони́ровать	exhibit
экспорти́ровать	export
экспроприи́ровать	expropriate

TABLE 33	INSERTED O AFTER PREFIX									
	во	взо	изо	надо	низо	обо	ото	подо	разо	со
брать	✓	✓ся				✓	✓	✓	✓	✓
гнать*	✓					✓	✓	✓	✓	✓
гнуть	✓		✓	✓		✓	✓	✓	✓	✓
-гревáть						✓	✓	✓	✓	✓
греть						✓	✓	✓	✓	✓
дви́гать							✓	✓		
дви́нуть							✓	✓		✓
драть*		✓	✓	✓		✓	✓		✓	✓
ждать						✓		✓		
жрать						✓				
звать*						✓	✓	✓		✓
злить						✓			✓	
-зревáть						✓		✓		✓
зреть						✓				✓
-йти́	✓	✓	✓		✓	✓	✓	✓	✓ся	✓
красть*						✓				
лгать			✓			✓	✓ся			✓
льстить						✓		✓		
-льщать						✓		✓		
-мкнуть							✓		✓	✓
-млевáть						✓			✓	
млеть						✓			✓	✓
мстить							✓			
мчать	✓									✓
-превáть							✓	✓	✓	✓
преть		✓					✓	✓	✓	✓
рвать	✓ся	✓	✓	✓		✓	✓	✓	✓	✓
слать							✓	✓	✓	✓
спать							✓ся		✓ся	
стлать				✓				✓	✓	
ткать	✓		✓					✓	✓	✓
ткнуть	✓							✓		

* no o in present/future tense
ся only used with the suffix -ся

CHAPTER 17. THE USE OF VERBAL PREFIXES

1) INTRODUCTION

This chapter lists all the prefixes in alphabetical order with the spatial meanings given first. Many of the meanings of the prefixes have already been discussed in chapter 14: *Verbs of Motion*. Only the major meanings of each prefix are given. Other less common uses are discussed in chapter 18.

The foreign prefixes listed in table 32 at the end of the previous chapter are omitted as their meanings are obvious. Table 34 lists the meanings of the prefixes in alphabetical order and gives a reference to the prefix and section where the meaning is discussed.

2) THE PREFIXES

A) <u>В (ВО)</u>

The main meaning of this prefix is: *motion into*. This is used in a wide variety of verbs in both literal and transferred meanings. With the verbs of motion е́хать *go (by vehicle)*, лезть *climb*, нести́ *carry (on foot)*, везти́ *carry (by vehicle)*, кати́ть *roll*, тащи́ть *drag* the prefix takes on the meaning of *motion upwards*. With verbs with the meaning: *listen, look, think, read* the prefix takes on the meaning of a thorough action: such verbs are always have the suffix -ся.

The preposition *в + A* is used for the first and third meanings, *на + A* in the second meaning.

I) <u>Motion into</u>

Мы въе́хали в столи́цу.	We drove into the capital.
Он вста́вил карти́ну в ра́му.	He framed the picture.
В Англию ввозят мно́го япо́нских маши́н.	There are a lot of Japanese cars imported into England. (literally: *carried into*)
Он включи́л телеви́зор.	He switched on the television. (literally: *keyed into*)

II) <u>Motion upwards</u>

Ма́льчик влез на де́рево.	The boy climbed up the tree.

Студе́нт внёс ве́щи на пя́тый эта́ж. — The student carried the things up to the fourth floor.

III) Thorough action

Я вду́мался в то, что он сказа́л. — I thought carefully about what he had said.

B) ВЗ (ВЗО, ВС)

This prefix is restricted in its usage. It is found with some verbs of motion and a few other verbs with the meaning of: *motion upwards*. This develops in non-literal uses into ideas of *a thorough or intense action.*

In literal meanings, the prefix is often accompanied by the preposition *на + A*.

I) Motion upwards

Мы взошли́ на верши́ну горы́. — We climbed to the top of the mountain.

Он вски́нул рюкза́к на пле́чи. — He threw his rucksack up over his shoulders.

II) Thorough, intense action

Пе́ред приёмом взболта́ть миксту́ру. — Shake the bottle before taking.

Террори́сты взорва́ли мост. — The terrorists blew up the bridge.

C) ВОЗ (ВОС)

This prefix is found in a few verbs of Church Slavonic origin. Many of the verbs are extremely formal and little used in everyday language. Like its Russian counterpart, it retains the idea of *motion upwards*, although not usually in a literal sense. Some verbs have the meaning of *beginning an action*; others have a meaning close to the English prefix *re*.

I) Motion upwards

В Москве́ возвели́ мно́го высо́тных зда́ний. — A number of skyscrapers have been erected in Moscow.

II) Start of an action

После́ этого собы́тия ма́льчик его́ возненави́дел.	After this event, the boy began to hate him.

III) Re-

Он стара́лся восстанови́ть хозя́йство страны́.	He tried to restore the country's economy. (literally: *stand up again*)
Он возврати́лся домо́й о́чень по́здно.	He returned home very late.

D) ВЫ

The main meaning of the prefix *вы* is to express the idea of *motion out of*. It is the opposite of the prefix *в*. The idea is often used in a transferred sense. The prefix is also used to suggest *an exhaustive action*. The idea of *out* is often clear. If the verb does not have an object, the suffix -ся will be used.

The prefix *вы*- is accompanied by the preposition *из* + *G*. In the perfective, the prefix is always stressed.

I) Motion out of

Заключённый вы́прыгнул из окна́.	The prisoner jumped out of the window.
Врач вы́рвал у меня́ зуб.	The dentist pulled my tooth out.
Он вы́чел семь из десяти́.	He subtracted seven from ten. (literally: *counted out of*)

II) Exhaustive action

Он вы́слушал расска́з до конца́.	He listened to the story right through to the end.
Я так уста́л, я вчера́ не вы́спался.	I feel so tired, I didn't have a good sleep yesterday.

E) ДО

The prefix *до* expresses the idea of *action to a certain point*. With motion verbs it states how far you have got; compare this with *под*, which merely suggests *motion towards*.

With other verbs it either indicates the point to which you have got or stresses completion of the action. It can also express the idea of an additional action. A few verb roots (звони́ть *ring*, звать *call*, буди́ть *wake*, стуча́ть *knock*, ждать *wait*, ду́мать *think*, etc) are used with this prefix and the suffix -ся to suggest the idea: *achievement of a goal (after a great effort)*.

The prefix is accompanied by the preposition *до* + *G*.

I) <u>Motion as far as</u>

Мы добрали́сь до го́рода.	We got as far as the town.

II) <u>Action to a specific point</u>

Хотя́ я до́лжен отда́ть кни́гу, я дочита́л её то́лько до середи́ны.	Although I must take the book back, I have only read half of it.

III) <u>Completion of an action</u>

Это зда́ние на́чали стро́ить ещё в про́шлом году́, а достро́или его́ то́лько сейча́с.	This building was begun last year, but it has only just been completed.

IV) <u>Additional action</u>

Он доли́л в стака́н молока́.	He poured some more milk into the glass.

V) <u>Achievement of goal</u>

К вам о́чень тру́дно дозвони́ться, вас никогда́ нет до́ма.	It is very difficult to get you on the phone, you are never at home.
Я договори́лся встре́титься с ним во вто́рник.	I agreed to meet him on Tuesday. (literally*: to speak and after discussion to come to a conclusion)*

F) <u>ЗА</u>

The prefix *за* is extremely versatile and has a great many commonly used meanings. Its spatial meaning is linked with its prepositional usage: *motion behind, beyond.* This meaning as a prefix is, however, much less common than the other meanings. In a few verbs this idea is extended to mean: *motion beyond normal limits, for a very long way.* The idea is further developed with a number of verbs into that of *an excessive action*, sometimes with unfortunate consequences. It is the equivalent of the English prefix *over*. Many verbs with this meaning have the suffix -ся.

With a few verbs of motion it has the idea of *calling in on*: you are going to a place on the way somewhere else. Though some of the verbs are very common (eg заходи́ть/зайти́ *call in on*), this use is highly restricted. This is linked with the prepositional usage of *за +I*: *to go for, to fetch something.* With some verbs of motion the prefix *за* is used to indicate *action in a specific direction*: the direction will be obvious from the verb. Further details of the two preceding uses are given in chapter 14.

за can also mean: *action covering the surface*, *filling*, the means by which you perform the action depends on the verb root. A development of this idea is the idea of *joining* two things together: it is used with verbs expressing *tying, buttoning, wrapping, etc.*

за is commonly used to indicate *the start of an action.* This usage is very close to the perfectivising use of the prefix (see section P).

With a few verbs the prefix *за* has the meaning of *acquiring something by the action expressed in the verb.* It is used with such verbs as: рабо́тать *work*, хвати́ть *seize*, воева́ть *wage war on*, служи́ть *serve*, брать *take*.

In its literal meaning of: *motion behind, beyond* the prefix *за* is followed by the preposition *за + A.*

I) Motion behind, beyond

Он заложи́л ру́ки за́ спину.	He put his hands behind his back.

II) Motion beyond normal limits

Куда́ же ты нас завёл?	Where on earth have you taken us?
Си́льным уда́ром футболи́ст заби́л мяч в воро́та.	The footballer with a powerful kick got the ball into the goal.

III) Excessive action

Не сто́ит захва́ливать дете́й, они́ мо́гут стать сли́шком самоуве́ренными.	You should not give children too much praise, they might get too self-confident.
Он засиде́лся в гостя́х и опозда́л на после́дний по́езд.	He stayed too long and missed his last train.

IV) Calling in on

По доро́ге домо́й он зашёл в магази́н за во́дкой.	On the way home he called in at shop for some vodka.

V) Action in a specific direction

Он загна́л коро́в в хлев.	He chased the cows into the shed.

VI) Covering the surface, filling

Он зали́л весь стол ча́ем.	He spilled tea all over the table. (literally: *poured and covered the table with tea*)
Он засы́пал ров землёй.	He filled the ditch with earth. (literally: *sprinkled and filled*)

VII) Joining

Продаве́ц заверну́л поку́пки и завяза́л их верёвкой.	The assistant wrapped up my purchases and tied them up with string. (literally: *turned and joined/ tied and joined*)
Закро́йте дверь, пожа́луйста!	Close the door, please. (literally: *cover and join*)

VIII) Start of an action

Он вошёл в ко́мнату и запе́л.	He came into the room and started singing.

IX) Acquisition

Мы завоева́ли Фра́нцию.	We conquered France.

Он зарабо́тал мно́го де́нег на заво́де.	He earned a lot of money at the factory. (literally: *worked and acquired money*)

G) <u>ИЗ (ИЗО, ИС)</u>

In its spatial meaning this prefix is the Church Slavonic equivalent of *вы*. It retains the meaning of *motion out of* but never in a literal sense. It is often the equivalent of the English prefix *ex*. In this meaning, the prefix *из* is not productive. The other meaning of this prefix is that of *an action to all of the object*. It is similar to the second meaning of *вы: exhaustive action*.

I) <u>Motion out of</u>

Ле́нин был и́згнан из Росси́и за революцио́нную де́ятельность.	Lenin was exiled from Russia for his revolutionary activity. (literally: *chased out)*
Институ́т ру́сского языка́ изда́л но́вую кни́гу о ру́сском глаго́ле.	The Russian Language Institute published a new book on the Russian verb. (literally: *gave out*)
Студе́нты бы́ли исключены́ из университе́та.	The students were excluded from the university.

II) <u>Action to all of an object</u>

Она́ исписа́ла всю тетра́дь стиха́ми.	She filled her exercise book with poems. (literally: *wrote all over her exercise book*)
Он изрисова́л сте́ну ме́лом.	He covered the wall with chalk. (literally: *drew all over the wall with chalk)*

H) <u>НА</u>

This prefix retains the meaning of the preposition: *motion onto*. However, unlike the preposition it is restricted to a small number of verbs. In some verbs it develops a the meaning of *collision*. It is used with the suffix -ся to indicate *an exhaustive action*; in this meaning it is very similar to *вы* (II). With a negative verb the meaning is: *to never tire of performing the action.*

The prefix *на* may also indicate *quantity*. With intransitive verbs, a quantity of the subject is performing the action; with transitive verbs the action is being performed to a quantity of the direct object, which is often in the genitive case expressing a partitative idea.

In its literal meaning, the prefix *на* is accompanied by the preposition *на + A.*

I) Motion onto

Де́вушка набро́сила на пле́чи пальто́ и вы́шла в коридо́р.	The girl threw a coat over her shoulders and went out into the corridor.

II) Collision

В темноте́ я натолкну́лся на стол и чуть не упа́л.	In the darkness I bumped into the table and almost fell over. (literally: *pushed myself and collided with*)

III) Exhaustive action

Он нае́лся и напи́лся и пошёл да́льше.	He ate and drank his fill and went on his way.
Мать не могла́ насмотре́ться на сы́на.	The mother never tired of looking at her son.

IV) Quantity

Пе́ред пра́здником мы пошли́ в гастроно́м и накупи́ли мно́го проду́ктов.	Before the holiday we went to the grocery shop and bought a lot of food.
К ме́сту происше́ствия набежа́ли любопы́тные.	Lots of curious people ran over to where the incident took place.

I) НАД (НАДО)

This is a little used non-productive prefix, having no spatial meaning. It can mean that *an additional extra action* is being performed: this bears some relationship to the meaning of the preposition *над + I.* It can alternatively indicate *an incomplete action* and is used with verbs of *cutting, breaking, biting, etc.*

17. THE USE OF VERBAL PREFIXES

I) Additional action

В э́том до́ме надстро́или ещё два этажа́.	This house had two extra storeys built on.

II) Incomplete action

Ма́льчик надкуси́л я́блоко и бро́сил его́, потому́ что оно́ оказа́лось ки́слое.	The boy took a bite out of the apple and threw it away, because it was sour.

J) НЕДО

This prefix suggests the result of the action was not fully achieved. It is the equivalent of the English prefix *under*. It is the opposite of the prefix *пере* (V).

I) Under-achievement

Мы все недооце́ниваем свои́ си́лы!	We all underestimate our strength.
Во вре́мя войны́ они́ недоеда́ли.	During the war they did not get enough to eat.

K) НИЗ (НИЗО, НИС)

This prefix of Church Slavonic origin is rarely used in Modern Russian and all the verbs with this prefix are very formal or old fashioned in character. It is non-productive. The equivalent Russian prefix is *с*. It has one meaning: *motion downwards*. The verbs are figurative in meaning.

I) Motion downwards

Бесконе́чные во́йны возвы́сили Наполео́на. Они́ же его́ низве́ргли!	Innumerable wars brought Napoleon to power. It was they too which brought him down!

L) О/ОБ (ОБО)

The prefix *о/об* has a variety of meanings, none of them the same as the preposition *о + P*. Its spatial meaning is: *motion around*. It develops several different strands of meaning: it can mean literally *motion in a circle round an object* or it can convey the idea of *surrounding* an object. It can also mean *motion around and avoiding*. The idea of *movement round many objects* can also be conveyed by this prefix: compare this with *из* (II).

From these spatial meanings some verbs connected with *thinking, speaking, writing* develop the idea of a thorough action. The prefix *о/об* can also mean: *a mistaken action.* It is used both with and without the suffix -ся. The non-reflexive forms mean: *to make a mistake and harm the object*; the reflexive verb forms indicate a mistake of a mechanical nature. Compare *про* (VI).

Finally the prefix *о/об* is used to form verbs from adjectives and nouns. If the verb has the suffix *ить* in the perfective, the meaning will be: *to give the object the quality in the root*; if the verb ends in *еть* or *нуть* the verb will have the meaning: *to become the quality in the root.*

If the verb has the meaning of *motion in a circle* the verb will be accompanied by the preposition *вокруг + G.* Otherwise, verbs with the meaning *round*, which are otherwise intransitive, will take a direct object when prefixed with *о/об.*

I) <u>Motion round (in a circle)</u>

Космона́вт облете́л вокру́г земли́.	The astronaut flew around the earth.

II) <u>Motion round (surrounding)</u>

Зда́ния МГУ обсади́ли больши́ми деревья́ми.	The buildings of Moscow University have been surrounded by big trees. (literally: *have been planted around with*)

III) <u>Motion round (avoiding)</u>

Теплохо́д, обойдя́ райо́н непого́ды, возвраща́лся в порт.	The boat, avoiding the area of bad weather, was returning to port.

IV) <u>Motion round many objects</u>

В по́исках ре́дкой кни́ги я обошёл все магази́ны.	In search of the rare book I went round all the shops.

V) <u>Thorough action</u>

Он осмотре́л дре́вний го́род.	He examined the ancient town. (literally: *looked thoroughly at*)

Он обсуди́л план рабо́ты с нау́чным руководи́телем.

He discussed the work scheme with his supervisor. (literally: *judged thoroughly*)

VI) <u>Mistaken action</u>

Касси́р обсчита́л меня́ на 20 копе́ек.

The cashier cheated me of 20 copecks. (literally: *counted and made a mistake*)

Он оговори́лся и назва́л непра́вильно после́днюю ци́фру своего́ телефо́на.

He made a slip and gave the last figure of his phone number incorrectly.

VII) <u>Give quality to</u>

Алекса́ндр II освободи́л крепостны́х в 1861 году́.

Alexander II liberated the serfs in 1861. (literally: *made free*)

Он осво́ил прочи́танный материа́л.

He assimilated the material he had read. (literally: *made his own*)

VIII) <u>Become quality</u>

Но́ги у него́ ослабе́ли.

His legs weakened.

Лицо́ опу́хло от слёз.

His face swelled up from crying.

M) <u>ОБЕЗ (ОБЕС)</u>

When combined with the suffixes *ивать*^{i} /*ить*^{p} this prefix means: *to deprive a person or object of the quality in the root*. If the verb ends in *еть* the verb means: *to be deprived of the quality in the root*. The verbs are usually formal, often technical.

I) <u>Deprive of a quality</u>

Врач обезбо́лил десну́ пе́ред удале́нием зу́ба.

The dentist anaesthetised the gum before extracting the tooth.

II) Be deprived of a quality

Больно́й обесси́лел по́сле присту́па гри́ппа	The patient had grown weak after an attack of flu.

N) ОТ (ОТО)

When used with motion verbs, this prefix indicates: *motion a certain distance way from*. This prefix is used with vehicles departing from a terminus. Verbs of *separating, dividing, cutting* have the meaning of *separating one piece from the whole*. Verbs of *tying, connecting* with the prefix *от* have the meaning of *untying, disconnecting*. They are the opposite of the prefix *при*. *от* is also used to suggest the idea of performing the *opposite action* to that suggested in the verb root. It can also be used to stress that the action in the verb is *complete*.

This prefix is frequently used with the preposition *от + G.*

I) Motion a certain distance away

Па́рень оттолкну́л ло́дку от бе́рега и пры́гнул в неё.	The boy pushed the boat off from the bank and jumped into it.

II) Motion away from (vehicles from terminus)

По́езд отхо́дит в 10 часо́в.	The train leaves at 10-00.

III) Separation

Отре́жьте мне ещё кусо́чек хле́ба, пожа́луйста.	Cut me another piece of bread please.

IV) Untying

Он отвяза́л ло́шадь и вскочи́л в седло́.	He untied his horse and jumped into the saddle.

V) Opposite action

Я стара́лся отговори́ть его́ от э́той пое́здки.	I tried to dissuade him from this journey. (opposite of *уговори́ть*)

Во вре́мя кани́кул я отвы́к ра́но встава́ть. — During the holidays I grew unaccustomed to getting up early. (opposite of *привы́кнуть*)

VI) Completion of an action

Мы то́лько что отобе́дали, когда́ го́сти прие́хали. — We had just finished dinner when the guests arrived.

O) ПЕРЕ

The spatial meaning of the prefix *пере* is of *motion across* or of *motion from one place to another.* This idea is also used in a transferred sense and can be the equivalent of the English prefix *trans.*

It is widely used in two other meanings: *performing the action again* and *performing an action excessively.* It is the equivalent of the English prefixes *re* and *over* respectively. In the latter meaning it is the opposite of the prefix *недо.* In both of these meanings the prefix *пере* may be added to an already prefixed verb.

With verbs of *cutting, tearing* it suggests *division into two parts.* With many verbs it suggests action to *a series of objects.* With some verbs it conveys a *reciprocal action*, an action done to each other. Such verbs are usually imperfective, have the suffix -ся and end in *иваться* or *ываться. пере* can also indicate the idea of *supremacy*, that one action is performed better than all the rest.

In the meaning of *motion across* the preposition *че́рез + A* is usually used: some common verbs of motion may be used with a direct object. In the meaning of *motion from one place to another* the appropriate prepositions meaning *to* and *from* are used.

I) Motion across

Мы перешли́ (че́рез) у́лицу. — We crossed the street.

Мы перепры́гнули (че́рез) кана́ву. — We jumped across the ditch.

II) Motion from one place to another

Ну́жно переложи́ть э́ти ве́щи из чемода́на в шкаф. — You will have to take these things out of the suitcase and put them in the cupboard.

III) Trans (non-literal)

Он переводи́л текст с английского языка́ на ру́сский.	He translated the text from English to Russian. (literally: *led from one language to another*)
Мы то́лько что перее́хали в но́вый дом.	We have just moved to a new house. (literally: *gone from one place to another*).

IV) Repeated action, re-

Он до́лжен пересдава́ть экза́мен по ру́сскому языку́.	He must retake his Russian language examination.

V) Excessive action, over-achievement

Ва́жность э́того откры́тия тру́дно переоцени́ть.	It is difficult to overestimate the importance of this discovery.

VI) Separation into two parts

Провода́ перере́зали и связь прекрати́лась.	The wires have been cut and communication has ceased.

VII) Action to a series of objects

За год я перечита́л все рекомендо́ванные кни́ги.	During the year I have read all the recommended books.

VIII) Reciprocal action

Мы с дру́гом перепи́сывались три го́да.	My friend and I corresponded for three years.

IX) Supremacy

Мой друг перекрича́л всех нас.	My friend shouted louder than all of us.

P) ПО

The main use of the prefix *no* is to make verbs perfective. In most cases this presents no problems and has been discussed in chapter 8, section 2A.

17. THE USE OF VERBAL PREFIXES

If the verb is of the type where the perfective indicates *to start to perform the action* the prefix *по* may be used. In such cases the prefix *по* is often considered to be the perfective form of the verb. Dictionaries produced in Russia often disagree on aspect pairs: eg *Ozhegov Слова́рь ру́сского языка́* does not consider *чу́вствовать* and *почу́вствовать* to be aspect pairs whereas the 4 volume *Слова́рь ру́сского языка́* compiled by the *Russian Language Institute* in 1981-4 does. The idea of *starting to perform an action* is therefore included as a meaning of this prefix. A similar problem also exists with the prefix *за*: see section F.

The prefix *по* has no spatial meaning connected with the preposition *по + D.* In addition to the meaning of *starting to perform an action по* is used to make a perfective verb with the general idea of *performing the action in a reduced fashion.* The most common meaning is: *to perform the action for a short time.* Less commonly, it suggests *performing the action to a limited extent.* The prefix *по* can also combine with some imperfective verbs ending in *ивать* or *ывать* with the meaning: *to perform a brief action from time to time.* It can also indicate action to a series of objects.

I) <u>Start of an action</u>

Он полюби́л чита́ть ру́сскую литерату́ру.	He grew to like reading Russian literature.

II) <u>Action for a short time</u>

Посиди́те у нас ещё пять мину́т.	Stay with us for another five minutes.

III) <u>Limited action</u>

Она́ попу́дрила нос.	She powdered her nose a little.

IV) <u>Action from time to time</u>

Он сиде́л в кре́сле и посма́тривал на часы́.	He sat in his armchair and kept on glancing at his watch.

V) <u>Action to a series of objects</u>

Она́ поброса́ла ве́щи в чемода́н.	She threw the things into the suitcase.

Q) ПОД (ПОДО)

The prefix *под* may have the same spatial meaning as the preposition *под + I*: *motion under*. A secondary spatial meaning has developed with some verbs: *motion upwards, from under*. With verbs of motion and a few other verbs expressing movement the prefix may mean: *motion towards*.

The prefix *под* also has the following meanings: *additional action*; *incomplete action* and *secret action*.

In the meaning of *motion under* the verb is accompanied by the preposition *под + A*, in the meaning of *motion towards* it is accompanied by the preposition *к + D*.

I) Motion under

Змея́ подползла́ под ка́мень и сверну́лась там клубко́м.	The snake crawled under the stone and curled up in a ball there.

II) Motion upwards, from under

Он подня́лся́ по ле́стнице и позвони́л.	He went upstairs and rang the bell. (literally: *took himself upwards, from under*)

III) Motion towards

Ма́льчик пододви́нул к себе́ таре́лку и стал есть.	The boy moved the plate towards him and started to eat.

IV) Additional action

Суп недосо́лен, на́до его́ чуть-чуть подсоли́ть.	The soup has not got enough salt in it, you must put a little more in.

V) Incomplete action

Бы́ло заме́тно, что де́вушка подкра́сила гу́бы.	It was clear that the girl had touched up her lipstick. (literally: *painted incompletely*)

VI) Secret action

Мать наказа́ла ма́льчика за то, что он подслу́шал разгово́р ста́рших.	The mother punished her son for eavesdropping on the grown-ups' conversation. (literally: *listening in secret*)

R) ПРЕ

This prefix is the Church Slavonic equivalent of *пере*. It is used with a limited set of verbs and is non-productive. The verbs with this prefix are always less literal in meaning. It is either the equivalent of the English prefix *trans*, conveying the idea of movement from one state to another or it has the meaning of an *excessive action*.

I) Trans (non-literal)

Горбачёв преобразйл совéтское óбщество.	Gorbachev transformed Soviet society.

II) Excessive action

Он преувелúчил своё знáние рýсского языкá.	He exaggerated his knowledge of Russian. (literally: *increased to an excessive degree*)

S) ПРЕД

This prefix is of Church Slavonic origin and is non-productive in the modern language. Its meaning is related to the preposition *пéред + I*. As a prefix it is more commonly used to indicate *action in advance* and is often the equivalent of the English prefix *fore*; with a few verbs it retains the spatial idea of the prepositional meaning of *motion in front of* but in a non literal sense.

I) Action in advance

Он предсказáл изменéние погóды.	He forecast the change in the weather.
Эти дéньги мы предназнáчили на покýпку автомобúля.	We have set this money aside for the purchase of a car. (literally: *fix in advance*)

II) Motion in front of (non-literal)

Он предложúл нам нóвую рабóту.	He offered us a new job. (literally: *put in front of us*)

T) <u>ПРИ</u>

The spatial meanings of the prefix *при* develop from the idea of *attachment* present in the preposition. It is used with a large number of verbs in this meaning. With verbs of motion it acquires the idea of *arrival at a place*.

Like the prefix *под* it can also have ideas of an *additional action* and an *incomplete action*. This latter meaning is found with some very common verbs of movement: встать *get up*, лечь *lie down*, поднять *lift* and the verb: открыть *open*.

In the meanings of *attachment* and *additional action* the verb is usually accompanied by the preposition: *к + D*; in the meaning of *arrival* the prepositions *в + A*, *на + A*, or *к + D* are used depending on the following noun phrase.

I) <u>Attachment</u>

Он привязáл лóшадь к столбý.	He tied the horse to the post.
Онá пришúла пýговицу к рубáшке.	She sewed the button on the shirt.

II) <u>Arrival</u>

Он приéхал в Санкт-Петербýрг в шесть часóв.	He arrived in St Petersburg at 6-00.
Он принёс стул в столóвую.	He brought the chair into the dining-room. (literally: *carried and arrived*)

III) <u>Additional action</u>

Он приписáл нéсколько строк к письмý, напúсанному мáтерью.	He added a few lines to the letter written by his mother.

IV) <u>Incomplete action</u>

Приоткрóйте чуть-чуть окнó.	Open the window a little.

U) <u>ПРО</u>

There is nothing in common between the meaning of the preposition and the prefix *про*. The preposition used with the accusative case has the meaning: *about, concerning*; the main spatial meaning of the prefix is: *motion through*. This idea can also be seen in a non-literal sense in a number of verbs. It can also mean: *motion past*: either simply going past or going past and avoiding.

The prefix *про* is also commonly used to form perfective verbs with the meaning: *to perform the action for a specific time or a specific distance.* It can also be used to indicate a *mistaken action*: unlike a similar use with the prefix *о* (section L VI) the prefix *про* indicates a mistake due to carelessness. *про* can also indicate that something has been lost as a result of the action in the verb.

In the meaning of *through* verbs prefixed with *про* are accompanied by the preposition *чéрез + A* or *сквозь + A*, *сквозь* suggesting greater difficulty than *чéрез*. In the meaning of *past* the preposition *мúмо + G* is used if it the sentences simply conveys the idea of *motion past*; if the added nuance of *motion past and avoiding* is present, the verbs are used with a direct object in the accusative case. In the meaning: *action for a specific time or distance* the verb is accompanied by a time or place phrase in the accusative case.

I) Motion through

Они́ проложи́ли доро́гу сквозь лес.	They built a road through the forest.
Он проре́зал отве́рстие в доске́.	He cut a hole in the board.
Он куда́-то пропа́л.	He has disappeared somewhere. (literally: *fallen through*)

II) Motion past

Он прошёл ми́мо до́ма и вошёл в сад.	He went past the house and came into the garden.

III) Motion past and avoiding

Он прое́хал остано́вку на авто́бусе, потому́ что спал.	He went past his bus stop because he was asleep.

IV) Action for a specific time

Мой оте́ц прорабо́тал на фа́брике 25 лет.	My father worked in the factory for 25 years.

V) Action for a specific distance

Сего́дня он прошёл 25 киломе́тров.	He has covered 25 kilometres today.

VI) Mistaken action

Я не хоте́л никому́ говори́ть, что получи́л письмо́ от сестры́, но случа́йно проговори́лся.	I didn't want to tell anyone that I had got a letter from my sister but I accidentally let it slip. (literally: *spoke and made a careless mistake*)

VII) Loss

Мы проспа́ли ста́нцию.	We were asleep and missed the station.

V) ПРОТИВО

This prefix is found with a few verbs with the meaning of *against*. The meanings are not literal and the prefix is not productive.

Verbs with this prefix are accompanied by a dative case or both dative and accusative cases.

I) Against

Кри́тик противопоста́вил литерату́ру нау́ке.	The critic compared literature with science. (literally: *put against*)
Он всё противоре́чил ма́тери.	He was always contradicting his mother. (literally: *speaking against*)

W) РАЗ (РАЗО, РАС)

The prefix *раз* has the idea of *dispersal, movement in various directions*. Intransitive verbs of motion have the suffix -ся. A linked meaning of the prefix indicates *separation into parts*. *раз* can also indicate *performing the opposite of the action in the root*: it is often the equivalent of the English prefix *un*. In a few reflexive verbs, normally perfective only, the meaning is: *to start performing an action and get thoroughly involved in it*.

17. THE USE OF VERBAL PREFIXES

I) Motion in various directions

По́сле ле́кции студе́нты разъе́хались по дома́м.	After the lecture the students went home. (literally: *went in various directions*)
Всем прису́тствующим на ве́чере разда́ли па́мятные пода́рки.	All those present at the party were given souvenirs of the occasion. (literally: *given in various directions*)

II) Separation into parts

Мать разре́зала арбу́з на ра́вные ча́сти и дала́ ка́ждому по куску́.	Mother cut up the water-melon into equal portions and gave everyone a piece.
Ма́льчик разби́л ча́шку.	The boy smashed the cup. (literally: *beat it into many parts*)

III) Opposite action

Он бы́стро распеча́тал письмо́ и с волне́нием прочита́л пе́рвые стро́чки.	He quickly opened the letter and excitedly read the first lines. (literally: *unsealed*)
Он меня́ уже́ разлюби́л.	He has already stopped loving me.

IV) Start of an intense action

Снача́ла мой спу́тник неохо́тно отвеча́л на вопро́сы, но пото́м разговори́лся.	At first my companion answered my questions unwillingly but then he really got going. (literally: *started speaking and got thoroughly involved*)

X) С (СО)

The prefix *с* retains both major spatial meanings found in the preposition: it can either mean *motion downwards* (cf the preposition *с + G*) or *motion together, into one place* (cf the preposition *с + I*). In this last meaning it is the opposite of the prefix *раз*. As with that prefix, intransitive verbs of motion have the suffix *-ся*. A non-literal development of this last meaning is that of an *accompanying action*. Here the form is always *co*, as in this meaning this is the Church Slavonic variant of the prefix *c*. The verbs are all formal in character. *co* is also used to translate the English prefix *co/con* and verbs with this prefix are often imperfective (see chapter 15, section 2).

Verbs of motion with the meaning *motion there and back* have a perfective form with the prefix *c*. It is also used in a few verbs with the suffix -ся to express a *reciprocal action*: two (groups of) people discuss something with each other and come to an agreement.

In the meaning of *motion down from or from off the surface of* the prefix is accompanied by the preposition *c + G*.

I) Motion downwards

Пти́ца слете́ла с де́рева.	The bird flew down from the tree.
Он сбежа́л с ле́стницы.	He ran down the stairs.
Ма́ма стряхну́ла кро́шки со ска́терти.	Mother shook the crumbs off the tablecloth.

II) Motion together

В 1980 году́ лу́чшие спортсме́ны ми́ра съе́хались в Москву́ на Олимпи́йские игры́.	In 1980 the best sportsmen in the world gathered in Moscow for the Olympic Games.
Сложи́в учébники и связа́в их верёвкой, я отнёс их в библиоте́ку.	I put the textbooks together, tied them up with string and took them off to the library.

III) Accompanying action

В поéздке по стране́ президе́нта сопровожда́л мини́стр наро́дного образо́вания.	The president was accompanied on the journey round the country by the minister of education.
Он мне о́чень сочу́вствовал.	He was very sympathetic towards me.

IV) Co/con

Кварти́ра состои́т из трёх ко́мнат.	The flat consists of three rooms.

Это не соотве́тствует действи́тельности.	This does not correspond to the truth.

V) Motion there and back

Мой това́рищ заболе́л и мне пришло́сь сходи́ть в апте́ку.	My friend fell ill and I had to go to the chemist's.

VI) Reciprocal action

Мы с тобо́й созвони́мся об э́том.	You and I will arrange this over the phone.

Y) У

The prefix *у* has no connection with the preposition *у + G*. With verbs of motion and a few other verbs indicating movement, *у* has the meaning of *motion away from*. It is used to form verbs from adjectives and nouns in combination with the perfective suffix: *ить* and has the meaning: *to give an object the quality in the root*, cf о (VII). *In* a few verb roots (eg ста́вить, -ложи́ть *put*, ве́шать *hang*, сы́пать *sprinkle*) the prefix has the meaning of *covering the whole surface of an object*.

I) Motion away from

Он уе́хал из Москвы́ в 5 часо́в.	He left Moscow at 5-00.
Приводя́ ко́мнату в поря́док, я убра́л кни́ги в шкаф.	Tidying up the room, I put the books away on the shelf.

II) Give quality to

Ну́жно укрепля́ть дру́жественные свя́зи ме́жду Англией и Росси́ей.	We must strengthen the friendly ties between England and Russia. (literally: *make stronger*)
Число́ студе́нтов в на́ших университе́тах всё увели́чивается.	The number of students in our universities is increasing all the time. (literally: *making itself bigger*)

III) Covering the whole surface

Пра́здничный стол был уста́влен цвета́ми и блю́дами с фру́ктами.	The festive table was covered with flowers and dishes of fruit.

TABLE 34	PREFIX MEANINGS (PART 1)	
accompanying action	с III	
achievement	до V	
acquisition	за IX	
action for short time	по II	
action for specific distance	про V	
action for specific time	про IV	
action from time to time	по IV	
action in advance	пред I	
action in specific direction	за V	
action to all of object	из II	
action to series of objects	пере VII	по V
action to specific point	до II	
additional action	до IV	над I
	под IV	при III
against	противо I	
arrival	при II	
attachment	при I	
avoiding	о III	
calling in on	за IV	
co/con	со IV	
collision	на II	
completion	до III	от VI
covering	за VI	у III
excessive action	за III	пере V
	пре II	
exhaustive action	вы II	на III
filling	за VI	
fore	пред I	
incomplete action	над II	под V
	при IV	
joining	за VII	
limited action	по III	
loss	про VII	
mistaken action	о VI	про VI
motion across	пере I	
motion as far as	до I	
motion away	от I	от II
	у I	
motion behind, beyond	за I	
motion beyond normal limits	за II	
motion downwards	низ I	с I
motion from one place to another	пере II	
motion from under	под II	
motion in front of	пред II	
motion into	в I	
motion in various directions	раз I	
motion onto	на I	

TABLE 34	PREFIX MEANINGS (CONTINUED)	
motion out of	вы I	из I
motion past	про II	
motion past and avoiding	про III	
motion round	о I	о II
	о III	
motion round many objects	о IV	
motion there and back	с V	
motion together	с II	
motion towards	под III	
motion through	про I	
motion under	под I	
motion upwards	в II	вз I
	воз I	под II
opposite action	от V	раз III
over	за III	пере V
over-achievement	пере V	
quality (become)	о VIII	
quality (deprive)	обез I	
quality (be deprived)	обез II	
quality (give)	о VII	у II
quantity	на IV	
re	воз III	пере IV
reciprocal action	пере VIII	с VI
repeated action	воз III	пере IV
secret action	под VI	
separation	от III	пере VI
	раз VI	
start	воз II	за VIII
	по I	
start of intense action	раз IV	
supremacy	пере IX	
surrounding	о II	
thorough action	в III	вз II
	о V	
trans	пере III	пре I
un	от V	раз III
under	недо I	
under-achievement	недо I	
untying	от IV	

CHAPTER 18. THE SYSTEM OF VERBAL MODIFICATIONS

1) INTRODUCTION

This chapter will examine the system of verbal prefixation. It will explain the modifications in meaning of the basic verb caused by prefixation. Cross reference will be made to section 2 of chapter 17.

Modification of the basic verb by means of prefixation can be divided into the following groups:

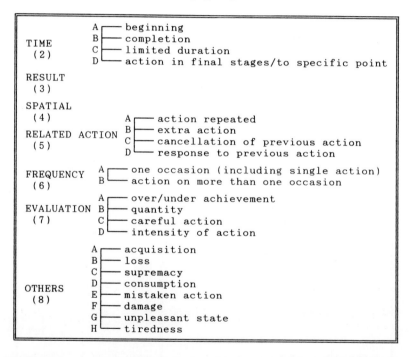

- TIME (2)
  - A beginning
  - B completion
  - C limited duration
  - D action in final stages/to specific point
- RESULT (3)
- SPATIAL (4)
- RELATED ACTION (5)
  - A action repeated
  - B extra action
  - C cancellation of previous action
  - D response to previous action
- FREQUENCY (6)
  - A one occasion (including single action)
  - B action on more than one occasion
- EVALUATION (7)
  - A over/under achievement
  - B quantity
  - C careful action
  - D intensity of action
- OTHERS (8)
  - A acquisition
  - B loss
  - C supremacy
  - D consumption
  - E mistaken action
  - F damage
  - G unpleasant state
  - H tiredness

Prefixation and suffixation are limited by both the form and the meaning of the verb. As far as the form of the verb is concerned, the presence of one prefix restricts the addition of a second one (see chapter 15, section 2). Cases where the addition of a prefix to an already prefixed form is possible are noted in the following sections. The meaning of the basic verb will indicate the types of modifications that are possible. This will be discussed in the remaining sections of this chapter.

2) TIME

The addition of prefixes to express the beginning, end or limited duration of an action are typical of intransitive verbs expressing an activity (рабо́тать^{i} *work*, шага́ть^{i} *step*) and state (боле́ть^{i} *be ill*, горева́ть^{i} *grieve*). Limitation in time is achieved by forming prefixed verbs, the majority of which do not form imperfective verbs by suffixation.

A) <u>BEGINNING OF AN ACTION</u>

I) <u>The prefix за-</u>

The prefix за- (see F VIII) is the most common prefix with the meaning of *the beginning of an action*. It is added to the following groups of verbs:

a) verbs of indicating sound

завы́ть^{p}	*start to howl*	загрохота́ть^{p}	*start to thunder*
заговори́ть^{p}	*start to speak*	закрича́ть^{p}	*start to shout*
запе́ть^{p}	*start to sing*	засвисте́ть^{p}	*start to whistle*

b) non-directional movement verbs

забе́гать^{p}	*start to run around*
замета́ться^{p}	*start to rush around*

c) physical and psychological state

заболева́ть^{i}/заболе́ть^{p}	*fall ill*
загорева́ть^{p}	*start to grieve*
запла́кать^{p}	*start to cry*
засмея́ться^{p}	*start to laugh*

d) verbs indicating a series of identical actions

заморга́ть^{p}	*start to blink*	зака́шлять^{p}	*start to cough*
зашага́ть^{p}	*start to walk*		

e) verbs denoting a process that is seen, heard or smelt:

запа́хнуть^{p}	*start to smell*	засвети́ться^{p}	*start to get light*

Other verbs of activity or physical process make use of the prefix за- less frequently. The idea of *beginning* is achieved by the use of начина́ть^{i}/нача́ть^{p}:

начина́ть^{i}/нача́ть^{p} руководи́ть^{i}	*start to lead*
начина́ть^{i}/нача́ть^{p} служи́ть^{i}	*start to serve*

Many verbs which have only an imperfective form, listed in chapter 9 section 4C, do not add the prefix за- in this meaning, nor do the majority of transitive verbs of action (eg стро́ить^i дом *build a house*).

In colloquial speech and in literature verbs prefixed with за- are found, which are not mentioned in dictionaries:

замечта́ть^p *start dreaming*   зашути́ть^p *start joking*

II) Other prefixes

The prefixes вз-, воз-, по-, раз- can express the idea of *the beginning of an action*: each of the prefixes is used with a small group of verbs:

a) вз- (see B II)

The prefix has the meaning of the beginning of a sudden intense action and is restricted to a small group of verbs:

взвыва́ть^i /взвыть^p	*start howling*
волнова́ться^i /взволнова́ться^p	*get excited*
взреве́ть^p	*roar*
вскипа́ть^i /вскипе́ть^p	*flare up (feelings)*

b) воз- (see C II)

возненави́деть^p *come to hate* воспыла́ть^p *blaze up (passion)*

With the exception of *возненави́деть*^{p} all verbs with this prefix are learned in style.

c) по- (see P I)

The prefix по- is used to express the start of an action with determinate verbs of motion and other verbs of movement:

пойти́^{p}	*set off*	помча́ться^p	*start to hurry*
потё́чь^p	*start to flow*		

With verbs of motion по- is considered to be perfective aspect of the verb.

Some other verbs use the prefix по- with the meaning of *to start to*:

полюби́ть^p *come to love*   почу́вствовать^p *start to feel*

почу́вствовать^p is often considered to be perfective aspect of the verb.

d) раз- -ся (see W IV)

This prefix indicates the beginning of an intense action:

разрыда́ться^{p} *burst into tears*
(cf зарыда́ть^{p} *start sobbing*)
рассмея́ться^{p} *burst out laughing*
(cf засмея́ться^{p} *start laughing*)

B) <u>COMPLETION OF AN ACTION</u>

Perfective verbs expressing the idea of *completion* add the prefix от- (see N VI). Such verbs are formed more frequently than verbs of beginning an action: they are formed from the majority of unprefixed intransitive verbs of activity and state:

отзвуча́ть^{p}	*be heard no more*	отобе́дать^{p}	*finish dinner*
отслужи́ть^{p}	*serve one's time*	отучи́ться^{p}	*finish learning*

There are two shades of meanings, which the following examples will illustrate:

Мы уже́ оттанцева́ли^{p}, тепе́рь ва́ше выступле́ние.	We have already finished dancing, now it's your turn.
Всё, я оттанцева́ла^{p}: нога́ по́сле перело́ма не гнётся.	That's it, I've finished dancing: my leg won't bend ever since I broke it.

In the first example оттанцева́ть stresses completion; in the second it conveys the idea that her dancing days are over for good.

In colloquial speech the prefix от- can be added to the majority of unprefixed and to some prefixed imperfective verbs of activity, state and action. It is especially common in verbs of the second type. Many of them are not listed in dictionaries.

Глаза́ у неё совсе́м плохи́е -- она́ отрисова́ла^{p}, отвышива́ла^{p}.	Her eyes are very bad -- she can't draw or sew any more.

The suffix -ся is optional and is typical of a more conversational style:

отбе́гаться^{p} *finish running* отрабо́таться^{p} *finish working*

C) <u>LIMITED DURATION</u>

There are two highly productive modifications that can be made to verbs of activity and state which set both the start and end of the action. They make use of the prefixes по- and про-.

I) <u>The prefix по-</u> (see P II)

This is a very common prefix that can be added to the majority of unprefixed imperfective verbs:

полежáть^{p} *lie* посмея́ться^{p} *laugh* порабóтать^{p} *work*

The use of the prefix по- to express limited duration is so common that dictionaries do not include the form for all verbs.

It is not possible for all imperfective verbs to add по-. The following verbs do not add по- in this meaning:

a) verbs of relationship: принадлежáть^{i} *belong*, содержáть^{i} *contain*;
b) modal verbs: хотéть^{i} *want*, намеревáться^{i} *intend*, желáть^{i} *wish*;
c) verbs expressing a lengthy state: люби́ть^{i} *love*, ненави́деть^{i} *hate;*
d) verbs where по- expresses a different meaning, for example:
   i) determinate verbs of motion: побежáть^{p} *start running*
   ii) change of state verbs: постарéть^{p} *have grown old*. Such verbs express result.

Verbs prefixed with по- may express an action within a limited time frame but of indefinite duration:

Мы вчерá хорошó повесели́лись^{p}.	We had a very good time yesterday.

The prefix по- often expresses the idea of an action which the speaker considers short:

Они́ немнóго помолчáли^{p}.	They were silent for a bit.

II) <u>The prefix про-</u> (see U IV)

The prefix про- also expresses the idea of an action limited in time. It can be added to the same verbs as по-:

пролежáть^{p} *lie* просмея́ться^{p} *laugh* проработáть^{p} *work*

The prefix про- is mostly used to indicate a lengthy action and includes a time phrase:

Дéти простоя́ли^{p} у шкóлы цéлый час.	The children stood outside the the school for a whole hour.

The use of the prefix is restricted, if it is used for another meaning:

прочитáть^{p} *read (perfective)* проли́ть^{p} *shed (tears, blood)*

Sound verbs prefixed with про- can have two meanings:

a) action completed (simple perfective)

Вдалекé прошумéл^{p} пóезд.	The train roared in the distance.

b) action considered to be lengthy

Стáрый паровóз прошумéл^{p} под óкнами стáнции цéлый день.	The old steam engine roared under the station windows the whole day.

D) <u>ACTION IN FINAL STAGES/TO SPECIFIC POINT</u>

Action verbs of the type: шить *sew,* стрóить *build* can add on the prefix до- to express the completion of the final stage of an action (see E III). Such verbs can in turn form imperfectives with the suffix -ыва-, expressing the action being in its final stage

Я довязáла^{p} (довя́зываю^{i}) сви́тер отцý.	I have finished (am finishing) knitting father's sweater.

The prefix до- can also indicate an action carried on up to a specific point, if this is included in the sentence (see E II):

Мáма дочитáла^{p} до сто двáдцать пя́той страни́цы.	Mother read up to page one hundred and twenty five.

3) RESULT

The addition of a prefix to an unprefixed verb may add the idea of *result.* If there is no other meaning present, this will provide the perfective aspect for the verb:

есть^{i}/*съ*есть^{p}	*eat*	стрóить^{i}/*по*стрóить^{p}	*build*
трáтить^{i}/*ис*трáтить^{p}	*spend*		

The perfective indicates that the result has been achieved, the imperfective that an attempt has been made to achieve the result.

The idea of result may be combined with a number of other meanings discussed in the following sections: spatial meanings (section 4), related actions (section 5) and evaluation (section 7).

4) SPATIAL

Spatial meanings are combined with the idea of result in verbs of movement and physical action. These meanings are examined in detail in chapter 17. A single verb can produce a whole series of spatial modifications. The prefixed perfective verbs regularly produce imperfectives with the same spatial meaning:

въезжа́ть^{i} /въе́хать^{p}	*go in*
выезжа́ть^{i} /вы́ехать^{p}	*go out of*
доезжа́ть^{i} /дое́хать^{p}	*go as far as*
заезжа́ть^{i} /зае́хать^{p}	*call in on*
наезжа́ть^{i} /нае́хать^{p}	*collide*
объезжа́ть^{i} /объе́хать^{p}	*drive round*
отъезжа́ть^{i} /отъе́хать^{p}	*go away from*
переезжа́ть^{i} /перее́хать^{p}	*go across*
подъезжа́ть^{i} /подъе́хать^{p}	*go up to*
приезжа́ть^{i} /прие́хать^{p}	*arrive*
проезжа́ть^{i} /прое́хать^{p}	*go through, past*
разъезжа́ться^{i} /разъе́хаться^{p}	*disperse*
съезжа́ть^{i} /съе́хать^{p}	*go down*
съезжа́ться^{i} /съе́хаться^{p}	*gather*
уезжа́ть^{i} /уе́хать^{p}	*leave*

5) RELATED ACTION

There are a series of modifications to the verb which combine result with relating the action under consideration to another action. The verbs are found in both perfective and imperfective forms.

A) <u>ACTION REPEATED</u>

The prefix пере- (see O IV) is used to convey the idea of an action being performed once again:

переде́лывать^{i} /переде́лать^{p}	*redo*
перестра́ивать^{i} /перестро́ить^{p}	*rebuild*
переиздава́ть^{i} /переизда́ть^{p}	*republish*
перечи́тывать^{i} /перечита́ть^{p}	*reread*

The first two suggest that the action will be done differently.

B) <u>EXTRA ACTION</u>

There are three prefixes used to express this idea: до- (see E IV), под- (see Q IV) and при- (see T III).

докупа́ть^{i} /докупи́ть^{p} прикупа́ть^{i} /прикупи́ть^{p}	*buy in addition*
подрисо́вывать^{i} /подрисова́ть^{p} пририсо́вывать^{i} /пририсова́ть^{p}	*add (to a drawing)*
долива́ть^{i} /доли́ть^{p} подлива́ть^{i} /подли́ть^{p}	*add (liquid) to*

C) <u>CANCELLATION OF PREVIOUS ACTION</u>

There are two prefixes used with this meaning: от- (see N V) and раз- (W III).

отгова́ривать^{i} /отговори́ть^{p}	*dissuade*
разу́чиваться^{i} /разучи́ться^{p}	*lose art of*

Pairs of verbs with opposite meanings are often formed from a single verb.

привя́зывать^{i} /привяза́ть^{p}	*tie up*
отвя́зывать^{i} /отвяза́ть^{p}	*untie*

The prefixes are sometimes added on to verb roots, which do not exist as unprefixed verbs:

одева́ть^{i} /оде́ть^{p}	*dress*
раздева́ть^{i} /разде́ть^{p}	*undress*
вооружа́ть^{i} / вооружи́ть^{p}	*arm*
разоружа́ть^{i} /разоружи́ть^{p}	*disarm*

D) <u>RESPONSE TO PREVIOUS ACTION</u>

The prefix от- can also indicate an action in response to a previous action:

Мы её зва́ли, но она́ не отозвала́сь^{p}.	We called her but she didn't answer.

6) FREQUENCY

A) ACTION ON A SINGLE OCCASION

Action on a single occasion is a feature of the perfective verb in Russian. This has already been discussed in chapter 9. Most of the perfective verbs discussed above indicate an action on a single occasion as well as expressing ideas of time or result.

The suffix -ну- can indicate one single action and is used with verbs that denote a series of identical actions. It has already been discussed in section 3A of chapter 8.

а́хатьⁱ	*sigh*	а́хнутьᵖ	*give a sigh*
глота́тьⁱ	*swallow*	глотну́тьᵖ	*swallow (once)*

In some cases the suffix -ну- is used as a means of forming the perfective:

привыка́тьⁱ/привы́кнутьᵖ *get used to*
достига́тьⁱ/дости́гнутьᵖ *reach*

The suffix -ану- combines the idea of a single action with an expression of the intensity of the action. It is used in colloquial speech.

дергану́тьᵖ	*pull strongly*	(= си́льно дёрнуть)
толкану́тьᵖ	*push strongly*	(= си́льно толкну́ть)

B) ACTION ON MORE THAN ONE OCCASION

Chapter 9 discusses the fact that an action on more than one occasion is most frequently expressed by the imperfective aspect. Some imperfectives cannot depict a continuous process and are usually used to indicate a repeated action (see chapter 8, section 4 B II):

съеда́ть† *eat* прочи́тывать† *read*

Repetition can be accompanied by a number of other meanings:

I) non-intensive irregular action

Unprefixed verbs having the meaning of a concrete action or a state form imperfective verbs with the suffixes -ивать or -ывать combined with the prefixes по-, под- or при-. The meaning of such verbs is that the action is performed non-intensively and not very frequently:

писа́ть^{i}	*write*	попи́сывать^{i}	*write (from time to time)*
боле́ть^{i}	*ache*	поба́ливать^{i}	*ache (on and off)*
ка́шлять^{i}	*cough*	пока́шливать^{i} or подка́шливать^{i}	*cough (intermittently)*
говори́ть^{i}	*say*	пригова́ривать^{i}	*keep on saying*

II) repeated action in the past

The use of the suffixes -ывать, -ивать or -ать with unprefixed verbs adds the meaning that the action *used* to happen but no longer does and is often accompanied by an idea of frequency. Such verbs are used largely in past tense and are a feature of literary prose:

Я у них си́живал^{i} це́лыми днями.	I used to sit with them for days on end.
В мо́лодости я знава́л^{i} мно́гих интере́сных люде́й.	I used to know many interesting people in my youth.

III) Reciprocal action

The prefix пере- combined with verbs ending in -ываться or -иваться is used to form new imperfective verbs with the meaning of a reciprocal action repeated between several participants (see O VIII). This is limited to a small group of verbs:

перегова́риваться^{i}	*exchange remarks with*
перепи́сываться^{i}	*correspond with*

A reciprocal action not necessarily indicating repetition may be conveyed by the suffix -ся alone (see chapter 15 section 5B):

Ребёнок слы́шал, как роди́тели ссо́рились^{i} .	The child heard his parents quarelling.

IV) action to a series of objects

The addition of the prefixes пере- (see O VII), по-, (see P V), раз-, об- (see L IV) convey the idea of a repeated action to a whole series of objects. The perfective verb expresses the event as a result of a series of identical actions to individual objects.

переби́ть^{p} (всю посу́ду)	*smash (all the dishes)*
поброса́ть^{p} (все ве́щи)	*throw (everything) around*
раскупа́ть^{i} /раскупи́ть^{p} (биле́ты)	*buy up the tickets*
объезжа́ть^{i} /объе́здить^{p} (всех друзе́й)	*visit (all one's friends)*

Imperfectives are formed from verbs prefixed in раз- or об-. They are less frequently formed from verbs with the prefix пере- and never from those prefixed with по-.

The prefix пере- may refer both to an action repeated to a whole series of objects and to an action performed by a whole series of subjects:

Он перепро́бовал^p всё, что пригото́вила хозя́йка.	He tried everthing the hostess cooked.
Все го́сти перепро́бовали^p э́то ку́шанье.	All the guests tried this food.

The prefix по- can be added to both prefixed and unprefixed verbs and to verbs of either aspect. The result is always a perfective verb, which is used in colloquial speech:

повыла́вливать^p *or* повы́ловить^p (всю ры́бу) *catch all the fish*
пооткрыва́ть^p *or* пооткры́ть^p (все две́ри) *open (all the doors)*

These verbs are not always found in dictionaries. A highly expressive variant is found in conversational language: it combines the prefixes по- and на- into verbs with the meaning: *a series of actions performed gradually to a large number of objects or by a large number of subjects:*

Из Москвы́ пона́ехали^p го́сти.	A lot of visitors have come from Moscow.
В го́роде за после́дние го́ды понастро́или^p мно́го одина́ковых домо́в.	In recent years they have built a lot of identical houses in the town.

7) EVALUATION

We have so far examined modifications to the verb which add dimensions such as space or time to the verb. This section will investigate a range of modifications which evaluate the intensity, duration and result of the action; in a number of instances they add an emotional value to the action.

In many cases the idea of evaluation is accompanied by the expression of a result (sections A, B, C, D). In such cases the formation of imperfective verbs usually by means of the suffixes -ивать and -ывать either not possible at all or if they are possible, they are often rarely used or cannot indicate a process but only repetition.

The following table lists the main prefixed (perfective) forms found in this section:

OVER-ACHIEVEMENT	переварить^{p}	*overcook*
UNDER-ACHIEVEMENT	недоварить^{p}	*undercook*
QUANTITY	наварить^{p}	*cook (a quantity of)*
CAREFUL ACTION	проварить^{p}	*cook thoroughly*
LESS INTENSIVE ACTION	подлечить^{p}	*have some treatment*
LONG INTENSIVE ACTION + RESULT	докричаться^{p}	до + G *shout till one is heard*
EXHAUSTIVE ACTION	начитаться^{p}	*shout to heart's content*
GREAT INTENSITY	разругать^{p}	*berate*
INCREASE IN INTENSITY	разговориться^{p}	*warm to one's theme*
OVER INTENSIVE (UNDESIRABLE RESULT)	докричаться^{p}	(до хрипоты) *shout (till hoarse)*
EXCESSIVE ACTION	изолгаться^{p}	*become inveterate liar*
EXCESSIVE ACTION (UNPLEASANT CONSEQUENCE)	залечить^{p}	*murder (by unskillful treatment)*
OVER INTENSIVE (TOTAL ABSORPTION)	зачитаться^{p}	*become engrossed reading*
OVER INTENSIVE (INTELLECTUAL ACTIVITY)	вчитаться^{p}	*get a grasp of a text*

A) <u>OVER/UNDER ACHIEVEMENT</u>

The idea of overachievement, an excessive action above the expected standard, is conveyed by the prefix пере- (see O V) and of underachievement, an incomplete action below the expected standard by недо- (see J I). Such verbs regularly form an imperfective with the suffix -ива- or -ыва-:

недоваривать†/недоварить^{p} *undercook*
переваривать†/переварить^{p} *overcook*

With intransitive verbs of activity and condition the prefix пере- is used more frequently to indicate an excessive action of great length and intensity:

перелёживать†/перележать^{p} *lie too long*
перерабатывать†/переработать^{p} *exceed fixed hours of work*

Table 35 provides examples of both transitive and intransitive verbs used with the prefixes недо- and пере-.

The prefix недо- should not be confused with prefix до- used in negative sentences:

Он ещё не дописал^{p} письмо. He hasn't finished the letter yet.

B) QUANTITY

The prefix на- is added to a verb to indicate that the action refers to a large quantity of the object, which is placed in the genitive case (see H IV)

BASIC VERB	QUANTITY VERB
вари́ть^{i} /свари́ть^{p} ка́шу cook porridge	нава́ривать†/навари́ть^{p} ка́ши cook a lot of porridge
гла́дить^{i} /погла́дить^{p} руба́шку iron a shirt	нагла́живать†/нагла́дить^{p} руба́шек iron a lot of shirts
де́лать^{i} /сде́лать^{p} игру́шки make toys	наде́лать^{p} игру́шек make a lot of toys
мыть^{i} /помыть^{p} я́блоки wash apples	намыва́ть†/намы́ть^{p} я́блок wash a lot of apples
печь^{i} /испе́чь^{p} пироги́ bake pies	напека́ть†/напе́чь^{p} пирого́в bake a lot of pies

The above verbs all express the idea of a large quantity and therefore cannot be combined with such words as: немно́го *little*, чуть-чуть *a tiny bit*.

The idea of a *large* quantity is sometimes absent in the following circumstances:

I) change of object

The unprefixed verb has the object affected by the action, the prefixed verb a related object:

давúть^{i} апельси́н — *squeeze an orange*
нада́вливать†/надави́ть^{p} со́ку — *squeeze juice*

II) future action

The prefixed verb expresses an action, the result of which will be used in the future:

соли́ть^{i} (капу́сту) — *pickle (cabbage)*
наса́ливать†/насоли́ть^{p} (капу́сты на́ зиму) — *pickle (some cabbage for winter)*

The prefix на- can also be found with an accusative object (see sections C and D III below):

нагла́живать^{i} /нагла́дить^{p} (руба́шку) — *iron (a shirt) carefully*
балова́ть^{i} /набалова́ть^{p} (ребёнка) — *spoil (a child) a lot*

C) CAREFUL ACTION

The prefixes вы-, на-, от-, про- are used if the speaker considers the action to have been carried out carefully. The following table gives examples of each prefix:

BASIC VERB WITH PERFECTIVE		CAREFUL ACTION
бели́ть[i] /побели́ть[p]	*whitewash*	выбе́ливать[i] /вы́белить[p]
мыть[i] /помы́ть[p]	*wash*	намыва́ть[i] /намы́ть[p]
точи́ть[i] /поточи́ть[p]	*sharpen*	отта́чивать[i] /отточи́ть[p]
жа́рить[i] /пожа́рить[p]	*roast*	прожа́ривать[i] /прожа́рить[p]

D) INTENSITY OF ACTION

I) Less intensive action

This idea can be conveyed by the prefixes под- (see Q V), при- (see T IV) and, less commonly, по- (see P III). Tables 36 and 37 give examples.

II) Long and intensive action + result

The prefix до- combined with the suffix -ся (see E V) or occasionally вы́- is used to express a long and intensive action with the achievement of a result. Table 38 compares other perfective forms with ones expressing a long intensive action with the achievement of a result.

III) Exhaustive action

The prefix на- combined with the suffix -ся (see H III) adds the meaning of an exhaustive action to the full satisfaction of the speaker. It can be added to any verb of activity or human condition:

говори́ть[i]	*speak*	нагова́риваться[†]/наговори́ться[p]	*talk oneself out*
есть[i]	*eat*	наеда́ться[†]/нае́сться[p]	*eat one's fill*

With verbs expressing unpleasant or undesirable states or activities, the prefix adds the meaning of *action to a high degree*:

пла́кать[i]	*cry*	напла́каться[p]	*have a good cry*
голода́ть	*starve*	наголода́ться[p]	*be extremely hungry*

A few verbs express the idea of an intense action with the prefix на- on its own:

баловáть^{i}	*spoil*	набаловáть^{p}	*spoil a lot*
мýчить^{i}	*torment*	намýчить^{p}	*torment a lot*

The prefix вы- combined with the suffix -ся (see D II) suggests that the exhaustive action brings the subject relief:

говори́ть^{i}	*speak*	выговáриваться^{i}/вы́говориться^{p}	*speak out*
спать^{i}	*sleep*	высыпáться†/вы́спаться^{p}	*have good sleep*

IV) <u>Action of great intensity</u>

This is conveyed by the prefixes раз- or, less commonly, из-:

ругáть^{i}/вы́ругать^{p}	*curse*		
	разругáть^{p} or изругáть^{p}		*berate*
критиковáть^{i}/покритиковáть^{p}	*criticise*		
	раскритикóвывать^{i}/раскритиковáть^{p}		*slate*
худéть^{i}/похудéть^{p}	*grow thin*		
	исхудáть^{p}		*become emaciated*

V) <u>Increase in intensity</u>

The prefix раз- is used combined with the suffix -ся (see W IV). Some common examples are:

разговори́ться^{p}	*warm to one's theme*
разбáливаться^{i}/разболéться^{p}	*become very ill*

VI) <u>Excessive intensity</u>

The following shades of meaning are found:

a) The prefix до- combined with the suffix -ся and the preposition до + genitive expresses an undesirable outcome:

докупáться^{p}	(до простýды)	*swim (until you catch cold)*
докричáться^{p}	(до хрипоты́)	*shout (until you are hoarse)*

b) The prefix из- combined with the suffix -ся expresses the idea of an excessive action:

исстрадáться^{p}	*become worn out (with suffering)*
изолгáться^{p}	*become an inveterate liar*

c) The prefix за- and an activity verb can express the idea of affecting a living creature to an excessively intense extent with unpleasant consequences:

заговори́ть^{p}	*talk someone's head off*
закорми́ть^{p}	*overfeed*

d) The prefix за- combined with the suffix -ся (see F III) is added to a limited group of activity verbs to produce verbs with the meaning of becoming totally absorbed in the action:

загова́риваться†/заговори́ться^{p}	*be carried away by talking*
заслу́шиваться†/заслу́шаться^{p}	*listen spellbound to*
засма́триваться^{i}/засмотре́ться^{p}	*be lost in contemplation of*

A few verbs stress that there will be unfortunate consequences:

зараба́тываться†/зарабо́таться^{p}	*tire onself out with work*
зау́чиваться†/заучи́ться^{p}	*overstudy*

e) The prefix в- combined with the suffix -ся (see A III) expresses the idea of intensive intellectual activity:

вчи́тываться^{i}/вчита́ться^{p}	*get a grasp of a text*
вслу́шиваться^{i}/вслу́шаться^{p}	*listen attentively to*

The verb спать *sleep* is listed below as an example of the range of meanings that a single verb can have with a variety of prefixes, all of which express different levels of satisfaction of a person's needs:

высыпа́ться†/вы́спаться^{p}	*sleep fully and well*
проспа́ться^{p}	= вы́спаться *after drinking and sober up*
отсыпа́ться^{i}/отоспа́ться^{p}	= вы́спаться *after work, a sleepless night, a journey*
заспа́ться^{p}	*sleep too long*
переспа́ть^{p}	*sleep too long with possible unpleasant result*
недосыпа́ть†/недоспа́ть^{p}	*sleep less than necessary*

8) OTHERS

The modifications discussed in this section are less regular. They often change the meaning radically, at times producing verbs with meanings which are substantially different from the basic verb. Many of the meanings in the perfective are combined with the idea of result.

A) ACQUISITION

Verbs prefixed with вы-, за- (see F IX), на-, от- convey the idea that something has been acquired or achieved. The following shades of meaning are observed:

I) Desirable acquisition after long intensive action

This is conveyed by the prefix вы-:

выпрáшивать^{i}/вы́проситьp	*obtain by begging*
вы́стоять (билéты)	*stand in queue and get (tickets)*

II) Desirable acquisition (length of action unspecified)

This is conveyed by the prefixes за-, от- or вы-:

зарабáтывать^{i}/зарабóтать^{p}	*earn*
завоёвывать^{i}/завоевáть^{p}	*conquer*
выи́грывать^{i}/вы́играть^{p} (дéньги)	*win (money)*
отсу́живать^{i}/отсуди́ть^{p} (учáсток)	*gain (piece of land) after a trial*

III) Acquisition (neutral)

The prefix на- conveys the idea of acquisition. Whether this is desirable or not depends on the object of the verb:

нагу́ливать^{i}/нагуля́ть^{p} (аппети́т, нáсморк)
get (appetite, cold) after walking
наживáть^{i}/нажи́ть^{p} (богáтство, врагóв)
acquire (wealth, enemies)

B) LOSS

The prefix про- (see U VII) is added to activity verbs and verbs of seeing, hearing to indicate loss:

прои́грывать^{i}/проигрáть^{p} (в кáрты дом)	*lose (house at cards)*
просыпáть$^{+}$/проспáть^{p} (пóезд)	*miss (train) by being asleep*
прослу́шивать$^{+}$/прослу́шать^{p} (отвéт)	*miss (answer)*

C) <u>SUPREMACY</u>

The prefixes пере- (see O IX), and, occasionally об-, can suggest the achievement of supremacy:

перекри́кивать†/перекрича́ть^{p}	*shout down*
перехитри́ть^{p}	*outwit*
обы́грывать^{i}/обыгра́ть^{p}	*beat (at a game)*

D) <u>CONSUMPTION</u>

The prefix из- can have the meaning of consuming the object by performing the action:

исстре́ливать†/исстреля́ть^{p} (патро́ны)	*use up (cartridges)*
испи́сывать†/исписа́ть^{p} (каранда́ш)	*use up (pencil)*
изна́шивать†/износи́ть^{p} (ту́фли)	*wear out (shoes)*

E) <u>MISTAKEN ACTION</u>

The prefixes о- (об-) and про- (see L VI and U VI) indicate an action carried out by mistake. Both can be combined with the suffix -ся. о-(об) + -ся usually indicates a slip of a mechanical nature, о- otherwise usually results in harm being caused to the object. про- (with or without -ся) usually indicates carelessness:

огова́риваться†/оговори́ться^{p}	*make a slip in speaking*
обве́шивать^{i}/обве́сить^{p}	*give short weight to*
проговáриваться^{i}/проговори́ться^{p}	*let something slip*
просыпа́ть^{i}/просы́пать^{p}	*spill*

F) <u>DAMAGE</u>

The prefix за- can indicate damage after a lengthy action:

заи́грывать†/заигра́ть^{p} (пласти́нку)	*wear out (record)*
зачи́тыва́ть†/зачи́та́ть^{p} (кни́гу)	*wear (book) out*
	fail to return (book)

If the verb is one of physical action, the *damage* will result in the death of the object:

забива́ть^{i}/заби́ть^{p}	*beat (to death)*
задави́ть^{p}	*knock down (in car)*

G) <u>UNPLEASANT STATE</u>

The prefix от- can convey the idea of pain or numbness caused to a part of the body after a prolonged action. It is used with verbs indicating position:

отлёживать[†]/отлежа́ть[P]	*make numb by lying*
отси́живать[†]/отсиде́ть[P]	*make numb by sitting*

H) <u>TIREDNESS</u>

The prefixes за- and у-, with or without -ся, can indicate tiredness:

зае́здить[P] (ло́шадь) уе́здить[P] (ло́шадь)	*exhaust (horse)*
забе́гаться[P]	*run oneself to a standstill*
загоня́ть[P]	*work to death*

9) THE VERB СТОЯТЬ

In the final section of this chapter we will examine some of the prefixed forms that the verb стоя́ть can have. This verb has been selected because it displays a great variety of the non-spatial modifications discussed in this chapter. Spatial prefixes have been discussed in chapters 14 (Verbs of Motion) and 17 (The Use of Verbal Prefixes).

A) <u>TIME</u>

I) <u>End of action</u>

ОТ-

Он уже́ отстоя́л[P] сме́ну.	He has finished his shift.
Мы своё отстоя́ли[P], тепе́рь вы посто́йте.	We've done our turn, now you do yours.

II) <u>Limited duration</u>

a) Indefinite time

ПО-

Он постоя́л[P] не́которое вре́мя у её до́ма, но так никого́ и не дожда́вшись, ушёл.	He stood for some time near her house, but left without waiting for anyone to come.

b) Not lengthy

ПО-

Дéти постоя́ли^{p} там всегó 10 минýт.	The children only stood there for 10 minutes.

c) Lengthy

ПРО-, ВЫ-, ОТ-

Онй простоя́ли^{p} здесь цéлый день.	They stood here the whole day.
Онй простáивали† здесь цéлыми дня́ми.	They used to stand here for days on end.
Мы два часá вы́стояли^{p}. (= простоя́ли^{p}, отстоя́ли^{p})	We stood for two hours.

III) <u>Action to specific point</u>

ДО-

Студéнты достоя́ли^{p} до пятй часóв.	The students stood until five o'clock.
Онй всегдá достáивали† до концá.	They always stayed till the end.

B) <u>EVALUATION</u>

Three prefixes are used to express the idea of *standing too long*. За- (+ -ся) has the meaning of complete absorption:

Нýжно егó позвáть, он застоя́лся^{p} пéред витрйной.	We must call him, he has been standing too long in front of the shop window.

До- + -ся assumes unpleasant consequences:

Мы достоймся^{p} здесь до тогó, что не попадём ни в кафé, ни в ресторáн.	We'll stand here so long that we'll not get in to a cafe or restaurant.

На- + -ся is used in colloquial language to indicate exhaustion:

Мы вчерá настоя́лись^{p} в очередя́х!	We were exhausted standing in queues yesterday!

От- in colloquial language indicates the idea of performing a lengthy action till one's legs are tired:

Все но́ги себе́ отстоя́ли^{p}.	His legs were tired with standing.

C) <u>OTHERS</u>

The verb вы́стоять^{p} can convey the idea of managing to stand for a specific time (and no longer):

Вы́стоял^{p} я там то́лько полчаса́: бы́ло о́чень ду́шно.	I managed to stand there for only half an hour: it was very stuffy.

The verb перестоя́ть^{p} can in colloquial language have the meaning of standing somewhere and waiting until something has finished:

Де́ти перестоя́ли^{p} дождь под а́ркой.	The children waited under the arch until the rain had finished.

The verb устоя́ть^{p} can have the meaning of managing to remain standing:

Ма́льчик получи́л тако́й толчо́к, что не устоя́л^{p} на нога́х и упа́л.	The boy got such a shove that he could not stay on his feet and fell over.

TABLE 35	UNDER/OVER ACHIEVEMENT			
A^i_p	вари́ть свари́ть	говори́ть сказа́ть	де́лать сде́лать	дава́ть дать
B	boil	say	do	give
$C^{\dagger}_p$	недова́ривать недовари́ть	недогова́ривать недоговори́ть	недоде́лывать недоде́лать	недодава́ть недода́ть
$D^{\dagger}_p$	перева́ривать перевари́ть	— —	— —	— —
A^i_p	грузи́ть погрузи́ть	жа́рить пожа́рить	лечи́ть вы́лечить	есть съесть
B	load	roast	treat	eat
$C^{\dagger}_p$	недогружа́ть недогрузи́ть	недожа́ривать недожа́рить	недоле́чивать недолечи́ть	недоеда́ть недое́сть
$D^{\dagger}_p$	перегружа́ть перегрузи́ть	пережа́ривать пережа́рить	переле́чивать перелечи́ть	переeда́ть перее́сть
A^i	гуля́ть	волнова́ться	загора́ть	спать
B	go for walk	be excited	sunbathe	sleep
$C^{\dagger}_p$	— —	— —	— —	недосыпа́ть недоспа́ть
$D^{\dagger}_p$	перегу́ливать перегуля́ть	— переволнова́ться	— перезагора́ть	пересыпа́ть переспа́ть

A basic verb B translation	C under-achievement D over-achievement

TABLE 36	LESS INTENSIVE ACTION I			
A^i	лечи́ть	расти́	стричь	та́ять
B	treat	grow	cut (hair)	melt
C^i_p	выле́чивать вы́лечить	выраста́ть вы́расти	пострига́ть постри́чь	раста́ивать раста́ять
D^i_p	подле́чивать подлечи́ть	подраста́ть подрасти́	подстрига́ть подстри́чь	подта́ивать подта́ять

A basic unprefixed form
B translation
C basic prefixed form
D less intense action

TABLE 37	LESS INTENSIVE ACTION II			
A^i_p	забыва́ть забы́ть	встава́ть встать	зараба́тывать зарабо́тать	открыва́ть откры́ть
B	forget	get up	earn	open
C^i_p	подзабыва́ть подзабы́ть	привстава́ть привста́ть	— подзарабо́тать	приоткрыва́ть приоткры́ть
A^i_p	размина́ться размя́ться	загора́ть загоре́ть	обсыха́ть обсо́хнуть	отстава́ть отста́ть
B	stretch	tan	dry	fall behind
C^i_p	— поразмя́ться	— подзагоре́ть	— пообсо́хнуть	приотстава́ть приотста́ть

A basic prefixed form
B translation
C less intense action

TABLE 38	LONG INTENSIVE ACTION + RESULT			
A^i	будить	ждать	звать	звонить
B	waken	wait	call	ring
C^p	——	подождать	позвать	позвонить
D^p	разбудить	——	——	——
E^i_p	—— добудиться	дожидаться дождаться	—— дозваться	дозваниваться дозвониться
F	succeed in waking	wait for	shout and get answer	ring and get answer
A^i	искать	кричать	стучать	требовать
B	look for	shout	knock	demand
C^p	поискать	прокричать	постучать	потребовать
D^p	найти	——	——	——
E^i_p	доискиваться доискаться	—— докричаться	—— достучаться	—— выгребовать
F	find	shout until heard	knock until heard	obtain on demand

A basic verb
B translation
C perfective indicating an action on one occasion with no indication of result
D perfective with neutral result
E long and intensive action: perfective = result; imperfective = attempt to achieve result
F translation of E.

BIBLIOGRAPHY

1) GENERAL

Словарь современного русского литературного языка, в семнадцати томах, *«Наука»*, Москва-Ленинград, 1948-65

Словарь русского языка в четырех томах, *«Русский язык»*, Москва, 1981-4

Ожегов, С. И., Словарь русского языка (23-е издание), *«Русский язык»*, Москва, 1991

Зализняк, А. А. Грамматический словарь русского языка, *«Русский язык»*, Москва, 1977

Борунова, С. Н., Воронцова, В. Л., Еськова, Н. А. Орфоэпический словарь русского языка (под редакцией Р. И. Аванесова), *«Русский язык»*, Москва, 1989

2) ASPECT

Рассудова, О. П. Употребление видов глагола в русском языке, *Издательство московского университета*, Москва, 1968

Forsyth, J. A Grammar of Aspect, *Cambridge University Press*, Cambridge, 1970

Rassudova, O. P. Aspectual Usage in Modern Russian, *Russky Yazyk*, Moscow, 1984

3) VERBS OF MOTION

Muravyova, L. Verbs of Motion in Russian, *Progress Publishers*, Moscow

4) PREFIXES

Барыкина, А. Н. и др. Изучение глагольных приставок, *«Русский язык»*, Москва, 1981

Ah Lin Tang's

CHINESE WHISPERS

COOKBOOK

To Alan + Pat

Selamat Makan

Ah Lin

Printed in Victoria, BC, Canada

Note for Librarians: a cataloguing record for this book that includes Dewey Decimal Classification and US Library of Congress numbers is available from the Library and Archives of Canada. The complete cataloguing record can be obtained from their online database at:
www.collectionscanada.ca/amicus/index-e.html
ISBN 1-4120-2659-8

TRAFFORD

This book was published *on-demand* in cooperation with Trafford Publishing. On-demand publishing is a unique process and service of making a book available for retail sale to the public taking advantage of on-demand manufacturing and Internet marketing. On-demand publishing includes promotions, retail sales, manufacturing, order fulfilment, accounting and collecting royalties on behalf of the author.

Offices in Canada, USA, UK, Ireland, and Spain
book sales for North America and international:
Trafford Publishing, 6E–2333 Government St.
Victoria, BC V8T 4P4 CANADA
phone 250 383 6864 toll-free 1 888 232 4444
fax 250 383 6804 email to orders@trafford.com

book sales in Europe:
Trafford Publishing (UK) Ltd., Enterprise House, Wistaston Road Business Centre
Crewe, Cheshire CW2 7RP UNITED KINGDOM
phone 01270 251 396 local rate 0845 230 9601
facsimile 01270 254 983 orders.uk@trafford.com

order online at:
www.trafford.com/robots/04-0487.html

10 9 8 7 6 5 4 3 2 1

Acknowledgements

I would like to thank my husband Max for helping me to persevere at writing this book and for all his comments on my food. Thank you for your continued support.
I also thank my son Matthew who helped me prepare and type the book and my son Jonathan who has tested all the dishes and helped me fold my serviettes.

Also many thanks to my assistant Ann who has consistently been superb at helping me behind the scenes. I am grateful to my friends and customers who have always praised my food and taken the time to write thanking me for a splendid meal.

Finally I thank my Chinese family members who have passed on to me their recipes and given me the chance to learn from them. This collection of wisdom has helped my 'Chinese Whispers' book to progress, and enabled me to pass my knowledge on to you.

Contents

Introduction

I was born the youngest of twelve children. From the age of two I was brought up by my Nonya godparents who took care of me until it was time to attend school. I was then raised back home by my Chinese parents. I remember the happy times I had when I was growing up and living with my godmother who involved me in her activities when it came to cooking. Watching her prepare the dishes for a mealtime or Chinese festival was a delight and made me realise just how important these meals were in bringing people together, thus playing an important part in my Nonya-Baba culture.

As my godmother sat down grinding the spices or cooking on the kitchen stove she would talk through the dishes she was preparing meticulously. As a Nonya they take pride in their cooking. The food is their passion and a full time job. Nonya cooking is generously spicy. Using coconut milk to balance out the taste of the hot and sour dishes. Her influence in using chillies, tamarind, pungent spices and fresh roots from exotic plants was essential.

My early interest was further fuelled as I grew by various trips to Penang to visit my uncle and aunt and see what was being cooked in their restaurant. This provided an early experience to see the hustling and bustling activities needed to prepare delicious meals.

At home, breakfast was a quick bicycle ride to a lively street store or food shop providing a complete variety of foods ranging from Chinese & Malay to Indian delicacies.

As Malaysia is a hot country school study is divided into two sessions; morning and afternoon. I was in the morning group. After school I hurried home for both the tasty food and to hopefully catch the intricate preparation. This time four or five dishes were served for lunch. One was usually a soup and one of the others a stir-fried vegetable dish, plus of course the commonplace plain boiled rice.

After lunch it was usual to take a nap or finish off the housework. In the early evening breeze we tended to sit around talking or revising work. We also enjoyed activities like shopping, visiting a *passa malam* night market and eventually making our way to a night food court to enjoy the exciting atmosphere and observe the care taken to produce the busy night's food.

Being brought up surrounded by people who have a passion for food I myself became a keen cook and studied cooking after leaving school. And so I came to England to stay with my sister, and married.
I spent some time teaching Oriental cooking at a college, and it was there that a pupil suggested that people would be interested in trying a new way to enjoy Oriental cooking and that I should go to people's houses to cook and inform guests about my cuisine. Instead of them going to a restaurant I prepared the food in their own home for a far more personal and enjoyable meal.
As well as preparing the dishes I also specialised in carving an assortment of animals and garnishes from vegetables and fruit to enhance the appearance of dishes or to provide a talking point for the table of guests.
I have since visited customers' homes, offices and social clubs where I prepared my meals, and could be cooking for ten to forty people. All having a thoroughly enjoyable meal.

I have divided my dishes into four main menus specialising on the area to which those dishes originate, each menu having its own story. These are the same menus which I have prepared for my customers. I have included copies of these menus before each of their particular introductions to their dishes. These menus are from Penang, Thailand, Singapore and Beijing. They produce lovely dishes using ingredients which are now readily available in England. Originally when I began I had to go to London to buy specific items, but now they can be purchased in local Chinese supermarkets which many major towns presently have.
With this book it will be possible to learn dishes from 'Fried Crispy Wonton' to 'Crispy Duck Aromatic style'. This collection of recipes will enable you to throw an outstanding dinner party where the guests are not just full of delicious food but are also asking you for the recipes and how you became such an excellent cook!

If any of my readers would like to discuss any of the recipes in this book or have any recipes from their travels they can always telephone me on *0117-9621101* or email at *ahlintang@hotmail.com*.

I call my book 'Chinese Whispers' because all the recipes have been passed to me by my relatives. They have been altered & improved to fit their choices, and I myself have enhanced them by incorporating the freshest ingredients, the finest spices, and ensuring the steps taken to produce a dish are followed as perfectly as possible. These 'methods of preparation' are what I refer to as 'true recipes'. They are the closely guarded secrets and the full ingredients and preparation necessary to properly produce a particular dish, as prepared in authentic restaurants or in their original countries designed to be the best styles of the recipes around. They are not cut down versions tailored for the masses which many recipe books or teachers feel is the best that they can offer. These are workable recipes as used by myself on a professional basis, and will produce real, original and most importantly delicious results.

Ah Lin Tang

EXPLANATIONS

I include here a list of descriptions for some of the more uncommon ingredients/terms which you, the reader, may not be familiar with. This list is by no means exhaustive as I feel that many once supposedly specialist Chinese ingredients are now far more readily available in the large supermarkets so that the average cook should be familiar with many of the products & terms used and would not benefit from such basic explanations. Also, where appropriate, I may comment on how easy, or indeed difficult, a certain item is to obtain.

I live in Bristol and bought the majority of my Oriental supplies from Michelle who runs an Oriental food specialists shop called *Kin Yip Hon* at 16A St Thomas Street, Bristol.

Al dente - To cook so as to be still firm when bitten. [Italian, literally 'to the tooth']

Belachan - Also known as *Shrimp Paste*, or the Thai *kapi*. Made from shrimps which are ground and fermented, thus providing an exotic fragrance to many dishes. It is used throughout Indonesia, Malaysia and Thailand, but in only small amounts. It can provide an impressive flavour to your dishes if handled correctly. It can be found in some large supermarkets, though a specialist Chinese grocer would definitely stock this.

Bamboo shoots - Are the young, edible shoots of the bamboo plant, native to Asia, and a popular item in Chinese cooking. Fresh bamboo shoots are the best, though in Britain they are usually only available in tins. They can be readily bought in most supermarkets. After opening the tin, they should be rinsed thoroughly. Unused bamboo shoots should be stored in the refrigerator in a jar of water, with the water changed daily. And can keep for a week.

Bamboo steamers - Come in several sizes of which 25cm is most suitable for home use. The food is placed in the steamer, and that in turn is placed above boiling water in a wok or pot. A tight-fitting bamboo lid prevents the steam escaping. Essential for preparing delicious *dim sum*.

Bean paste - Thick paste of crushed soy beans (black or yellow). Available from Chinese groceries, and is sold in jars.

Beancurd - Also known as *doufu* in China, and *tofu* in Japan. This soft, cream-coloured curd is prepared from yellow soy beans and is highly nutritious and full of protein. On its own it can have a bland taste but it has the ability to absorb the flavours of the food it is cooked with, and is thus used in a number of dishes, from soups to stir-fries. It is readily available in many supermarkets, Chinese grocers, and even health food shops. It has various forms, ranging from several dried varieties to a more firm 'cake' form.

Black beans – Fermented whole soy beans, preserved in salt and ginger. Chinese grocery shops sell them in a box container under the name of 'Preserved Beans with ginger'.

Blanch - Blanching is a process whereby the food is placed in hot/boiling water for a few minutes to cook it briefly but not entirely, and then plunged in cold water to stop this cooking process. It is a technique commonly used with Chinese vegetables prior to stir-frying. The goal is to slightly soften the ingredient and help to bring out its flavour without overcooking.

Candlenuts - A cream coloured, waxy, heart-shaped nut. Are usually crushed or ground before being mixed with other ingredients, and are especially popular in Indonesian dishes.

Chicken stock - Is an all-purpose base for many delicious dishes. It combines well with other foods. Prepared by mixing cold water and chicken bones in a large pan (you can use pork bones if you wish). Once boiled let it simmer for 5 minutes. Turn off heat. Pour into a clean container with a sieve to hold back the bones and froth.

Chilli oil - Can be bought from specialist Chinese grocers. I prefer to make mine by chopping dried red chillies and fresh red chillies. Put into a pan with vegetable oil. Cook slowly until the chilli oil oozes out usually about 10 minutes. Allow to cool and bottle.

Chillies - Are used extensively in Asian recipes. They are the seed pods of the capsicum plant and are widely available in fresh, dried or ground forms.

Chinese celery cabbage - Also called *Chinese leaves*. This Northern Chinese vegetable is popular among most Chinese due to its sweet, mild flavour and its versatility. It has a compact head of white stalks extending into yellow-white crinkled leaves. It has the ability to absorb flavours and its delicious crunchy texture makes a popular Chinese ingredient. It is usually only available in specialist Chinese groceries, or occasionally the larger supermarkets. It can be stored along in the vegetable section of the refrigerator, where it will keep for a week.

Chinese mustard green - There are different varieties but the commonest available has a green stalk which extends into a single, large, oval, ribbed leaf. It has a characteristic taste, and is usually only sold in specialist Chinese groceries.

Chinese white cabbage - Also called *Bok Choy*. There are many varieties, the most common has a long, smooth, white stem, and large crinkly green leaves. It has a light, fresh taste, and due to its popularity is available widely in supermarkets.

Cloud ears - Also called *black fungus*. A special type of edible tree fungus, common to Chinese dishes since the sixth century AD. Thin and brittle when dry, they expand to form thick brown clusters when soaked in water for half an hour. They absorb flavours well and provide a delicate crunchy texture, and are often added to hot and sour soup, and stir-fry dishes. Bought from specialist Chinese groceries.

Coriander - Also known as *cilantro* or *Chinese parsley*. Coriander leaves are mainly used as a garnish as one would use parsley. Coriander leaves have a distinctive taste, and are a popular addition to most dishes. Available widely in supermarkets. Avoid yellow and limp leaves, look for fresh, deep green leaves.

Coriander seeds, Cumin seeds - Usually these seeds are roasted. This is best achieved by spreading the required amount on an ovenproof dish, and heating in the oven for a few minutes, shaking the dish several times to ensure they are roasted evenly. When ready the seeds should have darkened and produce a pleasant fragrance.

Cornflour - Also called Cornstarch. This fine starch is extracted from maize and is used to thicken sauces or marinade and provide a velvety texture.

Dried prawns - Also called *Udang kering*. They are usually soaked before cooking. They provide a delicious flavour.

Fennel –Fennel Seeds have a sweet anise like flavour. To intensify flavour roast the seeds before use.

Fermented Red Beancurd - Brick red in colour, with a cheese-like taste, this type of beancurd is fermented with salt, red rice, and rice wine.

Fish sauce - This is a thin, savoury, delicious sauce made from salted fish. It can enhance many dishes, and is used extensively as seasoning in many Thai and Indonesian dishes, and can often be found in Chinese recipes. It is often sold under a variety of names depending on where it was made, with brands labelled with '*nuoc mam*' from Vietnam and '*nam pla*' from Thailand.

Fish-floss - Also known as ground fried fish. This has a distinct taste, and is usually only available in Chinese groceries.

Five-spice powder - This powder normally consists of star anise, cinnamon, cloves, fennel seeds and Sichuan peppercorns. N.B. there are variations which may contain cardamom. This packaged powder is available from specialist Chinese grocers, and is a common ingredient.

Galangal - This creamy-white root resembles ginger. It is only usually available in some specialist Chinese grocers or more commonly in London's Chinatown grocers. It has a delicate flavour.

Garam masala - A spice mixture often used in Indian cookery. Readily available from the large supermarkets.

Hoisin sauce - This reddish-brown, thick sauce is made from soy beans, sugar, vinegar, spices and other flavourings. It has a wide variety of uses and is valued for its unique combination of sweet and spicy flavours. It is readily available in the supermarket Hoisin sauce is available in both jars and tins. It is particularly delicious with aromatic duck in Chinese pancakes!

Jasmine tea –Is a speciality among Chinese teas. It is prepared from green tea of a chosen quality scented with fresh Jasmine flowers. I introduce the Jasmine flowers myself to obtain the correct flavour.

Julienne - Vegetables cut into short thin strips.

Kaffir lime leaves- The Kaffir lime citrus fruit is found in many parts of South-East Asia, but is not easy to find in the West. Its leaves, required for some of the dishes, are usually bought dried, and are available in specialist Chinese grocers and in many large supermarkets.

Lemon grass - This herb, which does indeed resemble a coarse, heavy type of grass, is used in many recipes for its sour-sweet, citrus flavour. It is readily available in grocery shops and is sold fresh in stems.

Mangetout - Also called *Snow peas*. Mangetout, French for *'eat it all'* are a frequent addition to stir-fry dishes. Their sweet flavour also goes well with seasoned meat or poultry. The French name comes from the fact that the whole pea, including the pod, is eaten. They are easily available in supermarkets.

Monosodium Glutamate (MSG) - This is a white crystalline extract of grains and vegetables, occasionally used in Japan, China, and Western food processing, to tenderise and develop the natural flavour of certain foods. Some people can have an adverse reaction to this. I believe that the freshest and finest ingredients need no altering and I therefore never use MSG in any of my dishes.

Mooli - Also known as *Chinese White Radish*. This popular Asian vegetable has no resemblance to the round red radishes we are used to. It is long and white, and resembles a large carrot. It is peeled before use, and is usually sliced or grated prior to cooking. Due to its popularity mooli is now able to be bought in many large supermarkets, and of course specialist Chinese grocers. They should be firm, and unblemished. And can be stored in the vegetable section of your refrigerator for up to one week.

Oyster sauce - This sauce is made from extracts of oysters, wheat flour, cornflour, glutinous rice, salt and sugar, all helping to form its distinct brown colour. This sweet and savoury taste is used in a wide variety of dishes and is delicious. Oyster sauce is normally sold in bottles, and must be refrigerated after opening. Available from specialist Chinese grocers.

Pancake skins - Made from a mixture of flour, water and sesame oil. I suggest that people buy these from specialist Chinese grocers. They are used for wrapping around crispy aromatic duck.

Pandan leaves - Also called *screwpine leaves*. Used for their distinctive fragrance and flavouring, these leaves are often available in large supermarkets.

Pawpaw - An elongated melon-shaped fruit with edible orange flesh and small black seeds. Readily available in most groceries.

Potato Flour - Is flour ground from cooked potatoes. It is used to help thicken sauces and can provide a more subtle and glossy finish than cornflour.

Rice vinegar - Also called *Rice wine vinegar*. This clear in colour vinegar is used in cooking and pickling. It is milder and less acidic than regular vinegar, and can be found in the large supermarkets.

Rock Sugar - Also called Crystal Sugar. This crystallised, pale cane sugar comes in chunks and has a 'pure' sugar taste.

Salted Soy Beans - Whole yellow soy beans fermented with salt and sugar. They are readily available from Chinese grocery shops.

Sambai - Also known as *Sambal*. Is a term for hot chilli sauces/relishes which have a number of variations but are based upon chilli plus another distinct ingredient, thus altering its particular flavour.

Samosa - A fried triangular 'pasty' containing either spiced meat or vegetables.

Sesame Oil - This rich, golden coloured, aromatic oil, made from pressed and toasted sesame seeds, is a popular ingredient in Chinese cooking. Not for use as a cooking oil, since it heats rapidly and burns easily. Instead, sesame oil is normally used as a flavouring. Readily available in most supermarkets and all specialist Chinese food shops.

Shaohsing wine - Also called *Shaoxing* wine. Is produced from fermented glutinous rice. Named after the town in which it originates, this golden wine is one of the oldest ever produced in China. Aged for ten years or more, this rich-flavoured liquid with low alcohol content is used both in drinking and cooking. It can be bought from specialist Chinese grocers. At home, store the rice wine at room temperature, preferably out of the light.

Sharon fruit – A persimmon

Simmer - To cook food gently in liquid that bubbles steadily, just below boiling point, so that the food cooks in even heat without breaking up.

Soy Sauce - Made from fermented soy beans, flour and water, this is one of the most ancient and essential seasoning in Chinese cookery. There are two main kinds of soy sauce: the dark (also called thick) and the light (also called thin). Both are used in general cooking, for marinating, and as dips. As the name implies, light soy sauce is lighter in colour and slightly milder than the dark variety. Many supermarkets will supply both varieties, and therefore be sure to check which one you are buying!

Soya Sauce - Also called *soy sauce*. Please refer to soy sauce.

Spring roll skins - Also called *Spring roll wrappers*. These are thin pastry squares necessary for making spring rolls. They come in several sizes; I use the 22cm square variety, usually with 30 sheets in each packet. They are bought in specialist Chinese grocers from the freezer-section. They do dry out very quickly and therefore attention and precision must be used when preparing them.

Star anise - This reddish-brown, hard, star-shaped spice is widely used in Chinese cooking to flavour meat and poultry. It has a characteristic liquorice flavour and fragrance. It is available in some of the major supermarkets usually sold in small packs.

Sugar-snap peas - Commonly available in supermarkets. These 'young' peas are picked early for their sweet flavour.

Tamarind - An important ingredient used in Asian cookery to give a dish a subtle sourness, often delicately enhancing a meal. It is most often prepared in my menus by simmering a chunk of this dried pulp in water for a few minutes, letting it cool, squeezing its juices and allowing its flavour to seep into the surrounding water. And it is this water/juice which is used in the actual cooking.

Water chestnuts - This white, crunchy vegetable can be bought fresh from many specialist Chinese food shops, but are also commonly sold tinned in large supermarkets. The water chestnut is valued both for its sweetness and its ability to maintain a crisp texture when cooked. Do peel them before use. Unused ones can be kept covered with cold water in a refrigerator for up to 2 weeks if the water is changed daily.

Wonton skins - Also called *wonton wrappers*. These are squares of especially thin pastry, and are made from the same dough as egg noodles i.e. wheat flour, egg and water. They are bought either fresh or frozen from Chinese grocers in small 7½ cm squares. Remember that they do dry out very quickly and become brittle therefore great care and attention must be paid to their preparation.

Notes on the Recipes

All the recipes in this book use United Kingdom measures in metric. Exact conversion from metric to imperial weights are only approximate, and I have appropriately rounded off the measurements as below.

Metric	*Imperial*
25g	1oz
50g	2oz
75g	3oz
100g	4oz
150g	5oz
175g	6oz
200g	7oz
225g	8oz
250g	9oz
275g	10oz
300g	11oz
350g	12oz
375g	13oz
400g	14oz
425g	15oz
450g	16oz

teasp = teaspoon
tabsp = tablespoon

½ teaspoon	2½ ml
	2½ g
1 teaspoon	5ml
	5g
3 teaspoons (1 tabsp)	15ml
	15g

Oven temperatures

Gas Mark	Centigrade	Fahrenheit
2	150	300
3	170	325
4	180	350
5	190	375
6	200	400
7	220	425
8	230	450
9	240	475
10	250	500

Notes on the Preparation

For those who enjoy cooking and are not afraid to take a chance to create a Far Eastern evening they will find this book invaluable. It contains a full banquet with all the suitable dishes supplied.

I have set out the recipes as I had prepared them for my dinner events, thus they are geared to serve ten people (the minimum I catered for). You can reduce the meal by cooking with half measures to suit four or five people as appropriate, but the order of preparation should remain the same to achieve the best results.

Once you have chosen your menu write down the things which you will need to order. If you have not heard of some ingredients search for them in my 'Explanations' list, and if they have to be specifically bought from a specialist Chinese food shop then plan exactly what needs to be purchased and don't be afraid to ask them for help!

Some of the dishes require quite extensive preparation before the evening's meal so make sure you have arranged a suitable amount of time free to ensure everything goes to plan. I suggest you initially start practising with one dish at a time, perhaps adding it to a normal family meal. Thus you can see exactly how long a particular dish takes for you to prepare. Over the years I have become quite adept at preparing multiple items and cooking particular dishes in a good time and so practice really is the key!

If you are cooking say the Taste of Penang menu. It would be best to prepare the starters in the morning, but for a dish such as 'Rasa Sayang Drunken Pear' which requires marinating it would ideally be started the evening before.
And once the big night comes round all your previous preparation will pay off, and you the host or hostess will provide an enjoyable evening with some truly delicious food.

Taste of Thailand

Beijing Banquet

Taste of Penang

Wonton soup

Hot & Sour soup

A Night In Singapore

Penang Fried Rice

Crispy Lemon Chicken

Pork with Ginger & Spring Onion

Prawns in Spicy Crab sauce

Beancurd & Vegetables stuffed with Fish

Stir-fried Vegetables in Oyster sauce

AH LIN TANG'S TASTE OF PENANG

Try my Oriental and Far Eastern dishes from my native land of Malaysia. All food will be prepared by me and served in your home with the host and hostess enjoying a relaxed care free evening. I also specialise in vegetarian dishes.

Whether celebrating a special occasion, entertaining some office clients or even just having a party but preferring something different, then let Ah Lin Tang create a taste of Penang to remember.

Starter

Satay: Tender slices of beef or chicken on sticks grilled, served with peanut sauce and cucumber

Sesame prawn toast and chicken and crab roll mini hors d'oeuvres

Wonton fry: Prawn dumpling fried Penang style

Nonya Spring Roll: Crispy pancakes filled with a delicious Nonya sauce

Main Course

Penang fried rice

Fried crispy chicken in lemon sauce

Sliced pork with ginger and spring onion

Prawns in spicy crab sauce Malaysian style

Beancurd and vegetable stuffed with fish in a sweet and sour sauce

Stir-fried vegetables in oyster sauce

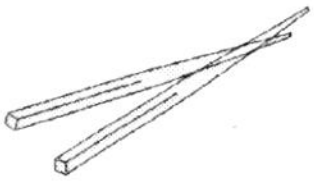

Sweets

Rasa Sayang drunken pear

Singapore Toffee Apple and Banana

All served with ice-cream or cream

Jasmine Tea

Chinese Tableware will be provided. Minimum 10 persons.

Try my Beijing, Singapore and Thai Menus

Ah Lin Tang's Taste Of Penang

When I first came to England in the 1960s Penang was a far off Island. Not many English people that I had met had actually been there except for those in the armed forces. Alternatively a few surveyors and those who had helped in dealing with Malaysian rubber or tin were the only other ones that I had the chance to speak with. Nowadays Penang is a five day tour advert in a Sunday newspaper or available on the Internet for £499. At present you can simply visit any large supermarket and pick up ready-made satay. It is so more easily accessible.

The purpose of my book is to put you in touch with the authentic local recipes, which I have come across whilst living in Malaysia and Penang.
The recipe is not made to a price; it is made because it tastes good and uses local ingredients.

Meals are important to the Chinese and it is common for entire families including aunts, uncles, cousins, nephews, and nieces, to all come together for a meal and sample a vast selection of dishes. Often when sisters and sister-in-laws get together there is an exchange of knowledge and new dishes are added to the table.

I first travelled to Penang (or *Pulau Pinang* as the Malays call it) in the late 1950s. My parents took me there from my home in *Telok Intan* (then called *Telok Anson*). We travelled by car. This was before the opening of the motorway, which provided a route from near my hometown to Butterworth. Butterworth is the port on the west coast of Malaysia, opposite to Penang.
In those days we used to drive on the road through the Malay villages (*kampongs*). Firstly we would stop in *Ipoh* for a delicious Dim Sum breakfast in one of the cafes. We would also travel past all the beautiful houses on Ipoh's 'Millionaire Road' where all the wealthy Chinese live. Continuing along we would visit the 'Ipoh Cave temple' and enjoy feeding the turtles in the inner temple pool with Chinese lettuce leaves bought for a few cents.
Next we are on our way to *Kuala Kangsar* which is the next large town. Throughout the journey there are various stalls at the roadside selling pineapples, durians (the king of fruits) watermelons, local mango, rambutan and many more fresh mouth-watering delights. We usually stop to purchase these

fruits because they are so sweet and refreshing and perfect for travelling in this hot weather.
Soon we arrive in Butterworth at the ferry terminal. This was before the bridge to Penang was built. The ferry runs twenty-four hours a day, and the ticket you purchase allows you the return journey.
The journey across is fascinating and it's great to feel the fresh sea air on your face which helps kill the humidity you have faced in an old non air-conditioned car.
After the ferry ride we drive along the coast road to Gurney Drive where my Aunt's house is. The house is an *attap* style bungalow. The front of the house in the early evening would be transformed into a hawker type café with food prepared my Aunt and her loyal *Penangite* workers. My Aunt is a Peranakan-Nonya and my uncle is originally from Canton in China.

One of the foods, which my Aunt makes is Nonya spring roll (known locally as *Popiah*). The Penangites who work for my Aunt specialise in making satay and other Gurney style dishes.
My wonton fried starter is from my Uncle's country. In Canton they prefer to either boil or steam their wontons. In Penang we tend to make this delicate little dumpling into a fried snack.

With regards to the main courses, of my Penang menu, these are standard dinnertime dishes used to feed the families who travelled to my Aunt's café.
The Malay Chinese tend to make as desserts dishes involving fresh coconut and other local products commonly known as *ice kachang* and *cendol*, which use green pea flour which at present you cannot buy in supermarkets in England, either normal or specialist.

For my sweets I have chosen desserts which are used in Malaysian restaurants and hotels that deal with a large number of Europeans and are thus geared to their tastes and requirements but are nonetheless authentic to that particular area and are commonly enjoyed and prepared by Malaysians.

The *Taste of Penang* menu is time consuming to prepare but is both visually appealing and delicious, and is always worth the effort for the excellent dishes which any host or hostess will be proud to serve.

Starter

BEEF AND CHICKEN SATAY

INGREDIENTS
500g sirloin or rump steak, cut into chunky strips
500g chicken fillets, cut into strips
5 lemon grass stalks
20g belachan
2 teasp fennel seeds
2 teasp cumin seeds
1 tabsp coriander seeds
1 pkt 15cm length bamboo sticks
3 teasp turmeric
3 tabsp sugar
6 tabsp vegetable oil
½ teasp salt
½ teasp pepper
2 tabsp coconut powder
1 tabsp coconut oil, melted (it starts off resembling butter)
2 teasp chicken stock powder
50g tamarind, soaked in 150ml warm water

Additionally for basting: 1 tabsp sugar, 2 tabsp coconut oil (melted)

METHOD
Firstly, prepare the lemon grass by cutting away the lower soft (more bulbous) part, about 4 cm in length. Then chop this lower part into chunks. Set this aside. Keep the remainder of the lemon grass for later.
Allow the tamarind to soak in the warm water for 15 minutes. Then squeeze the tamarind to remove any remaining juices. Drain this tamarind water into a separate container.
Put the fennel, cumin, coriander seeds and belachan into a baking bowl and roast for 10 minutes at 150-160°C. Take it out and leave to cool.
Next grind the roasted spices with the previously chopped lemon grass until very fine.
Empty these ground spices into a large bowl. Now add the turmeric, sugar (3 tabsp), salt, pepper, melted coconut oil (1 tabsp), coconut powder, tamarind

juice, chicken stock powder, and vegetable oil. Mix this well. Then divide this mixture into two separate bowls.
In the first bowl add the chicken strips, mix thoroughly and set aside. In the second bowl add the beef strips, mix thoroughly. Set aside. Allow these meats to marinate for two hours. Once marinated, thread the meat onto the bamboo sticks and finish up the threading until all the meat has been used up.
For basting - Use two of the remaining lemon grass pieces and squash their cut ends. This allows the lemon grass juice to be applied more easily. Set this aside. In a bowl add 1 tablespoon of sugar and 2 tablespoons of melted coconut oil. Stir and mix with the squashed ends of the lemon grass.
Begin to grill the satay. Baste the satay with the squashed lemon grass ends by dipping the ends into the coconut oil and sugar mixture. Wipe this mixture over the cooking satay, and grill until brown ensuring the meat is cooked.

Serve with Satay sauce *(see next recipe)* and cucumber.

Tip – The best flavours for my satay are achieved by cooking them delicately on a barbeque.

SATAY SAUCE

INGREDIENTS

12 dried chillies, soaked in water to soften
6 lemon grass stalks, use only the bulbous part about 4 cm, keep the rest for the sauce
120g shallots, medium sized
3 cloves of garlic
25g belachan (shrimp paste)
10 candlenuts
1 tabsp tomato puree
3 tabsp sugar
½ teasp salt
½ teasp pepper
1 vegetable stock cube
2 teasp turmeric
2 teasp coriander powder
2 teasp curry powder
1 tin coconut milk 400ml
1 piece galangal, squashed
180g tamarind, soaked in 250ml warm water, squeeze out the juice discard used tamarind
Vegetable oil for cooking
60g roasted ground peanut

METHOD

Cut into chunky pieces the soaked chillies, lemon grass, shallots, garlic, candlenuts and belachan. Put these into a grinder and grind until fine.

Heat a wok with oil on medium heat. Add the previously ground spices. Stir and cook slowly, making sure you stir the spices constantly to prevent them from burning.

Now add the coriander and curry powder and keep cooking for a good 10-15 minutes ensuring that all the spices mixed well.

Add the turmeric and tomato puree and the remaining parts of the squashed lemon grass (not used so far). Stir, add the sugar, salt, pepper, and galangal. By this time you should be able to smell the delicious cooked spices.

Turn the heat up and quickly add the tin of coconut milk. Remember to stir the sauce at all times. Add the tamarind juice and the crumbled vegetable cube.

Cook until the sauce bubbles, stir, and let it simmer for a few more minutes.
Taste it to confirm its sweet and sour flavour. Turn the heat off.
Pour the sauce into a container and allow to cool.
The sauce will thicken when you sprinkle in the peanut. Serve.

SESAME PRAWN TOAST

INGREDIENTS

250g fresh small raw prawns, chopped
125g belly of pork, sliced and minced
¾ tin 200ml bamboo shoots, chopped
2 egg whites
1½ tabsp cornflour
1 tabsp light Soy sauce
3 tabsp sesame oil
½ teasp salt
½ teasp pepper
2 teasp sugar
½ cube vegetable stock
1 tabsp fresh coriander, chopped
1 tabsp spring onion, chopped
sesame seeds
6 to 8 slices of bread
vegetable oil, for shallow frying

METHOD

In a big bowl add the prawns, belly of pork, bamboo shoots, egg white, cornflour, light Soy sauce, sesame oil, salt, pepper, sugar, vegetable stock cube, coriander and spring onion. Mix well and set aside.
Line a flat tray with cling film.
On a flat working surface lay the bread down, and spread the prepared mixture all over the upper surface of the bread. Now sprinkle some sesame seeds all over.
Press down lightly on the sesame seeds, and cut the bread diagonally (twice) into quarters.
Place them neatly on the tray. Finish off making the sesame toast by using up the rest of the ingredients in this way.

When needed heat the vegetable oil in a wok on medium heat and fry the sesame prawn toast with the filling side face down in the oil, therefore you know that the sesame toast will cook evenly. Finish off the cooking. Drain and serve.

CHICKEN and CRAB ROLL

INGREDIENTS
1 pkt Chinese rice paper (dry form)
150g fresh crabmeat
4 pieces of chicken thigh (boned and sliced)
3cm length of chilli (sliced)
2 cloves of garlic (sliced)
1 medium-sized carrot (grated)
a handful of transparent noodles (soaked and cut into 5cm lengths)
1 tabsp fresh coriander chopped
1 tabsp spring onion chopped
1 tabsp fish sauce
1 tabsp light Soy sauce
1 teasp chicken stock powder
½ teasp pepper
a pinch of salt
3 tabsp sugar mixed with 3 tabsp water (sugar water)
Oil for frying

METHOD
First soak half a packet of the Chinese rice paper in cold water until soft. Lift out slowly to prevent the soft rice paper from falling apart. Lay on a flat surface and cut it in half. Set aside.
Place the chicken, chilli and garlic into a blender. The filling should be blended until slightly coarse.

Next tip the filling into a large bowl. Add the carrot, crabmeat, chicken stock powder, the soaked transparent noodle, coriander, spring onions, fish sauce, Soy sauce, salt and pepper. Mix this well & set aside.
Line a flat tray with cling film to lay the finished product. On a flat working surface carefully lay a piece of the soft rice paper and brush it with the prepared sugar water.

Place a spoonful of the mixture into one of the corners of the paper, and roll this end along to form a tube. Place the prepared chicken and crabmeat roll onto the flat tray, and finish off preparing the rest of the chicken and crab rolls

Finally just shallow fry, and serve.

Tip - The Chinese rice paper must be purchased from a specialist Chinese food shop. Supermarkets do not supply the correct product.

Chicken & Pineapple with Mangetout (p135)

FRIED CRISPY WONTON

INGREDIENTS

1 pkt of pancake skins (normally used in spring rolls) - defrosted
250g small fresh prawns - chopped
120g belly pork - minced
½ tin (220g) water chestnut - chopped
½ teasp salt
½ teasp pepper
1 teasp sugar
1 tabsp light Soy sauce
1 tabsp ginger - chopped
½ vegetable stock cubes
2 eggs whites
3 tabsp sesame oil
1½ tabsp coriander - chopped
1½ tabsp spring onion - chopped
1 tabsp cornflour
Vegetable oil for frying

Cornflour paste:

> *2 egg yolks*
> *1 tabsp cornflour*
> *3 tabsp water*
> *Mix these three ingredients together well*

METHOD

In a large bowl add the prawns, belly of pork, salt, pepper, water chestnuts, sugar, light Soy sauce, ginger, egg whites, sesame oil, coriander, ½ vegetable stock cube, cornflour and spring onion. Mix well and set aside.
Line a flat tray with cling film, and set aside.
Prepare the cornflour mixture (mentioned in the ingredients). and place them into a bowl.

To make fried wonton:
Divide the pancake skins in half.
Keep one half in a plastic container to use later. With the other half fold a
cut them diagonally. Next separate these triangular pieces.

Arrange one piece of the triangle with the middle pointed tip facing you. Place a dessert spoon of filling onto the pointed end of the pancake skin. Brush the top part of the skin all over with cornflour paste and roll them up. You should now have a long piece of a wonton with a hump in the middle.
Next, lightly brush the top hump, of the central part of the wonton. Fold one side of the pastry skin on to the brushed hump. Now brush again on the folded pastry skin, and fold the other side of the pastry skin the other way to form the figure of a flying bird.
Place this finished product onto the prepared tray. Finish off all the wonton.

Fry them until cooked and golden brown.

Assorted Ah Lin Tang dishes

NONYA SPRING ROLL

INGREDIENTS
50g Dutch cabbage
75g green beans
75g Chinese celery cabbage
½ onion
2 cloves of garlic - chopped
1 tabsp ginger - chopped
2 celery sticks
2 carrots
½ chilli
100g Mooli
225g bean shoots tailed
100g bamboo shoots
10 Chinese mushrooms soaked in 100ml water
2 tabsp cornflour
1 tabsp oyster sauce
2 teasp dark Soy sauce
1 tabsp light Soy sauce
1 vegetable stock cube
½ teasp salt
½ teasp pepper
½ teasp sugar
4 tabsp sesame oil
2 tabsp fresh coriander - chopped
2 tabsp spring onion - chopped
1 pkt Spring Roll Pastry - size 250x250mm

Cornflour mixture:
1 egg
2 tabsp cornflour
4 tabsp water
Mix these three ingredients together

METHOD

Cut all the vegetables from the Dutch cabbage to the Chinese mushrooms into small bite-sized pieces.

You can now grate the carrots and Chinese Mooli, and leave them next to the vegetables.

Heat the oil in a wok and fry the ginger and garlic until you can smell the flavours of the spices.

Next add 2 tabsp of sesame oil, and then turn the heat to high. Add all the vegetables, and whilst stir-frying, add the crumbled vegetable cube, salt, pepper, sugar, oyster sauce, and both the dark & light Soy sauces.

Stir-fry this, and mix the mushrooms, water, and cornflour and add these to the vegetables.

The sauce will now thicken. Turn heat off.

Add the sesame oil and the coriander and spring onion. Set aside to cool.

To make the spring roll:

On a flat working surface, cut the pancake-skins in half.

Separate the rectangular skins into individual pieces. Now gather just 20 rectangular skins together and cut them again in half to form 40 small square pieces. Set this aside.

Place 1 piece of rectangular skin with its short side facing towards you.

Add 2 teasp of filling centrally, about one third of the skin from you. Brush the top half with egg-cornflour mixture.

Lift the lower flap over the filling and roll a quarter of the distance away from you, now tuck both sides inwards. Brush again with cornflour mixture and finish off the rolling. Set aside.

Now lay a small square piece on the working surface, brush all over with cornflour mixture. Place the prepared roll in the middle of this well brushed square pancake skin and keep away from the edges. Lift the lower flap over the spring roll and finish off rolling and tucking in both corners tightly, to form a compact parcel-roll. Arrange neatly on the tray. Repeat until all are done.

Deep fry until golden brown and serve

Ah Lin Tang's tip - Performing the wrapping of the spring roll twice is to create a double strength skin for deep frying, as normally it tends to burst open due to the juice weakening the skin. This prevents that.

Also to create the perfect spring roll requires a lot of practice but the delicious end results are definitely worthwhile.

NONYA SAUCE

INGREDIENTS
3 fresh chillies (sliced finely)
100mls light Soy sauce

METHOD
Mix together. Place into ten individual sauce dishes, and serve with Nonya Spring Roll.

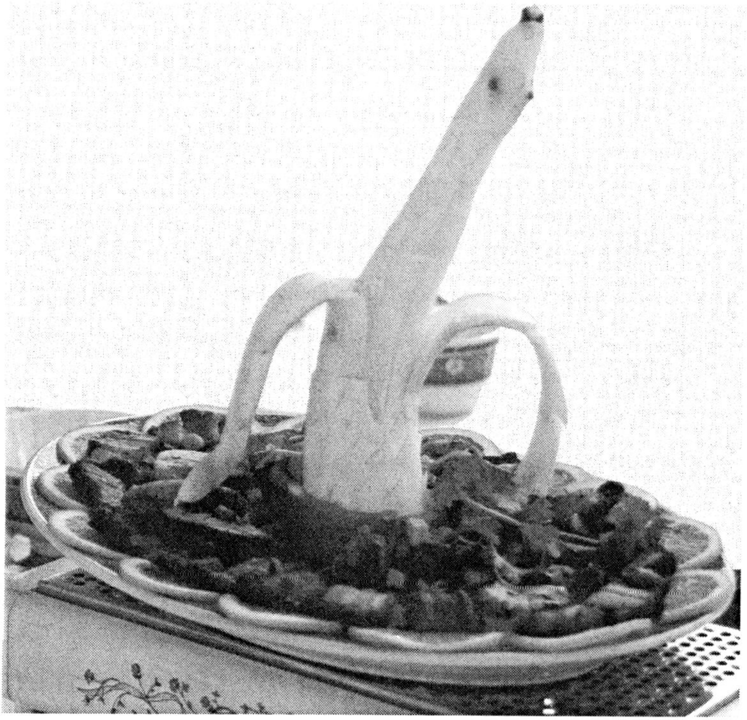

Palace Meat Platter (p68)

CHINESE CRISPY 'SEAWEED'

INGREDIENTS
1 to 2 packets of spring greens (600g total)
Vegetable oil for frying
125g almond flakes
¾ teasp salt
2 teasp sugar
2 tabsp Chinese fish-floss (optional)
Kitchen paper
Flat tray to dry the greens
1 sieve
2 woks

METHOD
Use only the dark green part of the spring greens. Cut out the hard stalk and discard. Wash and dry all the leaves.
Next gather a few green leaves together. Roll it up into a cigar-like shape and slice very finely. Use all the greens in this way.
Next spread the finely sliced spring greens on a large flat tray. Leave in a cool warm place to dry on its own. This method normally takes about three days to dry entirely. Alternatively dry them outside in the hot sunshine. This way takes about two days.
Do not cover the spring greens when drying as they will turn yellow. On the last day of preparation the greens will be dry, shrivelled up in size, yet still retain their green colour.
Heat the oil on medium, and firstly fry the almond flakes until light brown. Pour the whole amount of oil and the almonds into a sieve sitting on top of the second wok. Drain off the oil from the cooked almonds and pat them dry in kitchen paper. Set aside.
Divide the greens into two portions. Now heat the wok with the oil on medium, then fry the first patch of dried greens, by continually stirring and separating the greens in the oil making sure it is not too hot or it will burn the greens. Fry until crispy and the green colour turns to dark green.
Pour all the oil and crispy greens into the second wok with a sieve to catch the crispy greens. Shake dry the crispy greens and transfer them into kitchen paper. Leave aside.
Finish off frying the other portions to green.

Now add the sugar and salt into the crispy dried greens and mix them well. Taste to see if the sugar and salt is to your satisfaction. Set them aside.

To serve - divide the seaweed into small portions for your individual guests. Top with fish floss (optional) and almonds.

N.B. that the optional fish floss, bought specifically in Chinese supermarkets, is expensive.

Main Course

PENANG FRIED RICE

INGREDIENTS
1600g boiled rice (separate the grains)
½ small onion chopped
1 tabsp ginger - chopped
2 teasp garlic - chopped
1 level teasp salt
½ teasp pepper
½ teasp sugar
2 teasp dark Soy sauce
1 tabsp light Soy sauce
2 eggs
3 tabsp sesame oil
3 tabsp vegetable oil
4 shallots sliced
1 tabsp spring onion sliced

METHOD
In a large non-stick wok fry the shallots in vegetable oil until brown. Turn the heat off. Take the brown shallots out of the oil and keep in a container for later. Now heat the oil again and stir fry the onion. Cook lightly and add the ginger and garlic and fry for a few seconds until you can smell these spices.
Next add the rice. At this stage try to mix the rice evenly with the spices, do this for about 2 minutes in the wok. Increase the heat. and add the salt, pepper, sugar, dark and light Soy sauces. Mix again.
Make a hole in the centre of the rice and add sesame oil and the eggs. Cover it with the fried rice. Give it a good mix. Turn egg and rice over and turn off the heat.
Sprinkle with the spring onion and fried shallots and serve.

Ah Lin Tang's tip - Do watch the rice closely to ensure that it does not burn. I recommend a non-stick wok.
For decoration I also produce a coloured omelette. Made by dividing 1 beaten egg into two portions, adding a small drop of vegetable food colouring, stir, and shallow fry. Finally chop it into small pieces for garnishing.

CRISPY LEMON CHICKEN

INGREDIENTS
1kg chicken breast (cut into square bite-size pieces)
2 teasp chicken stock powder
5 tabsp lemon juice
½ teasp yellow food colouring (optional)
2 teasp lemon rind
½ teasp salt
½ teasp pepper
Vegetable oil for frying

Thin Batter:
75g flour
50g Custard powder
125ml milk
100ml water
½ egg

Cornflake crumbs:
100g Cornflakes
4 slices of bread (white or brown)
2 teasp lemon rind
1 teasp chicken stock powder
½ teasp pepper

Lemon Sauce:
2 tabsp of lemon curd
2 large lemons using the squeezed out juice
3 tabsp sugar
¾ teasp salt
½ teasp pepper
125 ml orange juice
½ teasp yellow food colouring (optional)
250 ml of chicken stock
2 tabsp vegetable oil
1tabsp cornflour (mixed with some of the chicken stock)

METHOD

First prepare the cornflake crumbs. Grind all the ingredients mentioned for these crumbs, and set aside.

Next make the thin batter by mixing and beating the batter ingredients until they are smooth.

To prepare the chicken - In a large bowl add the chicken pieces, chicken stock powder, lemon juice, lemon rind, salt, pepper, yellow food colouring (optional), and give it a thorough mix. Next add to this the thin batter.

To make lemon chicken:

First heat the vegetable oil for frying. Next take a piece of thinly battered chicken and dip it into the prepared cornflake crumbs. Now place this into the oil and fry until just lightly brown. Lift and drain. Set aside.

Lemon sauce:

Heat a saucepan on medium heat. Add the oil (mentioned in the ingredients) and the lemon curd and melt them lightly. Add the sugar, and stir. Add the lemon juice, salt, pepper, chicken stock and stir. Next turn the heat higher and add the orange juice and yellow food colouring (if used). Mix well before the sauce boils and finally add the cornflour mixture to thicken. Now allow to boil. Set aside.

Fry the lemon chicken again and pour the sauce over to serve.

Tip - The unused ½ egg can be saved for the fried rice or desserts which you can also be preparing.

SLICED PORK WITH GINGER AND SPRING ONION

INGREDIENTS
725g pork fillet - thinly sliced
1 tabsp bicarbonate of soda
120g ginger - thinly sliced
½ small onion - chunky cubes
2 cloves of garlic - chopped
1 tabsp dark Soy sauce
2 tabsp light Soy sauce
1 tabsp oyster sauce
1 teasp chicken powder
250ml chicken stock
¾ teasp salt
½ teasp pepper
½ teasp sugar
1¼ tabsp cornflour mixed into the chicken stock
1 long spring onion cut into 3cm lengths
3 tabsp oil and sesame oil mixed together
1tabsp Chinese wine

METHOD
In a bowl add the pork and bicarbonate of soda. Using your hand mix the two ingredients well. Leave this aside for at least 15 minutes, this helps the pork to tenderise quicker when cooking. Now wash the pork very well to remove any traces of the bicarbonate of soda. Drain off the water.
Heat the two types of oil in a wok on medium. Stir-fry the ginger and onion lightly and add the garlic. Stir-fry thoroughly, then turn the heat to high and quickly add the pork. Cook evenly and quickly, then add the dark and light Soy sauces, oyster sauce, chicken powder, salt, pepper and sugar. Stir fry this dish to distribute the spices into the pork.
Add the chicken stock mixed with the cornflour and let it bubble quickly. Turn heat off. Dish onto a serving plate.
Sprinkle with spring onion, and add the Chinese wine.

Ensure you do not over cook the pork. It should remain tender and succulent.

PRAWNS IN SPICY CRAB SAUCE *MALAYSIAN STYLE*

INGREDIENTS
800g raw fresh prawns (large size)
4 chillies - minced
2 teasp ginger - chopped
1 teasp garlic -chopped
2 teasp salted soy beans - chopped
1 tabsp tomato puree
2½ tabsp tomato sauce
1 teasp sugar
½ teasp salt
½ teasp pepper
1 vegetable stock cube
200ml water, mixed with 1 heaped teasp cornflour mixture
2 tabsp oil
1 egg white beaten
125g fresh crabmeat
spring onion and coriander

METHOD
First peel the prawns, then cut the back of the prawns quite deeply and take out the veins.
Heat wok on low, add the oil and cook the chillies Now add the ginger, garlic and salted soy beans. Turn to medium heat. Stir fry for five minutes or until you can smell the spices filling the air.
Add tomato puree, stir, add tomato sauce, stir, now increase the heat and add the prawns, stir and add the salt , pepper, vegetable stock cubes and sugar. Stir again and add the prawns.
At this stage make sure you stir-fry them continuously, one hand on the handle of the wok and the other nearer (but not touching) the metal, stir fry in all directions to enable the sauce to cover the prawns and stop the bottom of the wok from burning and sticking.
Now add the water combined with the cornflour, mix well. As soon as the sauce begins to bubble turn the heat to low.

Add the beaten egg white stirring at all times and lift off as soon as the sauce thickens and egg white turns white.

Serve and garnish with crabmeat and a sprinkle of julienne cut spring onion and coriander.

BEANCURD AND VEGETABLES STUFFED WITH FISH IN A SWEET AND SOUR SAUCE

INGREDIENTS
800g very fresh haddock fillet (sliced)
½ teasp bicarbonate of soda
½ teasp salt
½ teasp pepper
1teasp ginger - chopped
1 chilli - cut a 2cm portion & chop it up
1 tabsp fish sauce
2 teasp light Soy sauce
½ vegetable stock cube - crumbled
2 tabsp cornflour
1 coriander - cut finely
1 spring onion - cut finely
8 pieces of long French bean - cut finely

Vegetables
- *½ courgette*
- *½ aubergine*
- *2 chillies*
- *4 radishes*
- *4 soaked Chinese mushroom*
- *¼ piece of onion*
- *Three quarters pieces each of different colour peppers*
- *6 small button mushrooms*
- *One good sized piece of a flat sheet of dried beancurd*

Electric food chopper or blender
Vegetable Oil for shallow frying

Bowl of cornflour mixture
- *1½ tabsp cornflour*
- *4 tabsp water*
- ½ teasp salt

METHOD

Firstly prepare the vegetables.

Cut the courgette into 2 cm slices. Take a piece of the 2cm courgette and make a deep cut in the middle of it. Do not cut it too deep or it will split open when you try to stuff it with fish paste. Repeat making this cut to all the courgette slices. Set aside when it is finished. Repeat the same methods of cutting to the aubergine. For the radishes simply chop them into half pieces, cut the v-shaped groove, and then finally stuff them with the fish paste.

Slit open the chillies and take out the seeds.

Soak the flat beancurd in water for a few seconds and take it out as soon as the beancurd goes soft.

To make fish paste

Using a blender add the haddock and the next 9 ingredients mentioned from the list and blend until smooth. Scrape the fish paste into a large bowl. Add the last three ingredients i.e. the coriander, spring onions and French beans. Mix well.

Now place your right hand into the cornflour mixture and pick up all of the fish paste and throw it back into the bowl for six to ten times. This method of preparing the fish paste tastes good, firms up the meat and when cooked it produces a crunchy chewy texture.

Take one piece of aubergine, stuff 1 teasp of the fish paste into the slit part. Finish stuffing all of the vegetables in this way.

Lay the beancurd skin flat on a working surface. Take a handful of fish paste and roll it up like a sausage. Place the sausage-shaped fish paste onto the bottom end of the beancurd skin, lift the lower flap over the fish paste and roll the beancurd skin up. Now cut into 4 to 5 cm lengths.

Fill the hollow of each pepper with the fish paste, and repeat with the onions and chillies.

Heat a wok with oil on medium. Shallow fry the prepared vegetables with their stuffing side facedown until cooked and brown. Repeat for rest of the prepared vegetables and beancurd.

Arrange on a plate and pour sweet and sour sauce all over and serve.

SWEET AND SOUR SAUCE

INGREDIENTS
2½ tabsp of sugar
2 tabsp of tomato sauce
1 tabsp of tomato puree
2 tabsp oil
250ml stock mixed with cornflour
125ml pineapple juice
7 tabsp vinegar
1 teasp salt
½ teasp pepper
1 vegetable stock cube
1 tabsp cornflour

METHOD
Heat oil at a low setting in a saucepan. Add the sugar, stir, and add the tomato puree.
Cook slowly until the sugar is dissolved. Now add the tomato sauce, and stir for a few seconds. Next add the pineapple juice, turn heat to high, add the stock with the cornflour mixed in, still stirring add the rest of the ingredients. Turn heat to low and let it boil slowly until it bubbles.
Turn off heat. Taste and serve.

STIR FRIED VEGETABLES IN OYSTER SAUCE

INGREDIENTS
100g bean shoots (remove the tails)
70g mangetout (pre-trimmed)
70g Chinese white cabbage (cut into 4cm pieces)
½ courgette
¼ onion
10cm long celery
3cm in length chilli
7cm long leek
¼ pieces of mixed red, yellow, green pepper
¼ piece of broccoli (bite size blanched)
6 Chinese mushroom (soaked in 250ml water)
100g straw mushrooms
1 carrot
1 tabsp light Soy sauce
2 teasp oyster sauce
1 teasp dark Soy sauce
½ teasp salt
½ teasp pepper
½ teasp sugar
1 vegetable stock cube
1½ tabsp cornflour
1 tabsp of vegetable oil
2 tabsp sesame oil
2 teasp garlic - chopped
1 tabsp ginger - chopped
1 tabsp of Chinese Shaohsing wine
2 spring onion and 2 stalks of coriander (cut into 4cm lengths)
250 ml stock from the soaked mushroom water

METHOD
Place all the prepared vegetables onto a large tray in neat individual piles.

Skin the carrots. Cut a v-shaped groove into the carrot from top to bottom along its length. Repeat making 3 to 4 more v-shaped grooves. Now chop the carrot into bite size slices. Place them on the vegetable tray.

Chop the courgettes into 2cm thick slices. Now cut them into half pieces (i.e. semicircles). Set aside on the tray.

Prepare the celery, onion, pepper and chilli by cutting them into bite size. Leeks cut into eight pieces altogether. Leave it on the tray. Straw and Chinese mushrooms cut in half.

Heat the vegetable oil and sesame oil on medium, and stir-fry the ginger and garlic until the spices smell fragrant.

Now add the carrots, stir-fry, add the celery, onion, pepper, chilli, courgettes, leek and mangetout. Give it another stir fry, add the Chinese White Cabbage, the two different types Chinese mushrooms, broccoli and bean shoots. Stir & mix well. Add the oyster sauce, salt, pepper, sugar, dark and light Soy sauce. Stir-fry.

Mix the vegetable cube into the mushroom water, add the cornflour and mix. Pour this into the stir-fried vegetables, let it boil and the sauce thicken. Add Chinese Shaohsing wine. Turn heat off and serve.

Sprinkle the spring onion and coriander over the top.

Sweet

RASA SAYANG DRUNKEN PEAR

INGREDIENTS
10 pears (Conference variety - slightly soft)
½ bottle of red wine i.e. 375ml
3 tabsp sugar
5 tabsp lemon juice
4 whole cloves
4cm long piece of cinnamon
3 tabsp of Port
1 tabsp cornflour
3 cherries (cut into 10 pieces)
10 lychees (tin or fresh)
Selection of fresh fruit e.g. mango, pawpaw, cherries with their stalks intact, strawberries.
10 to 15 cocktail sticks.

METHOD
Skin and core the pears. Place these pears into a container. Pack them neatly alongside each other.
Add 1 tabsp of sugar, 1 tabsp of lemon juice, the cinnamon stick and cloves.
Pour red wine over the pears, cling film or cover, and leave aside in a cool corner for the pears to get 'drunk'. After 4 hours lift the lid away from the covered pears and check that the pears are thoroughly soaked in the red wine. You can tell this by their colour change i.e. they turn burgundy. Next turn the pears over and let the other side that may have not changed colour have the benefit of the red wine. Leave this aside for another four hours.
Pack as many drunken pears as possible into a large saucepan. Pour the red wine back onto the pears and cook on high until it boils. Now turn heat to medium and cook for another five minutes. Lift the cooked pears onto a plate.

Mix the cornflour and port together. Boil the wine syrup, add the Port mixture, sugar and lemon juice. Cook until the sauce begins to boil. Turn off heat.
Pour the sauce into a jug using a sieve to remove the cinnamon, cloves and lemon pips. Set this aside.

Place a cherry inside one of the lychees and stuff it inside a cooked pear. Repeat for the rest of the pears. Cut a selection of fruit into chunky square size pieces. Leave the cherry and strawberry whole.

To serve. Use two large plates and arrange 5 stuffed pears in a circle. Spoon the sauce generously over the pears. Now arrange the fruit around the pears, and place the cherries (still with their stalks). Place cocktail sticks into the fruit chunks and strawberries. Serve.

Ah Lin Tang's tip – It is best to prepare this dessert first thing in the morning, and store it in a cool place until the pear turns a burgundy colour.

SINGAPORE TOFFEE APPLE AND BANANA

INGREDIENTS
3 granny smith apples
3 bananas
400g sugar
2 tabsp sesame seed
Vegetable oil

For the batter:
250g plain flour
130g custard powder
1 egg
100ml milk
200ml water
4 clean dry tea-towels

Vegetable Oil for frying
Large bowl of very cold water
2 woks

METHOD
It is advised to read through this recipe thoroughly before preparing as the order is quite precise and requires care.

Prepare the batter - In a blender add the five ingredients mentioned for the batter ingredients. Blend this to a thick cream consistency. Set aside.

Peel the apples. Cut the three apples into quarters and each quarter in to three pieces so you should end up with about thirty-six pieces. Prepare the banana by cutting it into four or five pieces depending on its size. Add this fruit into the batter.
Heat the oil in the 1st wok and when it is ready for frying add the fruit covered with batter. One at a time fry until golden brown. Remove with a pair of chopsticks. Set aside.

To finish - Have the bowl of very cold water next to the 2nd wok. Now spread the tea towel fully open. Have a large serving plate ready for the finishing touch.

Work in this precise order. Heat the oil in the 1st wok and fry the battered fruit for the second time until dark brown and firm to touch. Whilst the fruit is frying heat the 2nd wok on medium, add the sugar, and then add just enough vegetable oil to completely cover the sugar. Stir at all times until the sugar melts and turns light brown. Now quickly turn the heat to low and add the sesame seeds and twice fried fruit (from the 1st wok) using a ladle held in one hand and chopsticks in the other, into the 2nd wok. Cover the toffee syrup all over the battered fruit.

Now pick the well-covered toffee fruit up with the chopsticks and drop them into the cold water. Work quickly and drop about six to eight pieces of the toffee fruit in to the water.

Put down the chopsticks and lift the toffee fruit from the cold water and into a dry clean tea towel. Wipe dry and place them on a serving plate.

Finish off all toffee fruit in this way and serve.

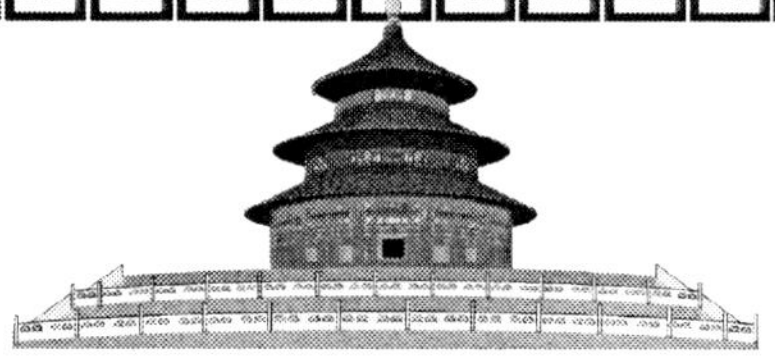

AH LIN TANG'S BEIJING BANQUET

A night to remember with these exciting dishes from Beijing (formerly Peking), the capital of China, as served at the Emperor's banquet held at the Summer Palace. All food will be prepared by me and served in your home with the host and hostess enjoying a relaxed care free evening. I also specialise in vegetarian dishes.

Whether celebrating a special occasion, entertaining some office clients or even just having a party but preferring something different, then let Ah Lin Tang create a taste of China to remember.

Starter

Soup of your choice: Wonton Soup, Chicken and Sweetcorn or Hot and Sour Soup

Stuffed Prawns with Crabmeat deep fried served in a Hot and Sour Sauce

Crispy Spring Roll

Aromatic Duck wrapped in salad and Pancake with a touch of Hoisin Sauce

Main Course

Emperor's fried rice

Sautéed Prawns Sichuan Style

Palace Platter consists of 3 kinds of Meat

Mongolian Lamb with Spring Onion

Chicken in Black Bean sauce and fried Pepper

Superior Monks delight of vegetable

Sweets

Royal Palace Fruit Soup flavoured with Chinese Spices

Dessert of the Day

All served with ice-cream or cream

Jasmine Tea

Chinese Tableware will be provided. Minimum 10 persons.

Ah Lin Tang's Beijing Banquet

I am a Malaysian born girl, but both of my parents are from China and my mother's family was from Beijing. My parents left China and lived in Hong Kong in the mid 1930s. Afterwards they came to live in Malaysia. Thus influences from Beijing cookery have been with me from a young age.

For centuries Beijing has been the capital of China. Emperors of different dynasties all had the best cooks at their service. Thus, Beijing cuisine is inevitably influenced by the Imperial cooking school. Today many fine restaurants boast of their authentic royal recipes. It should be noted each change of dynasty saw a diverse population and inflow from other parts of the country, accompanied by their different styles of cooking. For this reason Beijing cuisine is diverse in nature. Overall combining variety and quality ensuring that its cuisine is amongst the best in China.

Many of the dishes classified as Beijing style originated in the Imperial courts which had at the Emperor's command the best of all the food of China. The most famous dish being Beijing's *Aromatic Roast Duck*, in which the delicious duck meat and spices are wrapped in thin pancakes combined with lettuce, cucumber, onions and hoisin sauce.

Locals call Beijing cuisine 'capital city cuisine' as the city was also the capital during the Liao, Jin, Yuan, Ming and Qing dynasties. Apart from the Ming dynasty, the rulers of all the others were from northern nomadic tribes. Thus for all the 500-plus years spanning the other four dynasties Beijing dishes were dominated by meat - the staple of the ruling classes.
During those times Beijing was the gathering place of many of the literati and officials, and in their wake came countless skilled chefs from all over China. As you would expect they brought their differing local cuisines with them, greatly enhancing and inspiring the local dishes as then existed.
Sichuan and Jiangsu-Zhejiang cuisines are noteworthy for especially influencing the Beijing style. And since Sichuan is nearer to Beijing, more of its people than from elsewhere migrated to the capital in search of a living, many of them entering the catering divisions.

Within that period saw Beijing engaging in trade and cultural exchanges with many other regions of China. Thus many of the southern Chinese voyaged to the capital, with chefs amongst them. When this southern food was presented to the north, some of its flavours were altered to complement Beijing palates. This was because southern cookery was usually sweeter whereas in the northern territories the people had preferred saltier, rich flavours. Ultimately numerous dishes combined southern and northern characteristics to suit all tastes and influences.

In my Beijing menu I have incorporated some of the more famous and delicious speciality dishes of the region, all with accurate flavours and authentic recipe designs.

Starter

WONTON SOUP

INGREDIENTS
1 pkt wonton wrapper
180g small fresh Prawns (minced)
120g belly of pork (minced)
1 teasp ginger (chopped)
1 tabsp fresh coriander (chopped)
1 tabsp spring onion (chopped)
100g water chestnuts
½ teasp pepper
½ vegetable stock cube - crumbled
1 teasp sugar
1 egg white
1 tabsp cornflour
1 tabsp light Soy sauce
2 tabsp sesame oil

Mix together for broth:
3 pint chicken stock
1 teasp chicken stock powder
1 tabsp potato flour

1½ teasp salt
½ teasp pepper
1 tabsp light Soy sauce
2 tabsp sesame oil
Handful of 4cm in length Chinese flowering cabbage
Spring onion (chopped)

Hand strainer - equipment
2 saucepans

METHOD
Prepare the wonton dumplings:

In a large bowl add the prawns, belly of pork, water chestnut, ginger, spring onion, fresh coriander, pepper, sugar, crumbled ½ vegetable stock cube, egg white, cornflour, light Soy sauce, and sesame oil. Mix this all well.

To make wonton - Use 1 piece of wonton skin and add 1 teasp of the prepared filling in the centre. Gather together the corners of the wrapper with your other hand and give it a squeeze in the middle to secure the wrapping. Repeat until all the filling is used up.

Get 2 saucepans. In the first saucepan boil some hot water. As it simmers add the prepared wonton - no more than 20 at a time in each saucepan. Stir gently with a hand strainer to separate them. Once it starts to boil remove the cooked wonton with a hand strainer and place them onto a large plate. Finish off cooking all the wonton.

In the second saucepan heat the chicken stock. Add the salt & pepper. As it boils, add the Chinese flowering cabbage, wontons, light Soy sauce and sesame oil. Cook until the water boils usually in 5-10 minutes.

Turn off the heat, serve in an individual bowl with a sprinkle of spring onion. This is usually eaten with a dash of light Soy sauce mixed in.

CHICKEN AND SWEETCORN SOUP

INGREDIENTS
200g chicken breast (chopped)
650g creamy sweetcorn (tinned)
2 teasp ginger chopped
1 teasp salt
½ teasp pepper
1 tabsp light Soy sauce
2 tabsp sesame oil
2 egg whites (beaten)
2 tabsp vegetable oil
Spring onion finely sliced

Mix together for broth:
3 pints of chicken stock mixed together
1 teasp chicken stock powder
1½ tabsp potato flour

METHOD
In a large saucepan add the oil and stir-fry the chicken and ginger until it begins to change colour.
Add the sweetcorn, stir, and next add the stock mixture. Turn heat to high and add the salt and pepper. Allow this to boil, now turn the heat to low and cook slowly this way for 10 minutes.
Add the light Soy sauce and sesame oil. Stir in the egg white in a circular motion to allow the egg to set in white flaky pieces. Remove from the heat and sprinkle in the spring onion.
Serve.

HOT AND SOUR SOUP

INGREDIENTS
100g lean pork (chopped)
100g chicken breast (chopped)
A handful of cloud ears (soaked in 100ml water & sliced)
200g soft white beancurd (diced)
100g tin bamboo shoots (shredded)
1 tabsp fresh ginger (chopped)
2 tabsp minced chilli oil
2 tabsp vegetable oil
2½ tabsp sesame oil
3 pint chicken stock
1 teasp chicken stock powder
1½ teasp salt
½ teasp pepper
1½ tabsp potato flour
1 tabsp light Soy sauce
5 tabsp vinegar
2 egg white (beaten)
2 spring onion (chopped)

METHOD
In a large saucepan add the vegetable oil and turn the heat to low. Fry the ginger, pork & chicken.
Add the 3 pints of chicken stock and chilli oil, turn the heat to medium, stir, and add the cloud ears, and bamboo shoots. Let it boil for 3 minutes, then turn the heat to low. Whilst it simmers add the 1 teasp chicken stock powder, salt, pepper, vinegar, light Soy sauce, sesame oil, and then the sliced beancurd.
Stir the potato flour with the cloud ear water and add this to the simmering soup, and mix well. Taste and adjust seasoning.

Just before serving stir in the beaten egg white, making sure the egg is mixed well into the soup to form white flaky pieces. Add the spring onion and serve.

STUFFED PRAWNS WITH CRABMEAT DEEP FRIED, SERVED IN A HOT & SOUR SAUCE

INGREDIENTS
20 fresh jumbo King-prawns
500g fresh prawns (small - minced)
100g belly of pork (minced)
200g fresh crabmeat
2 teasp ginger (chopped)
3 tabsp spring onion - chopped
3 tabsp coriander - chopped
4 tabsp sesame oil
2 tabsp light Soy sauce
1 teasp pepper
2 tabsp cornflour
1 teasp sugar
½ vegetable stock cube crumbled
1½ eggs
100g water chestnut (tinned) – chopped

For coating
2 eggs beaten
250g cornflakes - make into crumbs
10 slices of bread - make into crumbs

Piping bag with a large nozzle.
Vegetable oil for frying

METHOD
Line a flat tray with cling-film.
Slice halfway down the back of the prawns. Take out the black veins. Finish off preparing the prawns this way (described as 'butterfly' prawns). Lay each

individual prawn on their back on top of the cling film tray, separate them apart. Set aside.
In a large bowl add the fresh small prawns, belly of pork, crabmeat, ginger, spring onions, sesame oil, light soy sauce, pepper, cornflour, sugar, crumbled vegetable cube, eggs and water chestnut. Mix this filling well. Set aside.

Have your tray of prepared prawns next to you. Fill the piping bag with the mixture. Now pipe a good spoonful of the mixture along the back, i.e. in the groove cut, of the butterfly prawns. Repeat with the rest of the prawns.
Gently lift the stuffed prawn into the beaten eggs, just bathe it lightly and now dip it into the cornflakes crumbs. This time cover the stuffed prawns fully with the crumbs.
Lay them neatly on the tray and repeat.

To fry:
Heat the oil to frying temperature and fry for 8 to 10 minutes until cooked inside.

Serve with Hot and Sour sauce

HOT AND SOUR SAUCE

This is made up from two types of chilli sauce. Note that this is used for dipping, i.e. in dipping the prawn/crabmeat. It is not for pouring over the dish.

For the first chilli sauce use the *Thai chilli sauce* (p93).
Second chilli sauce use the 'Chilli oil'

INGREDIENTS
To make chilli oil
4 red chillies (minced)
70mls vegetable oil

METHOD
Cook them together in a small saucepan until the oil oozes out of the chilli. Keep stirring this to stop the chilli sticking to the bottom of the pan and cook slowly. This takes about 5 minutes.
Keep the chilli oil in a screw top jar. It keeps in a fridge for a week.

Add a teasp of the Thai chilli sauce on to a small dipping dish, now add the chilli oil next to one another and serve.

CRISPY SPRING ROLL

INGREDIENTS
300g fresh small raw prawns (roughly chopped)
100g runner beans (chopped)
100g celery (chopped)
10 shallots (sliced)
100g Chinese celery cabbage (shredded)
100g Mooli (grated)
2 medium carrots (grated)
100g Yambean (optional) - grated
100g tinned bamboo shoots (shredded)
200g bean shoot (tails)
10 Chinese mushrooms, soaked in 100ml water (until soft)
2 tabsp spring onion (chopped)
2 tabsp coriander (chopped)
1 teasp garlic (chopped)
1 teasp ginger (chopped)
1 vegetable stock cube
2 tabsp cornflour
1 tabsp oyster sauce
2 teasp dark Soy Sauce
1 tabsp light Soy sauce
½ teasp salt
½ teasp Pepper
½ teasp Sugar
3 tabsp Sesame oil
2 tabsp Vegetable oil
1 pkt Spring roll pancake skin

Cornflour mixture:
2 eggs
2 tabsp cornflour
2 tabsp water
Mixed together and set aside

Flat tray, lined with cling film

Vegetable oil for frying

METHOD

Slice the soaked mushrooms. Set this aside.

Heat the vegetable oil in a wok on medium. Add the shallots. Stir-fry until brown in colour and crispy. Turn heat off. Now dish out all the crispy shallots, put this aside.

Turn heat back to medium. Add the ginger, garlic & the prawns. Stir-fry until the prawns change to a light pink colour. Now turn the heat to high and add all the vegetables. Stir-fry, and add the crumbled vegetable cube, Chinese mushroom, salt and pepper, oyster sauce, dark and light soy sauce, stir and let it cook thoroughly. Now add the cornflour mixture with the mushroom water. Stir, until the sauce thickens. Turn heat off. Add the sesame oil, coriander and spring onion, shallots. Set aside to cool.

On a flat working surface. Cut the pancake skins in half. Separate the rectangular skins into individual pieces. Now gather just 20 rectangular skins together and cut again into half to form 40 small square pieces. Set this aside.

Place one piece of the rectangular skin with its short side facing you. Add 2 teasp of filling centrally, about one third of the skin from you. Brush the top half with egg-cornflour mixture.

Lift the lower flap over the filling and roll a quarter of the distance away from you, now tuck both sides inwards. Brush again with cornflour mixture and finish off the rolling. Set aside.

Now lay a small square piece on the working surface, brush all over with cornflour mixture. Place the prepared roll in the middle of this well brushed square pancake skin and keep away from the edges. Lift the lower flap over the spring roll and finish off rolling and tucking in both corners tightly, to form a compact parcel-roll.

Arrange neatly on the tray. Repeat until all are done.

To serve. Heat the vegetable oil. Fry until golden brown, about 5-8 minutes.

CRISY DUCK AROMATIC STYLE

INGREDIENTS
2 whole ducks (each weigh ~2.25kg) - split the ducks in half
4 star anise
1½ tabsp of Five-spice powder
2 tabsp of ginger - chopped
3 tabsp of garlic - chopped
3 tabsp dark Soy sauce
1 tabsp salt
1 tabsp pepper
2 teasp of chicken stock powder
1 stick of cinnamon
2 tabsp of Chinese Shaohsing wine
Vegetable oil for frying

1 pkt of Chinese pancake skins (30 pieces)
Hoisin sauce
1 whole onion (sliced)
½ Cucumber (cut into matchstick sized pieces)
Cox lettuce (shredded)
Bamboo steam basket

METHOD
Into a large bowl place everything mentioned except the oil for frying. Using your hand rub the spices all over the duck. Cover and keep in fridge for a day to marinate.
Turn oven on medium-high about 200°C or gas mark 6 and cook duck in a covered casserole dish for a good 2 to 2½ hours or until the duck is tender. Let the duck cool down before removing it into another clean dish.

Put 1-2 tablespoons of hoisin sauce into individual saucers for each person. Steam the pancake skins for 10 minutes. Whilst they are steaming fry the aromatic ducks until crispy on both sides. Remove & drain.
Scrape the tender meat from the bone. Place on a serving dish.

To serve.
Place a pancake skin on a plate, smear on some sauce (usually hoisin), add some pieces of cucumber, onion, lettuce. Place on some crispy duck. Roll up the pancake and then eat!
Delicious.

Main Course

EMPEROR'S FRIED RICE

INGREDIENTS
1600g boiled rice (separate the grains)
½ small onion - chopped into bite size
1 tabsp ginger - chopped
2 teasp garlic - chopped
1 teasp salt
½ teasp pepper
½ teasp sugar
1 tabsp light Soy sauce
2 eggs (beaten)
3 tabsp sesame oil
2 tabsp vegetable oil
1 spring onion (cut into 3cm lengths)
1 fresh coriander (cut into 3cm lengths)
70g green peas
1 medium-sized carrot (diced into very small cubes)

To Garnish:
1 beaten egg, mixed with 1 teasp red vegetable food colouring,

METHOD
In a large non-stick wok fry the beaten eggs mixed with red food colouring to produce a flat omelette. Dish this out. Turn the heat off. Allow the omelette to cool, then slice it finely. Set aside.
Now turn heat back to medium. Fry the onion, ginger and garlic in vegetable oil until lightly brown.
Now add the rice and green peas. Increase this heat to high. Stir-fry for a few seconds, then add the salt, pepper, sugar & light Soy sauce. Mix again, make a hole in the centre of the rice and add the sesame oil and eggs. Cover it with the fried rice. Give it a good mix. Add the carrots. Turn egg and rice over and turn off heat. N.B. do watch the rice during preparation to prevent it burning.

To serve - Garnish with the omelette strips. Sprinkle with spring onion.

SAUTÉED PRAWNS SICHUAN STYLE

INGREDIENTS
800g fresh large prawns (shelled)
2 teasp roasted ground Sichuan peppercorns
1 tabsp tomato puree
1 tabsp Sichuan hot bean paste
1 tabsp minced red chillies
1 tabsp ginger - chopped
1 tabsp garlic - chopped
2 tabsp sesame oil
2 tabsp vegetable oil
2 tabsp light Soy sauce
½ vegetable stock cube
½ teasp salt
½ teasp pepper
½ teasp sugar
200ml water
2 tabsp cornflour
1 tabsp Chinese Shaohsing wine
2 Fresh coriander and spring onion - cut into 4cm lengths

METHOD
Firstly stir the cornflour into the 200ml water & mix well.
Make a deep cut at the back of the prawns, and take out the black vein. Set aside.

Heat oil on low, and add 1 tabsp sesame oil, then add the ground Sichuan peppercorns, hot bean paste, chillies, garlic, ginger and tomato puree.
Stir and cook until you can smell the spices and see the oil ooze out from the paste.
Now add the prawns, and turn the heat to high. Stir-fry quickly for a few seconds, then add the salt, pepper, sugar, vegetable stock cube, & light Soy sauce.

Take the cornflour mixture and add this to the prawns. Stir briskly until the sauce thickens, add the rest of the sesame oil, & Chinese wine. Turn heat off.

Sprinkle with spring onion and coriander, and serve

PALACE MEAT PLATTER CONSISTING OF 3 KINDS OF MEAT

AROMATIC CHICKEN

INGREDIENTS
4 chicken legs - boned
2 tabsp dark Soy sauce
1 teasp oyster sauce
1 teasp chicken stock powder
½ teasp salt
½ teasp pepper
1 teasp Five-spice powder
2 teasp ginger juice
2 teasp garlic juice
1 tabsp sesame oil
1 tabsp Chinese Shaohsing wine
2 fresh coriander and spring onion

METHOD
In a large bowl add the chicken and all the other ingredients.
Mix the chicken and these spices together. Cling film the bowl and leave in the fridge for at least 3 hours.

To cook:
Heat the oven on 200°C (Gas mark 6). Cook the chicken until done, it should take about 15minutes. Allow to cool and remove the chicken from its spicy juices.

When it is time to serve, deep fry the chicken for 5 minutes. And cut it into slices. N.B. that this should be served with 2 other meats, whose recipes follow on from this one.

Ah Lin Tang's tip – Do note that the garlic & ginger 'juices' are made by chopping them finely, then adding some water, and squeezing this mixture. Collect the juice squeezed out.

ROAST BELLY PORK - *CHINESE STYLE*

INGREDIENTS
500g belly of pork
1½ teasp salt
½ teasp sugar
½ teasp pepper
1 teasp chicken stock powder
½ teasp Five-spice powder
2 teasp yellow vegetable food colouring (optional)
100ml rice vinegar
2 star anise
2 teasp ginger - chopped

METHOD
First in a wok boil the rice vinegar on low heat. Add the belly of pork into the hot vinegar and blanch the skin side first, then the other side. Once the belly of pork changes colour and the skin shrinks, take it out, and allow to cool. Throw away the vinegar.

Now rub all the spices in the ingredients, except the salt and star anise, all over the belly of pork.
With the skin facing upwards now rub some salt all over the skin only and just a bit of salt on the underside. Place the star anise under the belly side and leave this prepared pork to marinate for a day in the fridge.

Turn oven on to 180°C or gas mark 4, and place the belly of pork skin side up on a rack in the oven. Roast for about 1 hour or until the belly of pork is cooked. To test whether the meat is done, pierce the meat with a skewer, if it goes in easily, and the juices which run out are clear and not pink then the belly of pork is not done.
Remove the belly of pork and place under a hot grill and let the skin bubble to form a crispy 'crackling' skin. Ensure the skin is not burnt.

Slice into pieces and set aside.

CHAR-SUI *BEIJING STYLE*

INGREDIENTS
800g of pork fillet
1 teasp fermented red beancurd
1 teasp of ground peanut butter
½ teasp Five-spice powder
½ teasp pepper
1 teasp chicken stock powder
½ teasp red vegetable food colouring powder
2 teasp ginger - chopped
1 teasp garlic - chopped
3 tabsp sugar
1 tabsp light Soy sauce
2 tabsp sesame oil
2 tabsp Chinese wine

For basting - mix together:
1 tabsp sesame oil
1½ tabsp honey

To make sauce:
120ml water
2 teasp cornflour
2 teasp Hoisin sauce
1 tabsp light Soy sauce

METHOD
Place the pork fillet into a large bowl, and add the first set of ingredients mentioned. Mix them well, cling film, and leave in fridge for a full day before roasting.
Preheat oven on 220°C or Gas mark 7.
Drain pork and place on a wire-tray with a baking tin underneath. Place this in the oven and roast for 20 mins. Next remove this from the oven, and apply the basting juice thickly all over the cooking char-sui.
Finish cooking this Char-sui making sure it produces a good red-brown sugary appearance.
Take out oven, and allow cool. Carve it into 1 cm slices.

To make sauce
Boil the sauce ingredients with the marinade juice i.e. the drained juice from the char-sui in a saucepan. Once it starts to boil, turn the heat off & allow it to pass through a sieve and serve this sauce in a separate bowl.

To Assemble the Palace Meat Platter

Using two very large oval Chinese plates, divide the sliced aromatic chicken into two piles and place one of the piles in the centre of one of the plates.
Surround this aromatic chicken with slices of char-sui overlapping each other, making sure you retain enough slices for the second plate.
Now take the pork slices and place them around the outer edge of the char-sui this time not overlapping.

Serve.

Ah Lin Tang's tip – Provided your oven is large enough you can cook all the 3 types of meat at once as long as you watch carefully the way each type of meat is roasting.

MONGOLIAN LAMB WITH SPRING ONION - *Tibetan style*

INGREDIENTS
800g boneless leg of lamb (sliced)
8cm long piece of leek
2 spring onions
3cm slice of chilli
2 teasp salted soy beans - chopped
2 cloves garlic - chopped
Small piece of ginger (thumb size) - sliced
1 teasp bicarbonate of soda
1 tabsp dark Soy sauce
1 tabsp light Soy sauce
1 teasp oyster sauce
½ teasp salt
½ teasp pepper
½ teasp sugar
1 teasp chicken stock powder
200ml chicken stock
2 tabsp sesame oil
1 tabsp vegetable oil
2 tabsp Chinese Shaohsing wine
2 fresh coriander cut into 4cm lengths

METHOD
Stir the cornflour into the chicken stock.
Mix the lamb with the bicarbonate of soda, and then leave aside. Cut leeks in half, then into four quarter pieces. Cut the spring onion diagonally into slices. Cut the chilli in to chunky bite size pieces.

Remove the bicarbonate of soda by running cold water onto the lamb. Wash this well, set aside, and leave it to drain.
Heat oil on low, add the ginger and yellow salted bean. Stir fry, add the garlic and 1 tabsp of sesame oil, cook for a few seconds.
Now turn heat to high, quickly add the lamb, stir-fry until it starts to change colour, now add the dark and light Soy sauce, chicken stock powder, salt, pepper, sugar, and oyster sauce.

Continue cooking, add the cornflour mixture, 1 tabsp sesame oil, Chinese wine, leek, chilli, spring onions, and coriander. Cook until the sauce thickens, turn heat off.
Serve.

Ah Lin Tang's tip – For a spectacular dish it is possible to serve this on a sizzling platter plate.

CHICKEN IN BLACK BEAN SAUCE WITH PEPPER & ONION

INGREDIENTS

700g chicken breast - cut into chunky bite size
2 tabsp whole black beans - chopped
250g total weight of green, yellow, red peppers - cut into bite size
100g red & white onions - chunky bite-sized
2cm fresh chilli - sliced
1 tabsp ginger - chopped
1 tabsp garlic - chopped
4cm length of spring onion - chopped
1 tabsp dark Soy sauce
1 tabsp light Soy sauce
2 teasp oyster sauce
2 teasp chicken stock powder
½ teasp salt
½ teasp pepper
1 teasp sugar
2 tabsp sesame oil
1 tabsp vegetable oil
1 tabsp Chinese Shaohsing wine
200ml chicken stock or water
2 tabsp cornflour

METHOD

Mix the cornflour into the chicken stock (or water).

Heat the vegetable oil on low, add the black bean, ginger, and garlic, and cook this all for a few seconds. Now add 1 tabsp of sesame oil. Turn heat to high, and add the chicken. Stir-fry quickly to stop the chicken and black beans becoming burnt at the bottom of the wok.

When the chicken changes colour to white, add the dark & light Soy sauce, oyster sauce, salt, pepper, sugar, and chicken stock powder. Give it all good stir, and add the fresh peppers, onions, chillies, 1 tabsp sesame oil and Chinese Shaohsing wine.

Add cornflour mixture. Cook until the sauce thickens, then turn heat off.

Serve, add the spring onions.

Ah Lin Tang's tip - Only use the black beans labelled with 'Preserved Beans with ginger' to ensure the best results. These are only bought from Chinese specialist food shops.

SUPERIOR MONKS DELIGHT OF VEGETABLE

INGREDIENTS

½ piece of broccoli
6 asparagus
250g Chinese mustard green vegetable
200g sugar-snap peas (trimmed)
1 medium-sized carrot
2 sticks of celery
¼ onion
¼ piece of red & yellow pepper each
Soak in 250ml water:
8 Chinese mushrooms
8 dry cloud ear fungus
1 clove of garlic - chopped
Thumb size piece of ginger - sliced
2 teasp dark soy sauce
2 teasp light soy sauce
1 teasp oyster sauce
4 cubes fermented beancurd
½ teasp salt
½ teasp pepper
½ teasp sugar
1 vegetable stock cube
2 tabsp cornflour
2 fresh coriander and spring onion, into 2cm lengths
2 tabsp vegetable oil

METHOD

Cut the broccoli into bite sized pieces. Blanch in boiling water until *al dente*. Set aside.

Cut the asparagus into 4cm lengths. Cut the carrot into 4cm lengths. Divide each carrot & asparagus piece lengthways into quarters. Next cut the celery into bite-size pieces, and also the onion & peppers into chunky sized pieces.

Prepare the Chinese mustard green vegetables by also cutting them into 4cm lengths.

Cut the soaked mushroom and cloud ear in half. N.B. the water that they are soaked in should be kept. Set the mushrooms & cloud ears aside.

Crumble the vegetable stock cube into the kept water and the cornflour. Mix well.
Heat the vegetable oil in a wok on low, add the fermented beancurd, ginger and garlic. Stir-fry for 3 minutes.
Turn heat to medium, add the carrots and asparagus. Stir-fry, turn heat to high, add the mushrooms and cloud ear, sugar snap peas, celery, chilli, onion, peppers and broccoli, and the Chinese mustard green vegetables.
Stir-fry for 3 minutes, add the dark and light Soy sauce, salt, pepper, sugar, oyster sauce.
Stir the cornflour mixture and add to the hot vegetables. Cook until the sauce thickens.

Serve and sprinkle on the top the coriander and spring onion.

Sweet

ROYAL PALACE FRUIT SOUP FLAVOURED WITH CHINESE SPICES

INGREDIENTS
Selection of fresh fruits, such as:
strawberries, raspberries, cherries, passion-fruit, apples, pears, sharon fruit, mangoes, pawpaw, melons, pineapple, lychees, oranges, grapes (white & red)

Spice-wine marinade:
½ bottle of white wine
5 pieces of lemon grass (10cm in length, ends squashed)
1 piece of cinnamon
20g cardamom seed
3cm long fresh ginger (squashed)
15 cloves

3 tabsp sugar
4 tabsp lemon juice

METHOD
Place all the five-spices mentioned inside the half bottle of wine. Seal the bottle and leave in the fridge for 1 week. This method helps the wine to absorb all the spices' flavour and when used on the fresh fruit it gives out a crisp spicy refreshing taste.
Prepare a varied selection of fresh fruits:
Melon - scrape into melon-balls
Grapes - cut into half
Other fruits cut into good chunky bite-size pieces. Arrange them in an attractive fruit salad bowl, and set aside.

Place a clean piece of kitchen-towel on a sieve and pass the marinated spice-wine and lemon juice through. Add the sugar, stir, taste to see if it is sweet enough.

Now pour the spice-wine syrup into the fruit salad. Decorate with raspberries, cherries, and passion-fruit.

Serve with a sprinkle of sugar.

MOCHA BAVARIAN MOUSSE

INGREDIENTS
¾ pint or 450ml milk
1 tabsp coffee granules
1 tabsp gelatine
5 tabsp water
5oz plain dark chocolate
100g sugar
3 large eggs
250ml double cream
1 or 2 moulds (for the mousse)

Chocolate flake to decorate.

METHOD
In a cup, add the water and sprinkle in the gelatine. Stir, leave aside for the gelatine to go spongy.
Warm the milk in a saucepan with the sugar and coffee powder until dissolved.
Now scrape the spongy gelatine and place the chocolate into the warm coffee milk. Stir until the chocolate is melted. This will form a Bavarian sauce. Turn heat off.

Place the yolk and egg whites into 2 separate bowls.
Beat the egg yolks until pale. Pour the beaten egg yolks into the prepared Bavarian sauce. And stir this over gentle heat to thicken, usually in about 5 minutes. N.B. Do not allow it to boil or the mixture will curdle.
Turn heat off. Pour this Bavarian sauce into a larger bowl and leave aside to set slightly.

In a separate bowl now beat the egg whites until stiff. Set this aside.
Next in another bowl beat the double cream until it can stand as a soft peak. Set aside.
Wait until the Bavarian sauce is about to set. Add the whipped cream and mix well. Now add the stiff egg white and mix it in gently.

Pour this Bavarian mixture into the moulds. Leave to set in the fridge until firm, usually about 2 hours or overnight if required.

To serve: Grasp the rim of the mould which holds the mocha Bavarian mousse. Immerse the mould carefully about ¾ of its depth in hot water for a few seconds, to help release the mousse from the sides of the mould. Place it on to a serving plate. Decorate with cream and top with flaky chocolate, and a jug of mocha sauce.

Mocha sauce

INGREDIENTS
½ tin evaporated milk
125g dark chocolate
2 teasp coffee granules
1½ teasp sugar
Empty screw top jar

METHOD
Add the 4 ingredients into a saucepan. Boil slowly to melt the chocolate. Turn heat off, leave to cool.
Now pour the sauce into the jar. Screw the top tight.
Give it a good shake for the mocha sauce to thicken up slightly and become full of froth.
Pour into a jug and serve.

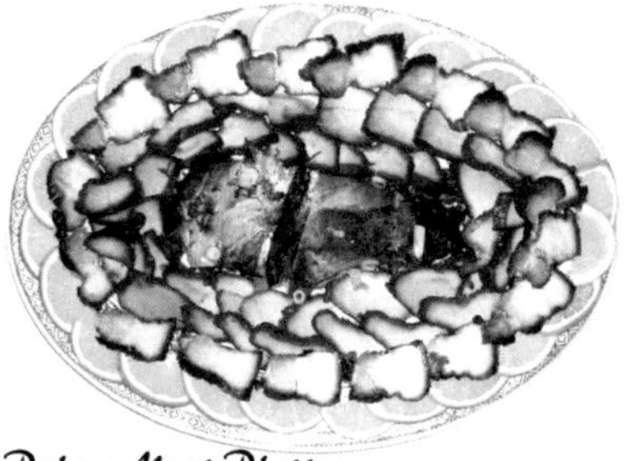

Palace Meat Platter

Mongolian Lamb
with Spring onion

Chicken in Blackbean sauce
with Pepper & Onion

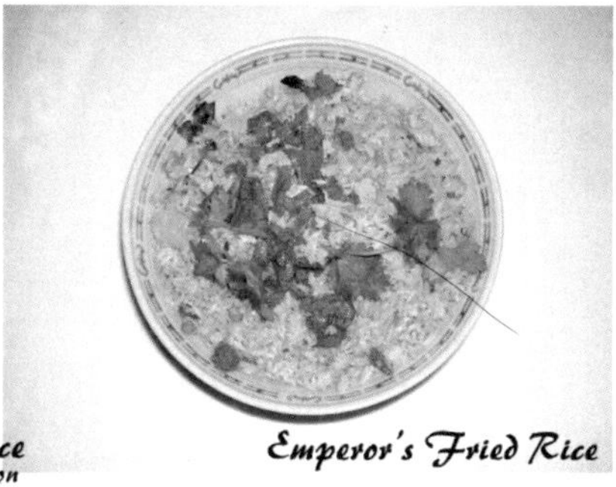

Emperor's Fried Rice

Superior Monks Delight of Vegetable

Sautéed Prawns Sichuan Style

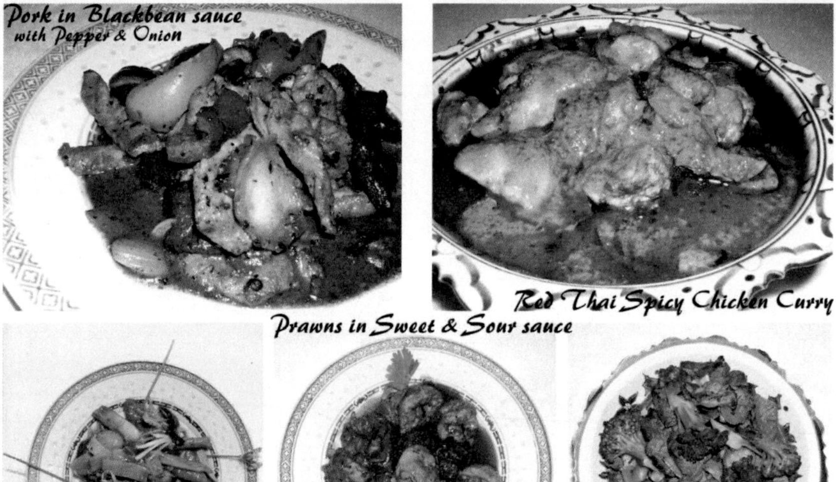
Pork in Blackbean sauce
with Pepper & Onion
Red Thai Spicy Chicken Curry
Prawns in Sweet & Sour sauce
Fresh Vegetables
in Oyster sauce
Beef in Oyster sauce
with broccoli & mushrooms
Spicy Thai Green Chicken Curry
Thai Boiled Rice

AH LIN TANG'S TASTE OF THAILAND

Exciting spicy dishes from the best of Thai cooking created to give you a night of delight. All food will be prepared by me and served in your home with the host and hostess enjoying a relaxed care free evening. I also specialise in vegetarian dishes.

Whether celebrating a special occasion, entertaining some office clients or even just having a party but preferring something different, then let Ah Lin Tang create a taste of Thai to remember.

Starter

Thai Satei: Tender slices of meat on sticks grilled served with a peanut sauce and cucumber

Chicken wings stuffed with Thai spice, minced chicken and served with Thai chilli sauce

Thai crispy little roll with a delicious filling of fine vermicelli, minced prawn and pork and spring vegetable

Thai mini hors d'oeuvres: Pepper spicy mushroom with plenty of garlic crispy fried served with chilli and thick garlic sauce

Main Course

Thai plain boiled rice

Spicy chicken curry

Sweet and sour Prawns

Slices of lean Pork fried with pepper and onion in Black Bean sauce

Tender slices of beef, fried in oyster sauce with broccoli and mushroom

A selection of fresh vegetables in oyster sauce

Sweets

Fresh fruit salad from afar and near

Creme Caramel

All served with ice-cream or cream

Jasmine Tea

Chinese Tableware will be provided. Minimum 10 persons.
Try my Penang, Singapore and Beijing Menus

Ah Lin Tang's Taste Of Thailand

My first trips to Thailand began when I was about fifteen. As I stayed with my aunt and uncle in Penang it was possible to catch large American-style taxi cars from a place in Georgetown which would take you over to Thailand. This journey took several hours. It would stop at the Thai border and there you would have to produce your passport and leave it with immigration whilst they checked you in. Security was strict and you were always glad to get through that part and be on your way to *Haadyai* which was a large town in southern Thailand where you were dropped off. This town has many good restaurants. It was also possible to then travel on to Bangkok by train.

Thailand, as the only country in Southeast Asia never to have been colonised has thus retained, built upon and cultivated its own substantial culinary traditions. The traditional foods all came about due to Thailand's natural wealth of ingredients. A stone inscription thought to be from *King Ramhkhamhaeng* of *Sukhothai*, the first independent Thai kingdom in the early 13th century, reads, "*In the water there are fish, in the fields there is rice*". It was recognised that these lands and waters were plentiful in produce. The central plains, watered by the *Chao Phraya River*, form one of the densest rice-growing regions on our planet.

These traditional foods however did benefit from selected imports from abroad. With the advent of Thai people migrating south from China, this promoted the usage of rice noodles in Thai cuisine. Europeans introduced the chilli pepper from South America. And the Indian traders established key ports along the southern peninsula, giving foreign spices to the Thai community.

Thailand has traditionally served both ends of the culinary spectrum, with on one end deliciously simple recipes, but on the other intricate & difficult methods. In the 1800s, vendors sold quick meals of noodles from boats along the country's network of canals. Today these meals are served by a multitude of pushcart traders on the streets of Bangkok. Meanwhile, '*royal*' or '*palace cooking*' developed among the upper classes – these included complex blends of Thai spices and artistically carved local produce, often vegetables & fruits.

The many cuisines of Thailand offer the culinary enthusiast a lifetime of exploration, ranging from the delights of '*palace*' food to the authenticity of hot street snacks. The extensive range of flavours that infuse the former kingdom of Siam are considerable - they include mouth-watering tangy green papaya, slippery rice noodles, fiery hot curries, and soothing lemon grass.

One of Thailand's best assets is its unique quality provided by the street kitchens. For 15 to 40 Baht, one can buy a full meal at a street kitchen, and for the bargain price the freshly prepared foods are superb. These street kitchens are frequented by both the lower and upper classes. For Westerners it is an incredulous sight to see a limousine chauffeured by a uniformed driver parking near the corner of Sukhumvit and Soi Rd, and a wealthy couple stepping out and taking a place at a fragile table. The setting doesn't seem to be of much importance. What counts is the quality of the food.

For my Thai menu I have incorporated both traditional, street kitchen style, and other delights prepared in a Thai style, to enable you to organise a range of dishes with a variety of delicious flavours & authentic tastes.

Starter

THAI SATEI *Pork and Chicken Satei*

INGREDIENTS
500g loin of pork
500g chicken fillets cut into strips.
3 lemon grass: use only bottom soft part of about 4cm (keeping rest for later use, squash one end)
1 teasp fennel seeds
1 teasp cumin seeds
1 tabsp coriander seeds
5 kaffir lime leaves
5 coriander roots
25g kapi (belachan)
3 teasp turmeric
3 tabsp sugar
6 tabsp vegetable oil
½ teasp salt
½ teasp pepper
2 tabsp coconut powder
1 tabsp ginger juice
1 tabsp coconut oil (melted, originally like butter)
2 teasp chicken powder
50g tamarind soaked in 150ml warm water
1packet of 15cm in length bamboo sticks

For basting:
1 tabsp sugar
2 tabsp coconut oil (melted)

METHOD
Put the fennel, cumin, coriander seeds and belachan into a baking dish and roast for 15minutes on gas 4, 180°C.
Cut finely the 3 lemon grass. Into a grinder add the cut lemon grass, the roast spices, the kaffir lime leaves, and the coriander roots. Grind until very fine.

In a large bowl add the above Thai satei spices, turmeric, sugar, salt, pepper, melted coconut oil, coconut powder and tamarind juice (needs to be squeezed out), vegetable oil, and ginger juice. Mix this well.
Now divide the satei mixture into two bowls - This is the marinade.
In the first bowl add the chicken strips and marinade.
In the second bowl add the pork strips and marinade.
Line a flat tray with cling film.
Thread the meat and place them in lines on the tray. In between the meat add the left over lemon grass.

For basting
Use two of the left over lemon grass pieces (see *ingredients*), squash the ends, add an extra 1 tabsp sugar, and two tabsp coconut oil (melted). Mix together in a bowl.

To serve
Grill the satei on high. Baste the meat satei with two crushed lemon grass ends. Dip into basting bowl and wipe the mixture over the cooking satei. Baste on both sides until brown and cooked.

Serve with satay sauce and cucumber.

Ah Lin Tang's tip – Ideally cooking the satei on a barbeque will add a delicious flavour which is well worth the extra preparation.

THAI SATEI SAUCE

INGREDIENTS

10 dried chillies (soaked in water to soften)
5 lemon grass: use only the bottom part about 4 cms, keep the rest for later use
100g shallots medium sized
3 cloves of garlic
20g Belachan (shrimp paste)
5 candlenuts
5 whole peppercorns
1 thumb-size piece of galangal (squashed)
5 kaffir lime leaves
5 coriander roots
1 tabsp tomato puree
3 tabsp sugar
½ teasp salt
1 cube of vegetable stock
2 teasp turmeric
2 teasp coriander powder
2 teasp curry powder
1 tin coconut milk 400ml
180g tamarind soaked in 250ml warm water, squeeze out the juice & discard the used tamarind
Vegetable oil for cooking
60g roasted ground peanut

METHOD

Cut in to chunky pieces the soaked chillies, lemon grass, shallots, garlic, candlenuts, belachan, coriander roots, whole peppercorn, and kaffir lime leaves. Place them into a grinder and blend until fine.

Heat a wok with vegetable oil on medium. Add the ground spices. Stir and cook slowly, making sure you continuously stir the spices to prevent them from burning.
Now add the coriander and curry powder and keep cooking for a good 10-15 minutes making sure that all the spices are covered in oil.

Add the turmeric, tomato puree and the rest of the squashed lemon grass. Stir, add sugar, salt, galangal. By this time the oil should be seeping through from all the spices and you should be able to smell their fragrance.
Turn the heat up and quickly add the tin of coconut. Remember to stir the sauce at all times. Add the tamarind juice and crumbled vegetable stock cube.

Cook until the sauce bubbles, stir, and let it simmer for a few more minutes. Taste for its sweet and sour flavour. Turn the heat off. Pour sauce into a container. Use the amount you want.

The sauce will thicken when you sprinkle in the peanut.

THAI CHICKEN WING

INGREDIENTS
10 chicken wings (boned)
100g fresh raw small prawns
225g chickens thigh (cut in slices)
1 tabsp spring onion (chopped)
1 tabsp coriander (chopped)
1 teasp chilli (chopped)
1 tabsp light Soy sauce
A pinch of salt
½ teasp pepper
1 teasp chicken stock powder
1 tabsp fish sauce
2 cloves of garlic chopped
Vegetable oil for frying
100g chopped carrots

Thin batter:
1 egg
50g flour
100ml cold water

4 slices of bread
125g of cornflakes.

METHOD
Place the chicken thighs and prawns into a blender and mince. Scrape all of this mixture into a bowl; add spring onion, coriander, chillies, light Soy sauce, salt, pepper, chicken stock powder, fish sauce, and garlic. Mix well. Set aside.
Line a tray with cling film.

Make the thin batter by mixing the eggs, flour and water. Set this aside.
Chop the bread and cornflakes into breadcrumbs. Set aside.

Lay the chicken wings on a flat working surface. Put the chicken mixture into a piping bag. Pipe this mixture into the insides of the boned chicken wings. Now

dip them into the thin batter and cover them well. And now place them into the breadcrumbs and cover them well again.
Lay these prepared chicken wings onto the lined tray. Repeat and finish stuffing the chicken wings.

To serve - deep fry until cooked for a good ten minutes until golden brown.
Serve with *Thai chilli sauce*.

Thai Chilli Sauce

INGREDIENTS
Need screw top jar
2 tabsp minced fried chilli
3 tabsp plum sauce
4 tabsp lemon juice
3 tabsp fish sauce
1 tabsp sugar
3 tabsp grated carrots

METHOD
Add all of these ingredients into the jar. Give it a good stir and mix thoroughly.
Put screw top back on. Keep it cool in the fridge. Serve.

THAI CRISPY LITTLE ROLL

INGREDIENTS

250g fresh small prawns (chopped)
125g belly pork (minced)
65g Dutch cabbage
65g green beans
65g Chinese celery cabbage (Chinese leaves)
65g leeks
½ onion
1 chilli cut to just 4cm
1 stick of celery
8 Chinese mushrooms (soaked in 100ml water until soft)
1 carrot (grated)
125g Chinese yambean or mooli (grated)
A handful of transparent noodles (soaked in water)
2 tabsp spring onion - chopped
3 tabsp coriander - chopped
3 tabsp fish sauce
3 tabsp light Soy sauce
½ teasp salt
1 teasp pepper
2 teasp chicken stock powder
1 vegetable stock cube
3 cloves garlic - chopped
3 tabsp vegetable oil
1½ tabsp cornflour mixed with the mushroom water
1 packet of pastry pancake skin (for spring-rolls)

Cornflour mixture:

1 egg mixed with 1 tabsp cornflour and 3 tabsp of water

Vegetable oil for frying
Flat tray lined with cling film

METHOD

Prepare the filling:

Chop all the vegetables including the Dutch cabbage, green beans, Chinese leaves, leeks, onion, chilli, celery and Chinese mushrooms into small bite size pieces. Set this aside.
Now cut transparent noodles into 4 cm lengths.
Heat a large wok on medium and add the 3 tabsp of vegetable oil, next add the garlic, stir fry, add the minced pork & prawns stirring continuously. Turn heat to high, add the vegetables including the carrots and Chinese yambean (or mooli). Keep stirring, and add the transparent noodles.
Add the crumbled vegetable cube, light Soy sauce, fish sauce, chicken stock powder, salt and pepper. Make a well in the centre of this mixture and add the stirred cornflour mixture. Mix thoroughly. The sauce should be thickened. Turn heat off and add the spring onion and coriander. Set aside to cool.

To finish the roll:
Set aside the lined tray and the egg cornflour mixture ready for use.
On a flat surface lay the pancake skins and cut them in half. Separate the rectangular pancake skins into individual pieces. Gather 20 rectangular pieces and cut again in half to form 40 small square pieces. Set these aside.

Place 1 piece of rectangular skin with its short side facing towards you.
Add 2 teasp of filling centrally, about one third of the skin from you. Brush the top half with egg-cornflour mixture.
Lift the lower flap over the filling and roll a quarter of the distance away from you, now tuck both sides inwards. Brush again with cornflour mixture and finish off the rolling. Set aside.
Now lay a small square piece on the working surface, brush all over with cornflour mixture. Place the prepared roll in the middle of this well brushed square pancake skin and keep away from the edges. Lift the lower flap over the spring roll and finish off rolling and tucking in both corners tightly, to form a compact parcel-roll. Arrange neatly on the tray. Repeat until all the Thai rolls are made.

To serve:
Heat oil in a wok and deep fry until golden brown, usually about 5 mins, and serve.

N.B. the double skin layers help the thin roll not to burst open when frying.

THAI CRISPY MUSHROOM

INGREDIENTS
600g button mushrooms

Thin batter – mix:
1 egg
125g of flour
125ml water

4 slices of bread
125g cornflakes
½ teasp salt
½ teasp pepper
½ vegetable stock cube (crumbled)
1 teasp chilli powder
3 cloves of garlic
1 tabsp coriander (chopped)
Vegetable oil for frying

METHOD
Wash the button mushrooms. Then prepare the batter in a bowl as mentioned above. Set aside.

Make the cornflake crumbs and breadcrumbs by placing the bread, cornflakes and garlic into a blender. Empty these crumbs into a large bowl, add in the salt, pepper, crumbled vegetable cube, chillies and fresh coriander and mix well.

First add a few mushrooms into the thin batter and cover them completely. Then dip these into the crumbs and cover well with this mixture. Place the prepared mushrooms on a tray.

To serve
Deep fry in hot vegetable oil until golden brown. This takes about five minutes. Serve with thick garlic sauce.

Thick Garlic Sauce

INGREDIENTS
4 tabsp mayonnaise
2 teasp minced fried chillies
1 tabsp garlic
3 tabsp lemon juice
3 tabsp double cream.

METHOD
Mix all the ingredients together. Keep this in a screw top jar in the fridge until ready to be served with the *Thai crispy mushrooms*.

This thick garlic sauce can be kept for a week if necessary.

MA HO - *(Thai galloping horse)*

INGREDIENTS
350g minced pork
2 tabsp coriander - chopped
2 tabsp spring onion - chopped
1 tabsp light Soy sauce
1½ tabsp fish sauce
1 chilli (4cm length) chopped
2 cloves of garlic - chopped
2 teasp of chicken stock powder
½ teasp salt
½ teasp pepper

Chopped peanut for coating
1 egg yolk (beaten)
pineapple pieces cut into small square chunks
vegetable oil for frying

Flat tray lined with cling film

METHOD
Add the ten ingredients mentioned, at the top of the list above, into a large bowl. Mix this thoroughly. Divide this mixture into ten portions.
Take one portion of the mixture, and it roll into a ball. Place a piece of pineapple in the centre. Cover the hole with the filling again by rolling it back into a ball.
Dip it completely into the egg yolk and lightly cover them in the peanut by rolling them in it.
Place the prepared *ma ho* on a lined cling film tray. Repeat until all the filling is used up.

To serve
Deep fry the *ma ho* until golden brown and cooked. Usually about 5 minutes.

Main Course

THAI BOILED RICE

INGREDIENTS
500g Thai fragrant rice
300g Basmati rice
½ tin of coconut (400ml) mixed with water, to 1300ml in total
100g butter
1 teasp salt
2 pandan leaves (screwpine leaves)

METHOD
Wash the two portions of rice with three changes of cold water. Drain the water away.

To boil the rice
Place the rice, coconut water, salt, butter and pandan leaves in a thick based saucepan. Boil, stir thoroughly often to stop the rice sticking to the bottom of the saucepan.
Once the water evaporates, stir once more. Cover and cook on a very low heat for 20 minutes.

Before serving fluff up the rice with a spatula. Throw away the Pandan leaves.

Ah Lin Tang's tip – For best results use a rice cooker for part of the rice preparation. They are readily bought in most home stores and are useful additions to the kitchen for perfectly cooked rice.

SPICY THAI GREEN CHICKEN CURRY

INGREDIENTS
800g chicken breast (cut into chunky bite size)
250ml chicken stock, mixed with 1 tabsp cornflour
2 teasp chicken stock powder
3 medium potatoes (boiled and cut into big cubes)
1 small onion (big cubes)
7 fresh coriander root (the dark root part) 3cm long
100g shallots (sliced)
20g shrimp paste

3 cloves of garlic
4 lemon grass
2 teasp of turmeric
1 tabsp whole peppercorns
7 fresh green chillies
1 tabsp of ginger (chopped)
1 tabsp of cumin seeds
1½ tabsp of coriander seeds
6 kaffir lime leaves
1 tin of coconut milk (400ml)
1 tabsp fish sauce
1 thumb-sized galangal (crushed)
2 teasp salt
10g fresh basil - chopped
25g fresh coriander - chopped
Vegetable oil for frying

METHOD
Ensure the fresh basil and coriander are both chopped coarsely. Set them aside.

Cut off the hard stump nearer to the soft part of the lemon grass. Cut from its plump side a 4cm length. This will be used in the curry paste. Squash the rest of lemon grass, it will be used later.

Place the whole peppercorns, coriander seeds, cumin seeds and shrimp paste in an oven, and roast for 10 minutes (do not let it burn) on temperature 170°C (or gas mark 3). Next grind the roast ingredients including the plump side of the lemon grass and kaffir lime leaves until fine.

Add these ground ingredients into a blender, and then add the shallots, garlic, chillies, coriander root, and ginger. Blend until fine.
Using a large pan on low heat add the Thai paste, cover it with oil, stir-fry and cook slowly (10 minutes). This helps the spices to mature and maintain their real flavour.
Add the squashed lemon grass and the galangal, stir, and add the turmeric and stir again. Increase the heat to high and add the tinned coconut. Mix, cook gently until it begins to bubble. Now add the chicken pieces, salt, fish sauce, and the chicken stock powder. Mix again. As it bubbles watch to see the chicken turn white, now turn the heat off.

Using another clean saucepan gently dish out the chicken into the second saucepan. Place on top of the second saucepan a hand-sieve, and tip the first saucepan of remaining curry sauce through the sieve into the second saucepan. Throw away the leftover scum (leaving the rich smooth sauce in the 2nd saucepan).

Turn heat to high, add the potatoes, basil, onions and cornflour mixture with chicken stock. Taste to ensure it is to your satisfaction. Finally allow it to boil quickly, turn off the heat.

Sprinkle some coriander on the top, and serve.

Ah Lin Tang's tip - To obtain the true dark coriander root, best to go to a specialist Chinese food shop where they stock the whole plant. Note that supermarkets will not supply the ideal material for this dish.

RED THAI SPICY CHICKEN CURRY

INGREDIENTS
800g chicken breast
85ml chicken stock, mixed with 1 tabsp cornflour
2 teasp chicken stock powder
3 potatoes (boiled) - cut into chunky pieces
1 small onion - cut into chunky pieces

100g shallots (sliced)
20g kapi (shrimp paste)
1 tabsp whole peppercorn
6 fresh red chillies
4 lemon grass
2½ tabsp whole coriander seed
1 tabsp cumin seed
6 kaffir lime leaves
7 fresh coriander root 3cm long
2 cloves garlic
1 thumb-size piece of ginger
2 teasp turmeric
½ tin 400ml plum tomatoes
1 tin 400ml coconut milk
2 teasp salt
1 tabsp fish sauce
Vegetable oil
1 tabsp tomato puree
25g fresh coriander - chopped

METHOD
Cut the chicken into thick chunks. Set them aside. Cut the onion into bite sized chunks, and the fresh coriander chop coarsely.

Cut off the hard stump nearer the soft plump part of the lemon grass. Now cut from the plump side a 4cm long length. This will be used in the curry paste. Squash the rest of the lemon grass, it will be used later.

Put the whole peppercorns, coriander seed, cumin seed, kapi (shrimp paste) and roast in an oven for10 minutes at 170°C (or gas mark 3). Do not let it burn.
Next grind these roasted ingredients including the plump side of the lemon grass and the kaffir lime leaves until fine.
Add the ground spices, shallots, chillies, kaffir lime leaves, garlic, ginger, and coriander root, all into a grinder, and blend until very fine paste.

Using a large saucepan add the ground red Thai paste, cover it with vegetable oil and cook slowly until the spices ooze out with bubbles.
Keep stirring to stop the spices burning at the bottom of the pan, and if cooked slowly this helps the spices to mature and retains its real full flavour. This will take about ten minutes. Now add the tomato puree. Mix.

The next step is to add the squashed lemon grass, stir, add the turmeric and the ½ tin plum-tomatoes. Increase the heat to medium and add the tinned coconut. Stir agian, cook gently until it begins to bubble. Now add the chicken pieces, salt, fish-sauce, and chicken stock powder. Turn heat to high, stir, cook until it starts to bubbles again and the chicken has turned white. Turn heat off.

Using another clean saucepan gently dish out the chicken into the second saucepan. Place on top of the second saucepan a hand-sieve, and tip the first saucepan (of curry sauce) through the sieve into the second saucepan. Throw away the scum (this makes the sauce look rich and smooth).

Turn heat to high, add the potatoes and onions and cornflour mixture with the chicken stock. Taste to insure it is to your satisfaction. Finally allow it to boil quickly, turn off the heat.

Sprinkle on top some coriander, and serve.

Ah Lin Tang's tip - If the curry sauce is too runny just add a touch of cornflour mixture to thicken.

PRAWNS IN SWEET AND SOUR SAUCE

INGREDIENTS
800g fresh Tiger-prawns
1 tabsp of chopped ginger
1 tabsp spring onion - chopped
1½ tabsp of fish sauce
½ teasp salt
½ teasp pepper
1 tabsp light Soy sauce

Thick batter:

1 egg
130g flour
100g custard powder
100ml milk
100ml water

Vegetable oil for frying

METHOD
Prepare the prawns:
Prepare prawns by shelling and de-veining them. Cut deeply in middle so prawns open up slightly. And remove the vein. Really open up the prawns for the best results - hence their name of 'butterfly' prawn.

To make batter:
Mix the eggs, flour, custard powder, milk and water, and then blend them into a smooth consistency similar to double cream.
Pour this batter into a large bowl and add all the ingredients mentioned except the oil.
Mix thoroughly. Heat the oil for frying.
Take the prawns and place them into the thick batter. Then place them into the hot oil and deep fry quickly to a light golden colour. Remove them, and set aside.

To serve:
Fry the prawns again until crisp and golden brown. Place them on a serving plate and pour the *Sweet and Sour sauce* all over.
Garnish with the spring onion.

Sweet & Sour sauce is detailed on p44.

PORK IN BLACK BEAN SAUCE WITH PEPPER AND ONION

INGREDIENTS
700g pork loin or pork fillet (sliced)
2 teasp bicarbonate of soda
2 tabsp whole black beans (chopped)
½ red pepper, ½ green pepper and ½ yellow pepper
½ a white and ½ a red onion
4cm long chilli
1 clove of garlic chopped
2 teasp dark Soy sauce
1 tabsp of light Soy sauce
1 teasp chicken stock powder
200ml water or chicken stock mixed, with 1 tabsp cornflour
½ teasp salt
½ teasp sugar
½ teasp pepper
2 teasp oyster sauce
1 tabsp fish sauce
A *thumb-size piece of ginger - sliced*
2 stalks of fresh coriander - cut into 3cm length
2 spring onions - cut into 3cm lengths
2 tabsp oil

METHOD
Using your hand rub the bicarbonate of soda all over the sliced pork. Set aside.
Cut the pepper, onion, & chilli into chunky bite sized pieces.
Now wash the pork in running cold water very well to remove any remaining bicarbonate of soda. Leave on a colander to drain.

Heat the oil on low, stir-fry the black bean, garlic and ginger until these spices produce a delicious smell, usually in about 5 minutes. Next add the pork, stir, and turn the heat to high. Cook until the pork changes colour. Add the dark Soy sauce, light Soy sauce, oyster sauce, salt, pepper, sugar and chicken powder. Mix these spices into the pork.

Now mix in the water (or chicken stock) and cornflour mixture. Stir and add the pepper, onions, and chillies.
Add in your fish sauce, taste and dish out.

Sprinkle with coriander and spring onion. Serve.

Ah Lin Tang's tip – For best results I use chicken stock instead of water, as it complements all the flavours well.

BEEF IN OYSTER SAUCE WITH BROCCOLI AND STRAW MUSHROOMS

INGREDIENTS
700g beef rump steak (sliced)
1 small broccoli
2 teasp bicarbonate of soda
125g of tinned straw mushrooms (cut into half pieces)
2 teasp oyster sauce
2 teasp dark Soy sauce
2 teasp chicken stock powder
1 tabsp light Soy sauce
2 tabsp Chinese Shaohsing wine
200ml stock or water
1 tabsp ginger chopped
1 tabsp garlic chopped
3 fresh corianders and spring onions cut into 4cm lengths
½ teasp salt
½ teasp pepper
½ teasp sugar
2 tabsp sesame oil
2 tabsp vegetable oil

METHOD
First mix the beef and the bicarbonate of soda with your hand. Set aside.
Cut the broccoli into good bite sized pieces and blanch quickly in boiling water until *al dente*.
Now wash the beef in cold running water to remove the bicarbonate of soda. Wash it well. Drain. Set aside.

Heat oil in a wok on low, stir-fry the ginger and garlic until the colour changes slightly. Add 1 tabsp sesame oil. Turn the heat to high, add the beef. Stir-fry and mix continuously to prevent the beef sticking to the bottom of the wok. Cook until the colour of the beef slightly changes.

Now add the oyster sauce, salt, pepper, sugar, dark and light Soy sauce and chicken stock powder. Mix well. Add the broccoli and straw mushrooms. Stir. Add the stock mixed with cornflour into the wok.
Cook this all quickly until the sauce thickens, add the Shaohsing wine and the remaining sesame oil, stir for a minute. Turn heat off.

Serve with spring onion and coriander sprinkled on top.

FRESH VEGETABLES IN OYSTER SAUCE

INGREDIENTS
100g bean shoots (tails)
70g mangetout (trimmed)
70g Chinese leaves - cut into 4cm lengths
½ courgette - cut into 3cm lengths
¼ onion - chopped
10cm long celery
3cm in length chilli (can be cut to this size)
¼ pieces of mixed red, yellow, green peppers
¼ piece of cauliflower (bite size & blanched)
125g oyster mushrooms
1 medium-sized carrot
1 tabsp light Soy sauce
2 teasp oyster sauce
1 teasp dark Soy sauce
½ teasp salt
½ teasp pepper
1 teasp sugar
1½ tabsp cornflour
2 teasp of salted soy beans
1 vegetable stock cube
2 tabsp of vegetable oil
1 tabsp fish sauce
2 teasp garlic - chopped
1 tabsp ginger - chopped
2 spring onion and 2 stalks of coriander (cut into 4cm lengths)
250ml water

METHOD
Place all the prepared vegetables onto a large tray in neat individual piles.
Cut a v-shaped groove along the length of the carrot. Repeat this, making 3 to 4 more grooves along different sides of the carrot. Now chop the carrots into 2cm slices and a slight flower shape should be formed. Slice the courgettes into strips 2cm wide. Now slice them in half again. Set aside on the tray.

Cut the celery, onion, pepper and chilli in to bite size pieces. Cut the oyster mushrooms into half.
Heat the vegetable oil on medium, and stir-fry the salted soy beans, ginger and garlic until the spices smell fragrant.
Now turn the heat to high. Add the carrots, stir-fry, add the celery, onion, peppers, chilli, courgettes, and stir fry again.
Next add the oyster sauce, salt, pepper, sugar, dark and light Soy sauces and fish sauce. Stir-fry. Add the oyster mushrooms, mangetout, cauliflower and bean shoots.

Mix the crumbled vegetable cube into the water, and add the cornflour and stir thoroughly. Pour this onto the stir-fried vegetables. Let it boil and the sauce thicken. Turn heat off.
Sprinkle the spring onion and coriander, and serve.

Sweet

FRESH FRUIT SALAD FROM AFAR & NEAR

INGREDIENTS
Selection of fresh fruits, such as:
Strawberries, Raspberries, Cherries, Passion-fruit, Apples, Pears, Sharon fruit, Mangoes, Pawpaw , Melons, Pineapple, Lychees, Oranges, Grapes (white & red)

Spice-wine marinade
¼ bottle of white wine
¼ bottle of Cinzano (white)
5 piece of lemon grass (10cm in length, ends squashed)
25g cardamom seed
2 long pieces of pandan leaves

3 tabsp sugar
4tabsp of lemon juice

METHOD
Place all the spices (including the leaves) mentioned inside the mixed bottle of wine & Cinzano. Seal the bottle and leave in the fridge for 1 week. This method helps the wine to absorb all the spices' flavour and when used on the fresh fruit it produces a crisp spicy refreshing taste.

Prepare a good selection of fresh fruits.
Melon - scrape into melon-balls
Grapes - cut into half
Other fruits cut into good chunky bite-size pieces. Arrange them on an attractive fruit salad bowl, and set aside.

Place a clean piece of kitchen-towel on a sieve and pass the marinated spice-wine and lemon juice through.
Add the sugar, stir, taste to see if it is sweet enough.

Now pour the spice-wine syrup into the fruit salad. Decorate with raspberries, cherries, and passion-fruit.

Serve with a sprinkle of sugar.

CRÈME CARAMEL

INGREDIENTS
Caramel Sauce:
4 tabsp water
300g Sugar
6 tabsp boiling water

Caramel:
750g Double cream
250g Milk
100g Sugar
7 egg yolks
3 whole eggs
70ml of Vanilla extract

2 square tins 12x12cm
1 large roasting tin (that can accommodate the 2 smaller tins)

METHOD
Make toffee:
Boil the cold water with the sugar in a heavy-base saucepan, with temperature on medium, until the sugar dissolves. Stir occasionally.
Now bring to the boil, but to do stir until the sugar turns a dark, golden brown.
Now remove from the heat. Add the 6 tabsp of boiling water. Be careful of the spitting when you pour in the boiling water.
Stir. Allow to cool slightly.
Pour this caramel sauce into two tins. Leave aside.

In the same saucepan add the double cream, milk, sugar, and bring to a boil. Turn heat off and leave to cool slightly forming a 'custard' mixture. In the meantime beat the egg yolk in a separate bowl. Add the vanilla extract into the cool custard, and then the beaten eggs into the mixture. Whisk well. Strain and pour into the 2 small prepared tins.
Now place these 2 smaller tins into a large roasting tin. Pour in the hot water to half fill the roasting tin. Cover the caramel tins with kitchen-foil. Cook in an oven on gas mark 6 or 200°C until the caramel is cooked, it takes about 1½ hours.

To test if the Thai caramel is done - Insert a piece of bamboo stick into the caramel and then quickly remove it again. If it comes out clean that indicates the caramel is cooked. Allow to cool and serve.

Decorate with strawberry fans (i.e. sliced strawberry spread out in fan shape) and a sprig of mint.

AH LIN TANG'S
A NIGHT IN SINGAPORE

A gourmet dream come true from the crossroads of Asia where the delicious foods of this multicultural island are at their best whether served from street stalls or in the surroundings of some of the world's most splendid hotels. Enjoy a Raffles style banquet in your own home.

All food will be prepared by me and served in your home with the host and hostess enjoying a relaxed care free evening. I also specialise in vegetarian dishes.

Whether celebrating a special occasion, entertaining some office clients or even just having a party but preferring something different, then let Ah Lin Tang create a taste of Singapore to remember.

Starter

Dim Sum: Mini hors d'oeuvres

Singapore fried noodles on lettuce leaves with Sambal

Stuffed deep fried crabmeat on a stick with chilli dip

Murtabak: Wrapped in roti filled with savoury curry Indian style

Main Course

Nasi Lemak (Fragrant Malay Rice)

Chilli Prawns Nonya Style

Sweet and Sour Fried Fish

Chicken and Pineapple with Mangetout

Raffles Roast Pork in an Island

Bugie Strip of Vegetable Stir Fried

Sweets

Singapore Style - Queen of Puddings

Dessert of the Day

All served with ice-cream or cream

Jasmine Tea

Chinese Tableware will be provided. Minimum 10 persons.

Ah Lin Tang's A Night In Singapore

Being one of twelve it is not surprising that I had a brother who lived in Singapore which was originally part of Malaya. Even from very early on the culture in Singapore was quite distinct from Malaysia.

Singapore cooking has multiple origins including Malaysian, Indonesian, Chinese and Indian influences. Here you will find the most authentic and tastiest of each of their cuisines. Singapore food is the development of these various cuisines since their first arrival over a century ago.

Nonya food has been previously mentioned by me. What I'd like to emphasize to you here are the equally superb but less acknowledged cuisines that have their origin in South-Eastern China. Apart from Cantonese cuisine that is renowned the world over, what is special in Singapore foods are these Southern Chinese cuisines not commonly found elsewhere.
Canton is where all the Chinese want to eat. Cantonese food is world famous especially its *Dim Sum* and *Wonton soup*. If you had eaten in a Chinese restaurant outside of China, it is most likely Cantonese food.

To most Singaporeans however, what *makan* is based upon is not the plush surroundings where the food is eaten, but more simply the quality of the food, the convenience and most importantly its delicious taste.
Singapore is undeniably a hot country and I have memories of sharing a hot plate of *Nasi Lemak* in a hawker centre amidst all the sweat and noise in the middle of an afternoon.

Seafood is especially popular in Singapore, eaten in many of the restaurants and hawker stalls. Singapore Chilli crabs, chilli prawns and deep fried baby squids are just a selection of some of the specialist dishes that one really shouldn't miss. If you do not know where to begin, East Coast Seafood Centre is definitely worth a visit.

Another place in Singapore you should not miss is Raffles Hotel. This was refurbished in the 1990s and is a popular place for the rich and famous. It is also where the well-known 'Singapore Sling', a gin-based cocktail drink, was invented. Raffles is also admired for its recommended tiffin and Chinese banquets which includes its celebrated roast pork.

The Singapore dishes which I have included in my menu are based on recipes which have been passed to me whilst staying with my brother and sister-in-law, and which I have learned on my travels around Singapore. The recipes are authentic & delicious and will produce excellent results if you take the time to properly prepare them.

Selamat Makan!
(enjoy your meal)

Starter

DIM SUM - *A SELECTION:*

HAR GAU (PRAWN DUMPLING PASTRY)

INGREDIENTS
2 pkt Har Gau wrapper (dumpling) - are plain white circular
200g fresh medium-sized prawns
500g fresh small prawns (coarsely chopped)
120g tin bamboo shoots (chopped)
1 tabsp spring onion (chopped)
1 tabsp fresh coriander (chopped)
1 teasp sugar
2 teasp light Soy sauce
3 tabsp sesame oil
½ egg white
½ teasp pepper
2 teasp cornflour

Wrapper dough:
350g wheat flour
2 tabsp cornflour
280ml boiling water
2 tabsp vegetable oil
Small pastry maker
Steamer basket

For the *har gau* pastry skin you can either buy them readymade in Chinese grocery shops or you can make your own wrapper dough which I have detailed below. You can also use a small pastry maker or try to master the Chinese technique of making the real *har gau*.

METHOD
In a large bowl add all the filling ingredients. Mix this well and set aside.

Making the Har Gau pastry wrappers:
In a mixing bowl add the wheat flour, cornflour and oil, then add the boiling water. Mix evenly, cover with a cloth for a minute or two for the dough to cool down. Knead the dough on a soft working surface. Add a little extra wheat flour if the dough is too sticky.
Roll into a long cylinder. Divide the cylinder into 36 individual portions. Working with one portion at a time, roll out the dough using a rolling pin into 9cm diameter circles. Set aside.

On a flat working surface place a piece of *har gau* wrapper skin inside the pastry maker. Add 1 teasp of the prepared filling. Fold over and seal tightly. Place prepared *har gau* in a steamer basket.

To make your own Har Gau using pastry wrapper dough.
Place a piece of home-made wrapper dough in your left hand, add a teaspoon of filling in to the centre of this wrapper. Fold over, pinch and press one end of the wrapper, and work with your index & thumb fingers to pinch all around to seal inside the filling, thus producing the dumpling.

Place the prepared *har gau* in a steamer basket and steam for ten minutes.
Serve with a dipping sauce consisting of light Soya sauce with a dash of sesame oil.

SIU MAI (PORK DUMPLING)

INGREDIENTS
200g belly of pork (minced)
200g fresh small prawns (coarsely minced)
½ teasp pepper
2 tabsp light Soy sauce
1 teasp chicken stock powder
2 tabsp sesame oil
¾ teasp sugar
2 teasp ginger (chopped)
100g tin of water chestnut - chopped
2 tabsp of chopped spring onion - chopped finely
2 tabsp cornflour
1 large egg white

1 pkt Chinese wonton skin (wrapper)
Steamer basket
A few Trout or Salmon roe - for garnishing (optional)

METHOD
In a large bowl add the ingredients (apart from the wonton skins and trout/salmon roe) and mix well. Set this filling aside.
On a flat working surface lay a piece of wonton skin. Put 1 tabsp of this filling into the centre of a piece of wonton skin. Draw all the sides of the wonton skin vertically upwards with the filling still in the centre of the wonton skin. Now squeeze lightly all around the outer skin, making sure the wonton skin sticks to the filling and at the same time forms a flat base for the Sui Mai to stand on. Smooth the surface. Put a small pinch of trout/salmon roe in the centre of the prepared *sui mai*.

To steam
Arrange the *sui mai* in a basket steamer. Cling film and steam over simmering water in a wok for 10 to 15 minutes.
Serve with light Soy sauce.

TURNIP CAKE

INGREDIENTS
700g mooli - grated
20g dried prawns (soak in 50ml water)
5 dried Chinese mushrooms (soak in 50ml water)
4 shallots (sliced)
1½ tabsp spring onion (chopped)
1 tabsp fresh coriander (chopped)
½ teasp salt
½ teasp pepper
1 tabsp sesame oil
½ vegetable stock cube (crumbled)
80g rice flour
2 tabsp vegetable oil

14x10cm rectangular tin - line it with baking foil.
A vegetable steamer

METHOD
Put the grated mooli into a bowl. Add 100ml hot water and leave for 5 minutes. Squeeze the water from the mooli. Save this water.
Put the well squeezed mooli into another large bowl. Set aside. With the saved mooli water pour this into a jug.

Dry the prawns, squeeze off their water and chop. Put the chopped prawns aside. Place the prawn water into the same jug as the mooli water. Squeeze excess water from the mushrooms, and place this mushroom water also into the jug. Chop the mushrooms. Set aside.

Fry the shallots until crisp, take them out and set aside. Heat the oil on low in a wok, add the prawns, stir-fry for a few seconds, now add the mooli and stir-fry again.
Turn the heat to medium. Add the mushrooms, spring onion, coriander, salt, pepper, sesame oil, vegetable stock cube and the rice flour. Mix well.
Turn heat to low. Now add 120ml of the saved water (from the jug) to the wok. Mix well again. Set aside.

Brush the insides of the kitchen foil with the vegetable oil. Dish the prepared mooli mixture into the well oiled tin. Compress the mixture tightly, and smooth the top evenly.
Cover this mooli mixture (in your tin) with kitchen foil.
Place the mooli mixture into the vegetable steamer and steam for 2 hours or until cooked.

The mooli cake should be firm and quite solid to touch once ready.
Allow to cool.

To serve
Slice the mooli (turnip) cake into 2cm wide portions.
Shallow fry the sliced mooli cake until golden brown on both sides. Serve with light Soy sauce with a dash of sesame oil or *chilli sauce dip* (p93).

SINGAPORE FRIED NOODLES - SERVED ON LETTUCE LEAVES WITH SAMBAI

INGREDIENTS
200g dry noodles
100g Chinese flowering cabbage - cut into 4cm lengths
½ onion chopped
500g bean shoots (tailed)
1 medium carrot
1 piece of celery
3cm length of chilli - sliced
6 dry Chinese mushrooms - soaked in cold water until soft, then sliced
100g mangetout (trimmed)
1 tabsp garlic - chopped
1 tabsp ginger - chopped
½ teasp salt
½ teasp pepper
2 teasp oyster sauce
½ vegetable stock cube - crumbled
1 tabsp dark Soy sauce
2 tabsp light Soy sauce
2 tabsp vegetable oil
2 spring onions and fresh coriander - cut into 4cm lengths
4 pieces of Cos lettuce

METHOD
Soak the noodles in warm water until soft and separable. Drain & set aside.
Cut the carrots, celery, chillies, mangetout, and mushrooms into thick matchstick sizes.
Heat the wok with the oil on low, and stir-fry the onion for a few seconds, then add the ginger and garlic.
Turn the heat to medium, add the noodle, give it a good stir-fry and now add the oyster sauce, and the dark & light Soy sauces. Crumble in the vegetable stock cube with the salt and pepper.

Turn heat to high, give the noodle a good stir-fry and add the rest of the vegetables. Now turn the heat off. Set aside.

Place the lettuce leaves overlapping in a circular pattern on a large serving plate. Pile the fried noodles on top in the centre. N.B. the lettuce leaves will still be visible poking out from underneath the noodles.

Sprinkle the spring onion and fresh coriander on the top & serve.

Ah Lin Tang's tip – Best results for many of my dishes are obtained by using a quality non-stick wok, which the keen chef should add to their kitchen's equipment.

Sambai (Dynamite)

INGREDIENTS
100g fresh red chillies
6g shrimp paste (grilled until its smell evaporates & it becomes dry)
20g dried prawns (washed)
2 shallots (sliced)
Vegetable oil

1 teasp sugar
3 tabsp lemon juice

METHOD
Add the chillies, shrimp paste, prawns and shallots into a blender and form a paste (medium coarseness). Heat vegetable oil on low, and add this paste. Stir-fry slowly until the oil oozes out of the paste and produces a lovely smell of *sambai*, this takes about 10 minutes. Now turn the heat off.
Allow to cool and place in a screw top jar. This can be stored for up to 1 week.

To serve
Take 3 tabsp of the prepared *sambai* and add to the sugar & lemon juice. Mix and place in a serving bowl next to the *Singapore Fried Noodle* (recipe above).

STUFFED DEEP FRIED CRABMEAT ON A STICK WITH CHILLI DIP

INGREDIENTS
20 small forks (made from wood are best)
200g fresh crabmeat
550g fresh prawns small (minced)
150g minced belly of pork (fatty side best)
1 egg
2 tabsp cornflour
½ teasp pepper
½ vegetable stock cube - crumbled
1 tabsp light Soy sauce
1 teasp sugar
2 tabsp sesame oil
1 tabsp ginger (chopped)
2 tabsp fresh coriander and spring onion (chopped)

Cornflake crumbs:
125g of cornflakes - made into crumbs
4 pieces of bread - made into crumbs

METHOD
Take a flat tray and line with cling film.
In a large bowl add all the ingredients (apart from wooden sticks!) Stir to form a paste until it is firm and sticky. Divide into 20 portions. Set aside.

Holding a small fork on the prong end. Press a portion of the paste onto the rounded-end of the fork (i.e. opposite to the prongs), press firmly and gently to form a crab-claw shape. This crab-claw appearance is formed by the prongs (resembling the pincers) and the crab paste on the fork resembling the meaty claw.

Cover the crab-claw entirely with cornflake crumb mixture. Place the finished crab-claw on the prepared lined tray. Repeat this with the rest of the filling to form the crab-claws.

Deep fry in oil and serve with *Chilli dip* (see below).

Chilli dip

INGREDIENTS
3 fresh chillies (chopped finely)
2 tabsp ginger (chopped finely)
100ml light Soy sauce

METHOD
Simply mix together well. Serve.

MURTABAK *(SISTER OF SAMOSA)*

INGREDIENTS
4 eggs (beaten, & mixed with 2 tabsp water)
1½ onions (chopped roughly)
3 pieces of celery (chopped roughly)
2 cloves garlic (chopped)
1 tabsp ginger (chopped)
4cm length of chilli (chopped)
½ teasp turmeric
1 tabsp of pkt curry powder
1½ tabsp Garam masala
1 vegetable stock cube - crumbled
½ teasp salt
½ teasp pepper
3 fresh coriander (chopped)
5 tabsp oil

1 pkt Chinese pancake skin (spring roll skin)

Mix together:
1 egg
2 tabsp cornflour
3 tabsp water

Vegetable oil for frying
Flat tray lined with cling film

METHOD
Heat the vegetable oil in non-stick wok on medium, and fry the Garam masala, curry powder, ginger and garlic. Cook slowly until spices produce a pleasant fragrance.
Add the onions, celery, chillies, and then turn the heat to high. Stir-fry well, add the salt, pepper, turmeric and the crumbled vegetable cube. Stir.
Now add the eggs, and quickly mix all the ingredients.
Add coriander, and again mix well.
When the scrambled egg is slightly cooked remove it from the heat.

Place this filling mixture into a bowl, and leave it to cool.

Take 10 pieces of pancake skin. Cut them into 3 equal pieces. Therefore producing 30 long pieces of pancake skin.
Have your cornflour mixture ready with a pastry brush, and the flat tray at the side ready as well.

To make the murtabak
Place 1 piece of the pancake skin in front of you, with its short side facing you. Place 2 teasp of the filling at one end and fold the pastry over diagonally, then fold again diagonally and again diagonally, still maintaining a triangular shape. Seal the murtabak end of the pastry down with the egg mixture.
Place the finished *murtabak* on the trays. Repeat this procedure until all the filling is used up.

Heat the oil and deep fry for about 5 minutes until lightly brown.

Main Course

NASI LEMAK (FRAGRANT MALAY RICE)

INGREDIENTS
400g long grain rice
400g Basmati rice
1 tabsp ginger (chopped)
0.25g saffron
½ tin of coconut (400ml) mixed with water, making 1300ml total
100g butter
1 teasp salt
2 pandan leaves (screwpine leaves)

METHOD
Wash the two portions of rice with three changes of cold water. Drain the water away.
To boil the rice - Put the rice, coconut water, salt, ginger, saffron, butter and pandan leaves into a heavy-based saucepan. Boil, and stir thoroughly quite often to stop the rice sticking to the bottom of the saucepan. Once the water evaporates, stir once more.
Now cover and cook on very low heat for 20 minutes.

Before serving fluff up the rice with a spatula. Discard the pandan leaves.

NONYA STYLE CHILLI PRAWNS

INGREDIENTS
800g fresh Tiger-prawns (shelled)
10 candlenuts
120g shallots (sliced)
3 cloves of garlic
5 chillies
4 lemon grass
2 teasp tomato puree
½ teasp turmeric
1 vegetable stock cube - crumbled
250ml prawn stock or water
1½ cornflour (add to the prawn stock/water)
¾ teasp sugar
½ teasp salt
½ teasp pepper
4 tabsp vegetable oil

METHOD
Prepare the tiger prawns by cutting quite deeply into their backs and de-veining. Set them aside.

The lemon grass should be cut into 10cm lengths. Then you should cut 3cm of this lemon grass at the plump end. The rest of the remaining lemon grass is to be crushed and saved for later.

Chop the candlenuts, shallots, garlic, chillies and lemon grass and then blend to make a fine Nonya paste. Heat the vegetable oil in a wok on low, and fry the Nonya paste stirring continuously until the oil starts to ooze out from the paste, and it should also start to change colour. The smell of the spices should now be apparent - this takes about 10 minutes.

Add tomato puree, crushed lemon grass, turmeric and the crumbled vegetable cube. Stir, turn heat to high, and add the prawns. Stir-fry, now add the salt, pepper and sugar. As soon as prawns turn pink add the prepared stock mixed with cornflour.

When the sauce thickens turn heat off and serve.

Ah Lin Tang's tip
Prawn stock is prepared by boiling the 250ml water with the tiger-prawn shells to capture some of the wonderful flavours.

SINGAPORE CHINESE STYLE SWEET AND SOUR FISH

INGREDIENTS
800g fresh Monk-fish (sliced into bite-sized chunks)
½ teasp pepper
1½ tabsp fish sauce
1 tabsp light Soy sauce
1 tabsp ginger - chopped
1 tabsp coriander - chopped
1 tabsp spring onion - chopped

Batter:

130g flour
100g custard Powder
1 egg
100ml milk
100ml water

Oil for frying

METHOD
Prepare the batter:
Using a blender add the egg, flour, custard powder, milk & water. Blend until a smooth consistency similar to that of double cream.

Pour this batter into a large bowl, add the fish, salt, pepper, fish sauce, light Soy sauce, ginger, spring onion, and coriander. Mix well taking care not to break up the fish.
Heat the oil until hot for frying. Hold a piece of fish, and place it into the hot oil. Fry quickly until light brown. Repeat this to finish off frying all the fish. Set aside.

To serve
Heat oil and deep fry again until crisp & golden in colour. Place on plate and pour *Sweet and Sour sauce* all over (p44).

CHICKEN AND PINEAPPLE WITH MANGETOUT

INGREDIENTS
800g chicken breast (cut into chunky bite-size pieces)
200g mangetout (trimmed)
200g fresh pineapple (into cubes)
3cm length of chillies (sliced)
½ teasp Five-spice powder
1 tabsp Worcestershire sauce
8 thin slices of ginger
1 teasp garlic (chopped)
½ teasp salt
½ teasp pepper
½ teasp sugar
2 teasp dark Soy sauce
1 tabsp light Soy sauce
1 tabsp oyster sauce
1 tabsp Chinese Shaohsing wine
1½ tabsp cornflour mixed with 200ml of chicken stock
1 teasp chicken stock powder
2 tabsp vegetable oil

METHOD
Cut each slice of ginger into 8 strips i.e. very finely.
In a bowl add the chicken, the chicken stock powder, Five-spice powder, and the Worcestershire sauce.
Mix and set aside. Heat the vegetable oil in a wok on medium, stir-fry the ginger, and garlic until it just starts to change colour. Now add the chicken, turn heat to high, stir fry and let the chicken cook slightly before adding the chillies, salt, pepper, sugar, dark and light Soy sauce and oyster sauce. Mix evenly and thoroughly.
Add the pineapple and mangetout, and cook for 2 minutes. Add the cornflour mix with the chicken stock. Let the sauce thicken.

Add the Shaohsing wine and serve.

RAFFLES ROAST PORK IN AN ISLAND - *incorporates 'Singapore Char Sui'*

INGREDIENTS
1kg leg of pork (boned)
Vegetable oil
To marinate:

4cm fresh ginger (squashed)
2 spring onion (squashed)
3 star anise (squashed)
1 tabsp Sichuan peppercorn (crushed)
2 tabsp dark Soy sauce
1 tabsp light Soy sauce
1 tabsp Chinese Shaohsing wine
2 teasp chicken powder
4cm long cinnamon stick

Gravy:

3 cloves garlic (crushed)
2 teasp cornflour
2 tabsp water

METHOD
Make several slashes in the pork skin to allow the marinade to penetrate.
Add the pork into a large bowl. Now add all marinade ingredients. Rub the spices all over the pork. Cover and leave in fridge for a day.

To cook
Heat the vegetable oil in a wok to medium. Lift the pork out of the marinade, shake off its excess juice and spices. Shallow fry, turning frequently, making sure the skin is brown all over.
Put the fried pork back into the marinade, and cover with foil.
Place the bowl inside a steamer or pan of hot water. Steam or cook in an oven for 2½ hours, 200°C (or gas mark 6).

Lift the pork out of the juices and allow to drain. Set aside.

Take one tabsp of the fatty oil from the liquid/juice and place into a saucepan. The remaining fat, scoop it up and discard. Heat the saucepan on low and fry the garlic with the removed oil until fragrant, the add the remaining skimmed juice.
Thicken the sauce with cornflour, and mix it with the water.

To serve
Cut the pork into bite size slices. Place and arrange the pork in the centre of a large plate. Pour and strain the gravy over the pork.

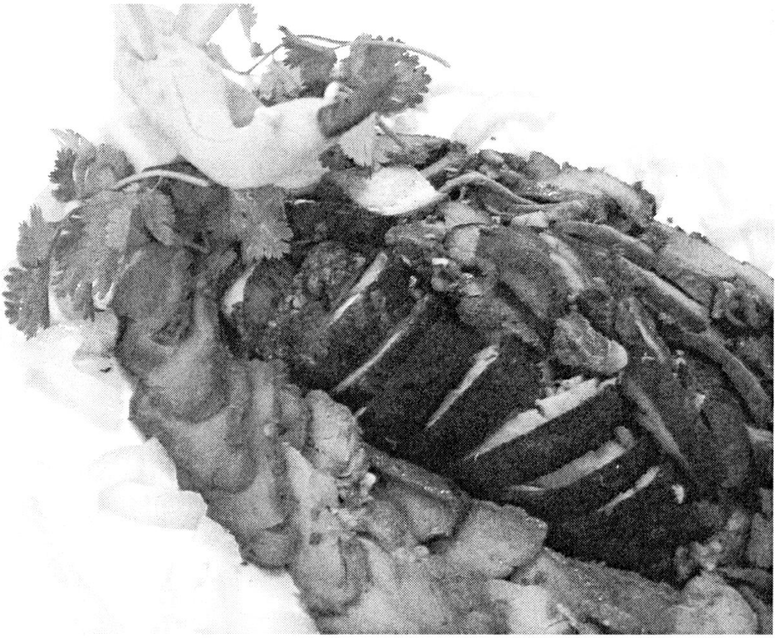

Singapore Char Sui

INGREDIENTS
600g pork fillet
50g rock sugar (crushed into fine pieces)
1 tabsp Hoisin sauce
1 teasp fermented red beancurd
½ teasp pepper
1 teasp chicken stock powder
2 tabsp Chinese wine
2 tabsp honey
½ teasp red food colouring (optional)
1 teasp garlic (chopped)
1 tabsp sesame oil

METHOD
Cut the pork fillet in half (if they are quite big). Place the fillet and all the ingredients into a large bowl. Rub these ingredients onto the pork fillet. Cling film, and keep in fridge for a day.
Preheat the oven on 200°C or gas mark 6. Drain the pork of its surrounding marinade, and keep this marinade in a separate bowl.
Place the pork on a wire-tray with a baking tin underneath to catch any dripping juices. Put all of this into the oven, and roast for 10 minutes. Take the pork out.
Now pour the marinade sauce (which was kept earlier) into a wok, turn heat to medium, add the half cooked *char-sui* and let it brown all over for another 5 minutes. Also let the thick sauce stick onto the *char-sui*. Allow this to cool.

To serve the Raffles Roast Pork in an Island incorporating Singapore Char Sui:
Firstly cut the *Singapore Char Sui* into slices. Place the *Raffles Roast Pork* into the centre of a large plate, and arrange the sliced *Char Sui* surrounding the central pork, into an overlapping design.

BUGIE STRIP OF VEGETABLE STIR-FRIED

INGREDIENTS
100g Chinese white cabbage (chopped into 2cm lengths)

Soak in 250ml water:
10 cloud ear
10 dry Chinese mushrooms
1½ tabsp cornflour

1 tabsp garlic (chopped)
3cm long ginger (sliced)
4 pieces beancurd puff
1 piece celery
1 medium-sized carrot
70g snap-pea (trimmed)
70g fresh oyster mushrooms (cut into bite-size)
70g tin bamboo shoot
200g bean shoots (tails removed)
3cm length of chilli (sliced)
70g fresh baby sweetcorn (chopped in half)
¼ onion (cut into chunky bite-sized pieces)
¼ red pepper (cut into chunky bite-sized pieces)
2 teasp oyster sauce
2 tabsp light Soy sauce
1½ tabsp sesame oil
1 vegetable stock cube
½ teasp salt
½ teasp pepper
¾ teasp sugar
2 tabsp vegetable oil

METHOD
Cut the celery and carrot diagonally into thick slices. Reach into the 250ml water and squeeze the soaked mushrooms and cloud ears and place them onto a

chopping board, and then cut them in half. Keep the water they had been removed from and crumble the vegetable stock cube into this mushroom water.

Heat oil on low in a wok and shallow fry the beancurd puff. Dish it out, allow to cool, and cut into quarters each.
Now fry the garlic and ginger in the same oil, stir-fry, turn heat to medium, add the carrots and baby sweetcorn, and stir. Now add the snap-peas, turn heat to high, add celery, red pepper, bamboo shoots, onions, and all the mushrooms and the cloud ears.
Mix evenly and thoroughly.
The heat should still be on high. Add the Chinese white cabbage, bean shoots, chilli, beancurd puffs, oyster sauce, salt, pepper, sugar, light soya sauce and sesame oil. Stir the mixed vegetables evenly and add the mushroom water, with cornflour.
Bring to the boil, and allow the sauce to thicken. Turn heat off and serve.

Sweet

SINGAPORE STYLE QUEEN OF PUDDINGS

INGREDIENTS
500ml double cream
200ml milk
2½ lemons (using just the rinds)
30g butter
75g sugar
A pinch of salt
120g white bread (into crumbs)
5 egg yolks (beaten)
7 tabsp seedless raspberry jam
1 punnet fresh raspberries
1 tabsp icing sugar - for decoration

For the meringue:
5 egg whites
25g Sugar
2 clear attractive pudding bowls

METHOD
Scrape as much of the lemon rind as you can and chop it finely. Set this aside.
In a saucepan place the double cream and milk with the sugar on medium heat. Stir, and add the lemon rind. Let it just start to boil, then turn the heat off and quickly stir in the butter and breadcrumbs. Mix well. Now allow to cool for 5 minutes.
Add in the egg yolks. Mix well again. Pour this mixture into the two pudding bowls.
Bake in a moderate oven 200°C or gas mark 6 for 30 minutes or until it just sets. Turn off the oven, and allow to cool. Set aside.

For the meringue

Beat the egg whites until stiff, and add in the 25g sugar.

Warm the jam in a saucepan until runny. Turn the heat off, and set aside. Spread the warmed jam over the pudding mixture, which had been in the oven. Now pile on the stiff meringue and spread evenly to cover the jam.

Sprinkle a little bit of icing sugar all over the meringue for a crunchy topping. Put it back in the oven on 150°C or gas mark 2, and allow it to cook until it is pale, golden, and the meringue is crunchy.

Leave to cool slightly before serving.
Decorate with raspberry, and dust with the remaining icing sugar.

MERLION PEACHES

INGREDIENTS
20 medium-sized ripe peaches
300g sugar
10 tabsp VSOP brandy
2 tabsp lemon juice
1 tin of rambutan stuffed with lychee (500g)
200ml double-cream (whipped)
A handful of pistachio nuts (crushed)

METHOD
Cut the peaches in half, remove their stones and skin. Place these prepared peaches into a large bowl, add the VSOP, lemon juice, and half of the sugar, and cover. Leave in a fridge for the day.
Lay the peaches on a shallow baking tray. Sprinkle the rest of the sugar on top, and grill on both sides until brown and hot.
Drain the stuffed rambutan and lychees.

To serve
Place the grilled peaches onto a serving plate with the cut side facing upwards. Pipe some whipped cream into the centre of the peach (in the slight groove where the stone had been removed). Lay a stuffed rambutan & lychee on top of the cream. Sprinkle with the pistachio nut. Serve.

Pour all the juice from the baking tray into a jug, and serve with the peaches.

Chicken & Pineapple with Mangetout

Raffles Roast Pork in an Island

Sweet & Sour Fish Singapore Chinese style

Bugie Strip of Vegetable Stir-fried

Nonya-style Chilli Prawns

Nasi Lemak

Rasa Sayang Drunken Pear

Royal Palace Fruit Soup

Singapore style Queen of Puddings

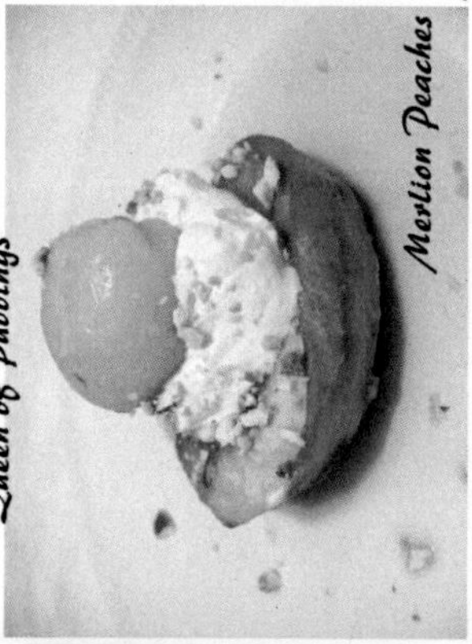

Merlion Peaches

Mocha Bavarian Mousse

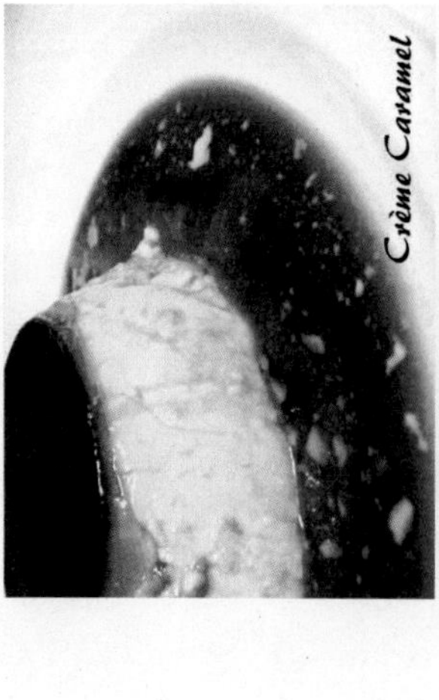

Crème Caramel

Fresh Fruit Salad from Afar & Near

Singapore Toffee Apple & Banana

INDEX

ISBN 141202659-8

9 781412 026598